Working in a Very Small Place

Working in a Very Small Place

The Making of a Neurosurgeon

Mark L. Shelton

Vintage Books
A Division of Random House, Inc.
New York

First Vintage Books Edition, May 1990

Copyright © 1989 by Mark L. Shelton

Grateful acknowledgment is made for permission to quote briefly from the following: John D. Hicks, *The Populist Revolt* (Minneapolis: The University of Minnesota Press, 1931); T. P. Morley, M.D., ed., *Current Controversies in Neurosurgery* (Philadelphia: W. B. Saunders & Co., 1976); the British Medical Association, *The Journal of Neurology, Neurosurgery, and Psychiatry* 46 (1983); The Congress of Neurological Surgeons, *Neurosurgery* 14, no. 5 (1984); The American Association of Neurological Surgeons, *Journal of Neurosurgery* 65 (November 1986); 66 (April 1987); 67 (October 1987).

Library of Congress Cataloging-in-Publication Data
Shelton, Mark L.
      Working in a very small place : the making of
a neurosurgeon /
   Mark L. Shelton.
         p. cm.
      Reprint. Originally published: New York : Norton,
© 1989.
      ISBN 0-679-72815-5 (pbk.)
      1. Jannetta, Peter J. 2. Neurosurgeons—United States
—Biography.
      3. Neuralgia, Trigeminal—Surgery. I. Title.
   RD592.9.J36S44   1990
   617.4'8'092—dc20   89-40484
   [B]   CIP

Manufactured in the United States of America
10 9 8 7 6 5 4 3 2

Dedicated to the memory
of Rose Shelton,
to Ross Shelton,
and, of course, to Eve

Contents

Acknowledgments

This book is the result of the cooperation of many people, far too many, perhaps, to name. Nonetheless, I should like to try.

First, I must thank Peter Jannetta himself for so graciously permitting me access to what is normally a closed and mysterious world. By allowing me in, he has by extension allowed many others to see what contemporary neurosurgery is and can be.

Just as important as Dr. Jannetta's own cooperation has been the cooperation of more than sixty of his patients, many of whose stories appear in this book. All let me enter their lives, their medical histories, and, in many cases, their hospital rooms, and made me feel at ease. I have used pseudonyms within the text and have changed certain identifying details as they pertain to individual patients—a ground rule that I made, rather than they. To a person, they told me that I should feel perfectly free to use their real names. I declined, because I worried that they were speaking out of the exuberance of the recovery from a chronic illness and that, by the time these words appeared, most would have forgotten about me and would have moved the memory of their own difficulties to some dark corner of the brain. All of the events and histories described within this book are presented as they were told to me or as I had observed, other than my use of invented names and geographical license to protect their privacy. Several patients deserve special mention for permitting me access to their entire medical records; I thank them for their trust in my ability to maintain a confidence and hope that that trust has been rewarded. And to the patients with which I spoke who do not recognize themselves portrayed here, I can only again offer my heartfelt thanks for their time and effort; I hope that the information and insight they provided me is reflected throughout the book, even if not recorded as individual cases.

Next, I thank the dozens of professionals at Presbyterian-University Hospital and the University of Pittsburgh School of Medicine for their time and patience, in particular Mary Lou Michel, Senior Vice-President of Development and Public Relations at Presby; Ann Metzger, Director of PR; Tom Chakurda, Assistant Director for Media Relations; and Diana Mathis and Mark Collins, Public Relations Specialists *extraordinaires.* I first proposed this project when Presby was under the excellent guidance of Daniel L. Stickler, who deserves much credit for assembling such a fine group of administrators as those mentioned above; his successor, Patricia Shehorn, continues to administer the hospital with care and grace. Shelley Gebar deserves my gratitude for several long and far-ranging discussions with me about what neurosurgery means to Presby.

At the University of Pittsburgh, Jane Duffield and her staff helped coordinate several of my visits.

In the front lines at Presby, I must acknowledge Patty Caldwell and Gail Schwartzmiller of the Department of Neurosurgery; Ellen Scott and Carol Schuit, the department's able administrators; Nancy Lippoldt, Clinical Coordinator;

Lisa Hawkins, Chief of Neurosurgical Nursing; Sharon Sell, Head Nurse of the neurosurgery patient units; and David Bissonette, the department's Physicians' Assistant.

Countless neurosurgeons, surgeons, residents, and specialists at Presby extended to me every courtesy and explained many of the finer points of their work: Rob Parrish, M.D., Ph.D.; Mark Dias, M.D.; Don Marion, M.D.; Eric Altschuler, M.D.; Paul Nelson, M.D.; Howard Yonas, M.D.; Laligam Sekhar, M.D.; L. Dade Lunsford, M.D.; Margareta Møller, M.D., Ph.D.; and Rosa Pinkus, Ph.D.—all gave of their time and energy. Fred Khalouf, D.O., and others in the Department of Anesthesiology explained that mysterious field to me; Viggo Kamp Nielsen, M.D., Ph.D., likewise introduced me to electromyography. John Moossy, M.D., and Julio Martinez, M.D., of the Division of Neuropathology, and Dachling Pang, M.D., and Leland Albright, M.D., specialists in pediatric neurosurgery, were invaluable in explaining many of the arcana of their respective fields. Aage Møller, Ph.D., gave me time, energy, answers, and journal reprints in large quantities.

I must also acknowledge Ronald Apfelbaum, M.D., of the University of Utah; Richard Paddison, M.D., of the Office of Preventive and Public Health Services in New Orleans; Steven Haines, M.D., of the University of Minnesota; Roberto C. Heros, M.D., of Harvard; Charles Wilson, M.D., of the University of California at San Francisco; Sol Erulkar, Ph.D., Brooke Roberts, M.D., and Leonard Miller, M.D., of the University of Pennsylvania; Abbott Krieger, M.D., of the University of Medicine and Dentistry of New Jersey; and Albert Camma, M.D., of Zanesville, Ohio. All responded to my requests for time and information with great courtesy and candor.

Special mention must be made of Carol Jannetta, M.D., and Joanne Jannetta, M.D., both highly regarded physicians in their own right, who shared their insights on their father and his work forthrightly and generously.

Others who provided assistance and advice include Judy Campbell, Monnie Lovas, Lori Hrico, Carol Anderson, and Ray Anne Lockard of the University of Pittsburgh, and the office and archival staff of the American Association of Neurological Surgeons. Bruce VanWyngarden and John Altdorfer, editors at *Pittsburgh Magazine*, helped immeasurably by allowing me to juggle my schedule around the writing of this book. Tim Seldes, of the Russell and Volkening Literary Agency, and Starling Lawrence, my editor at W. W. Norton & Company, helped me at every turn; Dick Allen, of the University of Bridgeport, and his wife Lori helped me in my initial excursion to the Big City. John Baskin and Mark Collins read the manuscript in its various incarnations and provided valuable advice. I used two reference books almost to the point of wearing them out: *Van Nostrand's Scientific Encyclopedia*, which was a gift to me from my mother, and *Dorland's Illustrated Medical Dictionary*. I owe a debt to the editors of both of these fine and finely done resources. In that regard, I must also mention the *Index Medicus*, published by the National Library of Medicine, which brings method to the apparent madness of the publication of literally thousands of medical journals. And thanks to the librarians and staff at the Falk Library for the Health Sciences of the University of Pittsburgh School of Medicine. If they didn't have it, they got it for me, which is the highest compliment I think anyone can pay to a library staff.

Finally, I would like to acknowledge the grace and good cheer of my wife, Eve Shelnutt, who supported me in every sense of the term throughout this project and without whom my work would mean little. She is the light of my life.

Laughlintown, Pennsylvania   1988

Note to the Reader

My use of the singular masculine pronoun in many places throughout the text of *Working in a Very Small Place* is not accidental, nor is it a conscious or unconscious slight. It is a choice I've made according to the following rationale: I am writing about a profession that is populated predominantly by males. I do not mean to suggest or imply that this is good or proper; this is simply the way things are right now in the world of neurosurgery. It seems artificial to me to suggest or imply otherwise, and so I use the pronoun "he" when referring to an unspecified member of the neurosurgical profession.

Working in a Very Small Place

Prologue

When Stanley Risk returned from his appointment with a prominent Phoenix neurosurgeon, he sat down and methodically planned his own suicide. Because he is a licensed pilot, the planning did not take long once the decision had been made. "I was going to file a flight plan, head for New Mexico, and just run out of gas in the mountains," he said three years later. "I looked very dispassionately at what I thought were all the pros and cons, and decided that it was the only thing to do."

What may seem unusual about Stanley Risk's decision is that he was not diagnosed as having a life-threatening tumor or a paralyzing disease—quite the contrary, in fact. He had been diagnosed as having trigeminal neuralgia, and trigeminal neuralgia is not fatal: it doesn't shorten one's life; it doesn't hold the prospect of life in a wheelchair; it doesn't affect mental capacity. It simply means that Stanley Risk would spend the rest of his life having episodes of excruciating facial pain.

But why suicide? He had a lovely wife, a beautiful daughter, a successful career as a television news director. Was it really as bad as all that?

"That's one of the *worst* things," he says, "because you don't look sick, you don't act sick. To the outside world, you seem just like you were before, and that's because no one who hasn't felt it can know how terrible it really is."

It had begun on a night in July 1981, and it ended on a bright morning in April 1986—but not with suicide. Stanley Risk's trigeminal neuralgia ended with a sophisticated neurosurgical procedure performed by a surgeon at Presbyterian-University Hospital in Pittsburgh, and his story is in many ways so typical as to be instructive. Some 15,000 people each year in the United States alone are thought to feel the first lightning bolt of pain that means trigeminal neuralgia, and what Stanley Risk endured before journeying to Pittsburgh to see Dr. Peter J. Jannetta is a sort of picture of contemporary medicine and what it can be. And it is the story of persistence on the part of both patient and surgeon—Stanley Risk changed his mind about suicide and instead doggedly pursued someone or something that could help him; and Peter Jannetta, ever mindful of the sometimes mysterious and subtle ways in which medicine changes, had the perspicacity and the courage (one fellow neurosurgeon called it, not unkindly, the "gall") to keep working in the face of adversity and to base his career on a chance observation he had made during an operation in 1966.

But Stanley Risk knew none of this in July 1981. He was, as are most people, blissfully ignorant of the existence of something called trigeminal neuralgia, ignorant of the existence of Peter Jannetta, and visiting a neurosurgeon was something that would have seemed so foreign to him as to be astonishing. "Two years ago, I didn't even know of the existence of the cranial nerves," said another of Jannetta's patients on the afternoon before her surgery, "and today, I could probably lecture to the medical students."

It was much the same for Stanley Risk. "I had always been

relatively healthy," he says. "I smoked too much, but I was never a malingerer. So that first episode was nothing more than an oddity. I had just left a television station in St. Louis to take a job as news and editorial director for a network in Phoenix, and I was living in an apartment alone—my wife was still in St. Louis because we were having trouble with selling the house. I was lying in bed and felt—you'll excuse the expression—gossamer wings tapping on my lower lip. There was no pain, just a tapping—it felt like a millipede trotting back and forth. It was odd, and I went to see the doctor the very next day. It was not painful that first time—it was a sort of pleasurable little buzzing. He didn't find anything wrong. But the next night, it was the same thing, only more insistent. 'I'm trying to tell you something,' I now think it was saying. And I told my wife the next night on the phone that I thought I was developing a cold sore or something, but there was no eruption. It just went away."

And it came back. "Four or five months later, I was at rest, and I got a similar feeling in my lower lip. But this time it was more electric—not pain, but it was a *charged* feeling. It frightened me, but, again, it went away.

"Six months passed with no recurrence, and then I woke up one morning with what I thought was a *helluva* toothache. I went to the dentist, he yanked a tooth, but there was still pain. It was episodic: it would hurt, and then it wouldn't hurt. I'd be free for a week or ten days, and then it would come back. Then it went away for another four or five months and came back with a *vengeance*. I thought, 'Uh-oh, something is really wrong here—an abscess, maybe?' I went to an *enlightened* oral surgeon, thank God, who said, 'I think you've got trigeminal neuralgia.' And—I'll never forget this—I said, 'Well, what is it?' He looked at me for a long time and then finally said, 'Well, it's not pleasant.' That was the first I had heard of trigeminal neuralgia. I still didn't know anything about it; the oral surgeon sent me to a neurosurgeon, who put me on the medication Tegretol.

"After ten days on four hundred milligrams a day, I just couldn't function. My work is mainly as a writer. I do a commentary every day on the news, and after ten days of Tegretol, I couldn't remember my own name, let alone sit and work at a typewriter. I'd sit down to type something and realize I had no idea what it was. So *back* to the doctor, and we tried Dilantin. This worked for about three weeks, and then it didn't. I almost went nuts this time—the pain would absolutely jolt me out of my chair. If you can imagine being touched on the cheek with a squadron of cattle prods, you can begin to imagine what an episode was like. And then it went away, and I thought, 'Well, we've beaten this, finally,' and *boom* it was back. I went back to the neurosurgeon, and this was when he finally sat down and explained to me what trigeminal neuralgia is. 'I want you to know what you're in for,' he said. He told me that no one knows what causes it; he told me about the various treatments being done, things that had names like alcohol injection and radiofrequency coagulation; and he told me about Jannetta's procedure, which he said was much more invasive and, consequently, sounded more dangerous. And he told me I'd have it for the rest of my life. That's when I went home and plotted my own demise."

A physician familiar with the onset of trigeminal neuralgia will recognize Stanley Risk's description as right out of a textbook: gradual onset of symptoms, periods of remission, some relief from medications, and finally a worsening. Not all sufferers have exactly this experience. Some are able to get relief from medication, and in some, their symptoms dissappear for years. But for many, Stanley Risk's story will sound painfully familiar.

"The reason I decided to do away with myself was not entirely selfish," says Stanley. "I could see my personality change. I had always been sort of gregarious, but I was rapidly becoming more emotional: quicker to argue, quicker to shout. I didn't want to *be* that way. But I ultimately decided that the easy way out—suicide—wasn't fair to my family, God love 'em, and I decided that I wasn't going to surrender without some kind of fight.

"So I didn't know what I was going to do, except keep trying to go on, when Fate stepped in. I was at the airport office talking to one of the mechanics, and I happened to see on his desk a sheet of paper that had on it, among other things, the words trigeminal neuralgia. I asked him about it. It turned out that his father had TGN and had gone to Texas for a procedure called percutaneous radiofrequency coagulation; his father had been symptom-free for eight months. *Zoom!* I called this doctor, made an appointment, and went down there for what is truly the most Godawful procedure ever devised by man. I was totally unprepared for it—I don't think there is any way *to* prepare for it. But I was there, so we did it. You're wheeled into a room, completely alert and cogent, and they give you a shot that's supposed to relax you (a fifth of Scotch wouldn't have relaxed me at that point). And then the needle." Stanley Risk leans back and closes his eyes. "Oh, Lord, what an experience."

Percutaneous radiofrequency coagulation involves the insertion of a long needle under the skin of the face (that is, percutaneously) and, simplified, uses electricity to burn the rootlets of the trigeminal nerve. "You're awake the entire time, and you can *hear* the needle moving around. The whole thing lasted two hours and forty-five minutes, after which I was limp as a rag—absolutely wiped out.

"And a year later, the pain came back."

Recurrence after radiofrequency coagulation is common; some studies show that 50 percent of those treated suffer from a recurrence after one year. The advantage of the procedure is that while it is uncomfortable to undergo, it is associated with very low risk (a common trade-off for "elective" neurosurgical procedures is risk versus benefits). For many, radiofrequency coagulation means freedom from the pain of trigeminal neuralgia, a return to a normal life. For Stanley Risk, the gamble didn't pay off.

"When the pain came back, I thought, 'No, this is impossible; it can't be back.' So I went to a dentist, who thought I needed a root canal, so I had a root canal, which was *nothing* compared to the other procedure. You hear people complain about root canals. Well, I went home and had steak and oysters for dinner—it just couldn't *approach* what I felt from that needle. And that night, the pain woke me up, and I spent three hours on my knees cursing God. I had never felt pain like that; it literally drove me to my knees. The next morning, I called the Texas surgeon and went back down to have the procedure again. As I was being wheeled down the hall, I was nervously making small talk with the girl who was pushing the cart. She asked me what I was going to have done, and when I told her, she said, 'Boy, I wouldn't have one of those for *anything.*' Right there, I asked them to turn around, but the doctor talked me into it. This one took three hours and seventeen minutes, and I came out of it with some numbness, which is not unusual, but no pain—for about six months."

In the fall of 1985, Stanley Risk and his wife were at a college football game when he opened his mouth wide to take a bite of a hot dog. "The pain hit me, and I remember thinking, 'No more, no more.' I talked to my wife about it, had no idea what I was going to do. So I went back to the Phoenix neurosurgeon, and we tried Tegretol again. No soap. The episodes now were coming maybe forty times a day and lasting for thirty seconds or more. There was a period of two weeks when I was completely at the mercy of the pain. If it struck while I was at the dinner table, I would throw my plate across the room involuntarily. It was like being in a boxing ring: it would hit me, and I'd try and hit back.

"During this time, I was becoming one of the world's leading authorities on trigeminal neuralgia. I would go the medical-school library once or twice a week and just read and read and read. Yasargil, Dandy, Spiller, Sweet—all the giants of neurosurgery, all doing battle with TGN. And this younger guy, Jannetta. I went to my neurosurgeon, and we talked about it. He was a little hesitant, because now we were talking about a full-blown operation (whenever anybody tells you about a brain operation, the first thing they say is 'Well, first they drill a hole in your skull . . .'). But the doctor said, 'If you're going to do it, go to Jannetta, because he's the guy who developed and refined it.' And he called and made the arrangements right then. And arms akimbo and braced like a sea dog, I got on an airplane and came to Pittsburgh."

The procedure that brought Stanley Risk to Presbyterian-University Hospital is called "microvascular decompression," and it is based on the theory that the cause of trigeminal neuralgia (and, as will be discussed later, a whole range of other diseases) is a tiny blood vessel compressing the trigeminal nerve where the nerve arises from the brain stem—in the back and at the bottom of the brain. One complication of the normal aging process is atherosclerosis—hardening of the arteries—which causes the blood vessels to lengthen slightly; this is a well-documented occurrence. Simplified, Jannetta believes that a combination of this lengthening and the configuration of blood vessels around the base of brain causes a blood vessel—generally an artery but sometimes a vein—to press against one of the "cranial nerves," the twelve pairs of nerves that arise from the brain and control our sight, hearing, taste, smell, the movements of the eyes and face. This compression "short-circuits" the nerve. And if a blood vessel presses against the fifth, or trigeminal, nerve, the symptoms are those of trigeminal neuralgia.

What Peter Jannetta does about these blood vessels, though, is where the controversy begins. In a procedure developed over a period of twenty years, he makes a small opening in the back of the skull, exposes the cranial nerves, and, with the aid of the operating microscope, inserts tiny bits of shredded felt in between the blood vessel and the nerve, making a pad that relieves—or "decompresses"—the pressure on the nerve. And the symptoms disappear.

As a treatment for trigeminal neuralgia, microvascular decompression has been controversial for several reasons. First, Jannetta began doing the procedure at a time when the operating microscope was still new to neurosurgery—and many of the offending blood vessels are invisible to the naked eye. Other surgeons, therefore, had difficulty verifying his results. Second, the procedure seemed a radical one for a non-life-threatening condition. Procedures such as radiofrequency coagulation, while not perfect, did not involve a sophisticated operation in one of the most delicate and dangerous areas of the brain: the cerebellopontine angle, which is where the cranial nerves are. Within the cerebellopontine angle lies the brain stem, along which are the involuntary centers for the control of heartbeat and respiration. Furthermore, retraction—moving—of the cerebellum is in itself a dangerous undertaking. Complications such as paralysis and stroke were not uncommon in 1966 from any operation that moved the cerebellum. And, finally, Dr. Peter J. Jannetta, when he made the initial observation that developed into a treatment for trigeminal neuralgia in 1966, was a neurosurgical resident—a graduate student, in a way—in a profession where the elders are revered and the younger members work quietly in their shadow. Jannetta, then age thirty-four, was seen as a child in the field, and he was claiming to have developed a definitive treatment for a condition that had stumped the giants of neurosurgery from the time of Harvey Cushing on down. And he made the solution sound so simple: remove the cause, and you remove the symptoms. For a profession that spent much of its time treating symptoms, having the cause be something so trivial as a blood vessel banging into a nerve—even a cranial nerve—was going to be scrutinized very carefully and welcomed grudgingly, if at all.

Stanley Risk, on his arrival in Pittsburgh, knew little of this part of the evolution of microvascular decompression. Much of what he knew was gathered from reading Jannetta's articles in medical journals and from talking to his Phoenix neurosurgeon, and neither of those would automatically lead one to suspect that his neurosurgeon was in any way a controversial figure. And anyway, Stanley Risk was more concerned about having an operation on what he had been assured was a most vital area of the brain. "I'm not sure what I expected when I went to Pittsburgh," he says. "I was mostly thinking about the operation, and I guess I expected that Jannetta would be some great egomaniac coming in on a cloud. (You have to remember that a person with trigeminal neuralgia is grasping at straws, and for someone to dangle the possibility of a cure in front of you is the most important thing in your life, and the person who dangles it is the most important person in your life all of a sudden.) Well, when he breezed in for the first time, I was never so *surprised*. I found him extremely warm, extremely easy to talk to, extremely generous and reassuring. He came in a couple of times, and we sat and just talked. But even with the pain, it was a hard thing to gird myself for. The morning of the operation, I told the nurse that I was getting dressed and going home. But I decided, sort of at the last minute, to stay. And the pain is gone."

On that morning, Stanley Risk was anesthetized and

prepped for surgery, and Jannetta performed a microvascular decompression of the fifth cranial nerve. The operation itself was uneventful and lasted about two and a half hours. Stanley Risk's postoperative recovery was complicated by his history of heavy smoking and his weight: he spent six and a half hours in the postanesthesia recovery room and two and a half days on oxygen in the neurosurgical continuous care unit. One curious development after the operation was his absolute disgust at even the idea of smoking. "I made a grand gesture of throwing my cigarettes in the wastebasket," he says, laughing. "I had no symptoms of withdrawal, no compulsion to smoke. It was as though my subconscious had told me that I didn't smoke. And the weight is going to come off, too. Before the TGN, I was always fairly active. But because of the pain, you become very self-protective: your life really changes. When I was having attacks of pain, I had Cream of Wheat through a straw for breakfast and baby food through a straw for lunch and milk shakes through a straw for dinner. The *thought* of chewing was enough to send a shiver through me. But now, I'm going to jog, box, take karate lessons, swim, make a lot of love to my wife—all the things I haven't dreamed of doing in the past few years. The pain is so debilitating that you don't have any energy for exercise. You become so pain-conscious—the pain is as familiar as putting on a pair of socks—it's something that you know is going to occur. You know you're going to have pain, so you tend to withdraw into yourself. But all that's going to change."

Because of the two previous radiofrequency procedures, Stanley Risk's chances of a total cure are lower than for others who undergo microvascular decompression—about 70 percent versus 92 or 93 percent for those who have never undergone a previous invasive procedure. "And that worries me a bit, you're always waiting for the other shoe to drop, waiting for it to start up again. They tell me that if I make it one year, then the chances are very, very good I'm cured." He thinks for a moment. "I've got two hundred seventy-nine days to go," he says, and laughs. "You see? It is so difficult to let yourself go, but I'm going to let myself go. You can count on it."

For Stanley Risk, that April morning was the most important event of his adult life. For Peter Jannetta, it was another day at the office: on the morning that he operated on Stanley, he did four other operations—two for trigeminal neuralgia, one for hemifacial spasm, and one for disabling vertigo. His surgery days tend to be like that. All told, there are about six hundred people waiting to be operated on by Jannetta, even though all across the country and around the world other neurosurgeons—many of whom he has trained himself—are performing microvascular-decompression procedures. For Jannetta, it is in the operating room where the really satisfying work occurs—"the fun part," he calls it. Although the procedure undergoes constant refinement, it is basically as he proposed it in 1966: gently retract the cerebellum, find the offending vessel with the aid of the microscope, move it away and hold it away with shreds of felt, and know that the symptoms will abate because their cause has been removed. Presbyterian-University Hospital has become a factory of sorts for the cure of cranial nerve disorders; Jannetta performs an average of eight procedures a week, and two other members of the staff also do the operations. The cumulative reports are published regularly: more than a thousand procedures for trigeminal neuralgia, more than five hundred for hemifacial spasm, more than two hundred for vertigo. And around the country and around the world, other surgeons publish their own findings, and the case reports mount. It is a universal human desire to leave a lasting legacy, and neurosurgeons are no different in this regard. Unless he discovers something even more prominent, Peter Jannetta will bequeath a definitive treatment for people, like Stanley Risk, with certain cranial-nerve disorders. "I said to Jannetta on the third day post-op," says Stanley Risk, " 'What a great feeling it must give you to relieve people's pain this way.' And just for a second there, he got this look—sort of an open look—and said, 'Yes, it does.' And I felt that I knew something then. I thought, 'Here is someone who is actually *doing* something for people, and he knows it.' It was an amazing experience from start to finish, an amazing journey."

For Stanley Risk, trigeminal neuralgia will eventually begin to fade from his daily consciousness. He will quit reading medical journals; he will return to his normal routines; he will take up karate and lose the weight he gained during his five-year odyssey. He has no more questions, as long as the pain stays away. He will not forget Peter Jannetta, but perhaps he will think about Jannetta less often as things return to normal. That's what being cured means. For Peter Jannetta, that's what makes it all worthwhile—all the research, all the conferences, all the hard questions and hard rebukes from other professionals. "*That's* what makes this different from ninety-nine percent of medical treatment," Jannetta says as he begins to tell the story of that first observation and all that came of it. "What we do is make people whole again, make them normal again. We don't cut something out or take something away, but, rather, we give something back: a normal life."

I

The Battlefield

In order for Peter Jannetta to cure a patient like Stanley Risk of trigeminal neuralgia, he must bore a hole in the back of the patient's skull and explore an area known as the cerebellopontine angle, a very small place on the underside of the brain. What Jannetta looks for is clinically described as "cranial nerve compression," which means pressure on one of the cranial nerves by one of the many blood vessels found in close proximity to the nerves at or near the point where they arise, or begin, at the brain stem. Cranial-nerve compression by a blood vessel—"vascular compression"—is caused, according to Jannetta, by a combination of unique anatomical relationships (some of us being born with our blood vessels close to our cranial nerves) and the aging process, which causes blood vessels, even the tiny blood vessels within the cerebellopontine angle, to harden and lengthen. When a blood vessel presses in a certain way and in a certain place along a cranial nerve, the nerve is stimulated and causes a wide range of conditions, depending on which cranial nerve is compressed—or so the theory goes.

A neurosurgeon who suspects vascular compression of, say,

the trigeminal nerve, as in Stanley Risk's case, will enter the cerebellopontine angle and, with the aid of a microscope, look for the offending blood vessel. When he finds it, he moves it away from the nerve and holds it there with a tiny pad. The trigeminal neuralgia should then disappear. Cases of vascular decompression of a cranial nerve are well documented; Jannetta and those neurosurgeons who perform the operation know what to look for. How Jannetta came to know what to look for, where to look for it, and why it is important to do so is a story that can serve as a metaphor for how revolutions in medicine happen—or almost don't. The story has high drama, painstaking patience, methodical perseverance, a dose (some say an *over*dose) of self-confidence, bits of luck, fate, timing, and serendipity. The theory can be summed up in a sentence or two, as most scientific theories finally are. But getting there, getting to that paragraph in a textbook, getting on the surgical schedule, getting a new idea to be not so new—there is the story. It is one thing for a surgeon to devise something new and try it himself; it may be successful, he may be eminently satisfied with the results, he may do it again and again and again. But it is another thing to get others to do it, too. Without that, a generation may pass before someone happens upon the same idea and tries his hand at having it catch on. One person cannot change medicine unless he changes the minds of enough of his peers for word to begin to get around. Only then is the revolution safe.

Jannetta's revolution is, well, revolutionary for several reasons, not the least of which is that it has taken place within the field of neurosurgery. Neurosurgery as a discipline is still much less than a century old. The first successful brain operations for the removal of tumors, for example, took place in the early 1900s; the Society of Neurological Surgeons, the first professional organization within the specialty, was not formed until 1920; and it wasn't until 1932 that the Harvey

Cushing Society (which is now the American Association of Neurological Surgeons) began holding regular meetings for the exchange of clinical and scientific information. In the early years, when virtually every procedure was new and standards of treatment and care were still in their most rudimentary stages, neurosurgeons had the worst of both worlds: their best efforts to treat patients, most of whom were terminally ill, resulted in very high rates of morbidity—sickness or deficit or loss, such as the loss of hearing, caused by an operation—and mortality—death. Because of the high rates of morbidity and mortality, neurosurgeons generally were only referred those patients who were beyond the help of any other specialty. Physicians in other specialties would send patients to neurosurgeons as a sort of last resort; and neurosurgeons, still learning what they could and could not do, had to do so while knowing that their peers considered referral to a neurosurgeon as something just short of a death sentence.

Thus, when an effective treatment for a condition was developed in the early years of the specialty, it was almost universally adopted, refined, and applied by neurosurgeons. After all, few enough of their procedures fit the definition of "effective," and a procedure that had acceptable levels of morbidity and mortality, and was reasonably successful, was going to rapidly become an accepted procedure, particularly if the condition was not a life-threatening one in the first place. The accepted treatments for trigeminal neuralgia in the early part of the twentieth century were pretty much the same as they were in the early 1960s. What turn-of-the-century neurosurgeons called "*tic douloureux*," or "painful tic," had a name change, but not much of a change in terms of treatment: either the nerve was killed by alcohol injection or electric current, or the nerve was cut. Surgeons might cut the peripheral branches of the nerve and call it "peripheral rhizotomy," or they might cut the sensory branches of the nerve

31

and call it "retrogassarian section." And even when retrogassarian section became known as the "Spiller-Frazier operation" in deference to the neurologist (Spiller) and the surgeon (Frazier) who developed it, it still was a procedure intended to destroy the nerve. The Spiller-Frazier procedure reached its apogee in the 1920s and has only in the last few years begun to fall out of favor, primarily as a result of improvements in radiofrequency coagulation and partially as a result of Jannetta's work. Radiofrequency coagulation still destroys part of the nerve and thus causes some sensory loss. Jannetta's procedure, which is much more involved and complex, is the only one that offers hope of relief from pain without losing nerve function.

But at the time the Spiller-Frazier operation was refined, it, and the destructive procedures such as alcohol injection and radiofrequency coagulation, represented the most acceptable solutions to a very vexing condition when alternatives such as opening the skull through the posterior fossa (the bony chamber at the back of the head that contains the cerebellum and the brain stem), as Jannetta does, to gain access to the cerebellopontine angle were almost inevitably accompanied by very high morbidity. Surgery within the cerebellopontine angle was until relatively recently considered almost unacceptably dangerous for any reason. The delicate physiology of the cerebellum, the fragility of several of the cranial nerves, less-than-ideal preoperative and intraoperative testing, the small size of many of the structures within—all combined to make surgery within this region very difficult and very risky. Thus, acceptable procedures, although producing less-than-perfect results, were better than the alternatives.

It is also worth noting here that the rank difficulty of brain surgery in its infancy played some role in the way that new procedures were developed and disseminated. Procedures that were accompanied by 50 and 60 percent mortality rates were not uncommon, and there are neurosurgery patient series chronicled in early twentieth-century surgical journals where mortality was 100 percent. It is not difficult to imagine the psychological toll such results exacted on the few neurosurgeons practicing at the time, as well as the toll from criticism by other physicians. Neurosurgeons developed a very thick skin very quickly, and the "vanadium-steel ego" still to some degree associated with the practice of brain surgery was in no small way born of the early frustrations that accompanied pioneers in the field.

Too, the stereotypical neurosurgery department, with its strong and dominant chief, its rigid hierarchy, the long unofficial apprenticeship when the new man in the department (there are only two dozen women in the United States who are board-certified neurosurgeons) handles the cases that the others above him pass over, still to some degree exists today. It is a carryover from those early years, when the chief was the chief because he was the best at the toughest cases and the best at maneuvering the department—and the specialty—through difficult times. Such an organizational structure does not always lend itself to the embracing of new ideas, of radical ideas, or of ideas that go against the common wisdom as well as against the best efforts of the giants of the field. And for such an idea to come from a *resident*, which Jannetta was when he made his initial observations of vascular compression, is asking a bit much from anyone, but especially from neurological surgeons. Residents don't make important discoveries, and any discoveries that are made by anyone are supposed to fit the conceptual framework of the field. The germinating idea for the whole theory of cranial-nerve compression as the cause of trigeminal neuralgia came to Jannetta while he was preparing cadaver dissections of the cranial nerves to be used in a class for first-year students at the Dental School, which is the kind of thing that residents are supposed to be doing. They are not supposed to be making signal discoveries or coming up with theories that, at first blush, do not seem to resemble anything that anyone thought was remotely plausible.

Jannetta's theory did not fit in with the traditional understanding of cranial-nerve disorders, nor, to be charitable, did it even fit a nontraditional understanding. Consider the symptoms of cranial-nerve disorders like trigeminal neuralgia and hemifacial spasm in the way that physicians have seen them for centuries, and contrast the persistence of the symptoms with the utter simplicity of Jannetta's theory. To have such intractable conditions be caused by a mere physical phenomenon is unlike almost any other clinical problem the neurosurgeon faces. Most neurosurgery is performed in response to anomalous growth (such as a tumor), a physical weakness or deformity of structure (aneurysms and arteriovenous malformations), or trauma (a bullet wound, a ruptured disk, a crushed or cut nerve). Vascular compression of the cranial nerves fits none of these catagories in at least two ways. First, it is not a growth or foreign body causing the compression, but rather occurs within "normal" physical relationships. The exceptions to this are when tumors themselves cause compression of the nerve. But improved diagnostic tests, such as the CT scan, make the discovery of an unsuspected tumor a rarer and rarer event. At any rate, tumors, if removeable, are removed as a matter of sound medical practice. Second, rather than treating the symptoms, which is what most of medicine, whether it is classical or contemporary, generally does, decompression of the nerve—inserting that tiny pad—purports to remove the *cause* of the disease, not just the symptom.

Think about that for a moment in the context of the most common medical treatments. High blood pressure, for example, has a dozen different causes, and careful physicians treat high blood pressure based on their understanding of what is causing it in a given individual. Hypertension that is treated with medication that lowers the blood pressure doesn't remove the cause, just the symptoms, which is often all that is necessary since it is the effects of high blood pressure on the kidneys, the circulatory system, the heart, that make it dangerous in the first place. Eyeglasses eliminate the symptoms of myopia, not the cause.

Surgeons are more accustomed to removing causes rather than treating symptoms, but the key word here is "remove." Appendicitis? Remove the appendix. Gall-bladder trouble? Thousands of people get along just fine after the accursed thing is removed. Tumor surgery is carried out under the same theory, except that a tumor is something that shouldn't be there in the first place; if it is a benign tumor, or even a malignant tumor removed early enough, the problems, both cause and symptom, generally go away. The most impressive extension of this might be transplant surgery, where not only is the cause of all the problems removed, but a functioning replacement is popped in to do the job that the original equipment had gradually failed to do.

But Jannetta doesn't remove anything: he just moves a few things around. A neurosurgery resident at Presby (as Presbyterian-University Hospital is jocularly called by everyone) once compared vascular decompression to, of all things, cosmetic surgery, because the symptoms of cranial-nerve compression, like the debutante displeased with her nose, is very private and personal, and the cranial-nerve surgeon, like the plastic surgeon, often realigns things the way Nature intended, if Nature were infallible.

Finally, Jannetta's work had to be a revolution because of the way it differs from those acceptable and accepted treatments. No neurosurgeon, privately or publically, is pleased when the most he can do is alleviate symptoms by damaging something that is working fairly well. The trade-off that a sufferer from trigeminal neuralgia faces when considering, say, radiofrequency coagulation is an unpleasant procedure, the possibility of some loss of nerve function, and the possibility of recurrence, which, objectively, is what Jannetta's procedure offers as well. Radiofrequency coagulation (the procedure for which Stanley Risk twice traveled to Texas), however, does not require an operation within the skull, does not require general anesthesia, and is associated with very low morbidity and mortality. About the only treatment less intrusive would be what is generically referred to as "medical" treatment—medications such as Tegretol, which is effective often enough so that it is the first treatment physicians usually try when a diagnosis of trigeminal neuralgia is confirmed. But, like all medications, it has side effects. And, like all medications, it doesn't work all the time and it doesn't work forever, so a sufferer must begin to consider more involved alternatives such as radiofrequency coagulation. It is widely accepted now that any interventional procedure, be it coagulation or sectioning or vascular decompression, must be attempted at or near the root of the trigeminal nerve, which is generally considered to consist of two parts, sensory and motor, or the "portio major" and the "portio minor." (If one wanted to make all the leaves fall off a tree, one would perform tree surgery at or near the roots.)

But the roots of the trigeminal nerve are surrounded by important neuroanatomical structures; there is no way in without moving something. The Spiller-Frazier procedure, for example, requires entering the skull through the temporal fossa, which is above and slightly behind one's ear, and retracting—moving—the temporal lobe of the brain. It is not an ideal approach for several reasons, primarily because the trigeminal nerve roots are difficult to reach. The advantage of an approach through the temporal fossa is that it was much less dangerous than an approach through the posterior fossa. Mortality associated with the procedure dropped from 22 percent in the 1890s to less than 1 percent in a series reported by Frazier himself in 1928. But while the imminence of death gradually receded for patients undergoing the Spiller-Frazier procedure, side effects such as paralysis of the facial muscles, loss of sensation, bleeding from broken blood vessels within the skull remained common.

Neurosurgeons, then, were already in much the same position that all pioneering specialists find themselves in at one time or another: one or two procedures had become well accepted within the professional community, despite their drawbacks. The leaders in the field did not so much attempt to portray their accepted practices as flawless as to accept these choices as being the best available ones, given what they saw to be the boundaries of the field: that surgery within the cerebellopontine angle was unacceptably dangerous, that destructive procedures such as alcohol injection and radiofrequency coagulation were much less so, and that the safest and most successful surgical intervention was the Spiller-Frazier operation. These boundaries were already solidly in place by the 1920s, and attempts to alter them then were met in much the same way as Jannetta's efforts were in the 1960s.

The neurosurgeon who tried to affect those boundaries was Walter Dandy at Johns Hopkins University, who published a report in 1925 outlining an approach to the trigeminal nerve within the cerebellopontine angle as a means of gaining exposure to the nerve roots and selectively sectioning them for relief of trigeminal neuralgia. For the rest of Dandy's career (he died in 1946 at the age of sixty), he performed the operation and reported on it. And although several other neurosurgeons also learned the procedure and did it themselves, for a variety of reasons it never caught on.

Some of those reasons were technical, some were political. Dandy himself stressed in his publications the need for consummate skill and the proper instruments for operations in the cerebellopontine angle; many neurosurgeons decided that the risks of the Dandy procedure as compared to the Spiller-Frazier procedure were too great. Dandy's work came at the time when neurosurgery as a specialty was trying to convince both the medical community and the general public that surgery on the brain was safe and necessary, and there was already wide documentation of safer procedures. Frazier himself, from his position as Professor of Surgery at the University of Pennsylvania, had declared in 1921 that the surgical problem of trigeminal neuralgia had been mastered. Given the long and difficult trials, refinements, and adaptations that the Spiller-Frazier procedure had undergone, it was not likely that the field would accept with open arms a more difficult and complex procedure, even if the operation demonstrated modestly improved results.

Another reason had to do with the interrelationships among the neurosurgeons themselves. References to Harvey Cushing invariably refer to him as "the Father of Neurosurgery," "the Master Brain Surgeon," "the First Brain Surgeon," some of which are more accurate than others. No one would dispute Cushing's skills nor his contributions to the field nor the influence he wielded from his position at the Harvard Medical School. And no one would dispute the fact that he had little regard for Walter Dandy, which had an effect on the acceptance of Dandy's work. Even though Dandy reported on hundreds of cases where he operated successfully within the cerebellopontine angle for relief of trigeminal neuralgia, and many of his peers no doubt read his articles and the articles of several others who reported on similar work, the procedure never caught on, and as late as 1959 the work of Dandy continued to be either forgotten, disregarded, or dismissed.

Why? Jannetta, when he made his initial observations, had

no idea but has had occasion in the intervening years to give it some thought—particularly when parallels could begin to be drawn between the reception of his own work and that of Dandy's. "Dandy wasn't able to do what he had to do *outside* the operating room," recalls Jannetta. "He was advocating a difficult procedure that was unsafe unless the neurosurgeon had been well trained in the technique. He didn't train a large number of surgeons to do the procedure, which is necessary if something is going to be kept alive. One surgeon, no matter how much he operates, has very little effect. But if he trains a group of surgeons who go forth and multiply and train others, then the ripple effect is tremendous. And it didn't help that the Cushing-trained people had also been trained to disregard him. But, then, he didn't have much regard for them, either."

Also, it must be remembered that Dandy was doing essentially what practitioners of the Spiller-Frazier procedure were doing—severing one of the branches of the nerve. Because of the improved access within the cerebellopontine angle, he was able to be much more selective in how he severed the nerve and, as a result, had far fewer patients with loss of sensation, facial paralysis, and loss of the motor branch of the nerve. What is interesting to note, however, is that Dandy observed the same physiological phenomenon that led Jannetta to the concept of vascular decompression, although Dandy continued to section the nerve branch to relieve the symptoms of trigeminal neuralgia.

Given this history, it is perhaps easier to understand why it has taken Jannetta's work so long to be accepted within the neurosurgical community.

Sectioning branches of the nerve, as in rhizotomy and the Spiller-Frazier operation, guarantees some loss of sensation but offers a chance at relieving the pain. Radiofrequency co-agulation is relatively safe and, when skillfully done, often provides relief for months or years. Jannetta's operation is much more involved. Even with the dramatic improvements in anesthesia, the development of techniques for gentle movement of the cerebellum, the use of intraoperative monitoring, it is still an operation in a very risky area, an operation that is not foolproof, an operation where many things can go wrong very easily. Some neurosurgeons say—as their predecessors did in Dandy's time—that this alone is reason enough to abandon the whole business. Even if the theory is correct, it doesn't make sense to do a full-scale operation in a very small and dangerous place if there are other "acceptable" alternatives. "Why," they ask, "would anyone perform such an operation, let alone counsel patients to undergo it?"

The answer, finally, is simple: because there is a chance, a very good chance if one looks at the percentage of successful operations done by Jannetta and others, that the pain, the twitch, the vertigo will go away and never come back. To those people, that is enough. To many neurosurgeons, it was the ultimate in egocentric surgery. See Peter Jannetta in *Newsweek* magazine. See Peter Jannetta on television talk shows. Read about Peter Jannetta in the newspaper. Read yet another article in the *Journal of Neurosurgery* about this fantastic *cure* for trigeminal neuralgia, for disabling vertigo, for hemifacial spasm. The world of neurosurgery was not particularly ready for Peter Jannetta nor for his brand of revolution, which is one reason, or part of one reason, why he has been called a quack and a fake, why some neurosurgeons think and say—loudly—that the whole business is an embarrassment and a fraud perpetrated by an arrogant youngster who thinks a tiny blood vessel, in just the right place, causes everything from trigeminal neuralgia to plagues of locusts, or so it seems.

Jannetta didn't know at the time that he was not the first to theorize on the basis of a series of clinical observations that certain disorders were caused by vascular compression, nor was he the first, as it turned out, to surgically decompress the nerve. He was the first to use the operating microscope to advantage in observing the relationships between vessel and nerve and is undoubtedly the first to make note of the importance of *where* the nerve is pressed by the blood vessel, both of which played a large—a crucial—part in the gradual acceptance of his work by his peers. What is finally important about Jannetta's work is not that he was a Columbus, but rather a Marco Polo or an East India Trading Company, because he opened the trade routes for other surgeons. He had to do this because the work of predecessors like Walter Dandy, which was based on the same kinds of observations, had for forty years been ignored or ridiculed or simply forgotten by the neurosurgical community at large.

That this had happened, and indeed that it happened on more than one occasion, is monument to the nonclinical side of medicine, which was also something that Jannetta was unaware of at the time of his initial observation. He was, as he recalls, more involved with what he had thought he found that he was with how it would be professionally received. Only after what he at first thought was a curious response on the part of his peers to the work he was doing did some inkling of what he could expect from the neurosurgical community at large occur to him.

Jannetta's first operations for vascular decompression were just that—*his* first cases; his first observations were just *his* first observations. Dandy was probably *the* first, in the sense of the first man in space. But between Dandy, in the 1920s, and Jannetta, in 1966, there were others. And the procedure, the theory, never caught on. That it finally has is a credit to a certain persistence on the part of Jannetta, as well as an understanding of scientific revolutions and how they come about.

The story of this revolution must begin with a map of the battlefield, and no battlefield has been so intimately and lovingly mapped as has the nervous system. Neuroanatomy as a discipline demands rigor of its disciples for the two standard reasons that make any endeavor involving the nervous system so rigorous: the nervous system is extraordinarily complex, and the subtlest distinctions are often of the utmost importance. The naming of the structures of the brain, for example, which includes systematic nomenclature, idiosyncratic nomenclature, and a host of places named, like mountains, for their discoverers, is the necessary first step in appreciating the various functions of the brain and in beginning to understand them. Neuroanatomists live in a world of names, names of places within structures within larger structures; a neuroanatomist strives to strain the soup ever clearer. All anatomy sometimes seems complicated by a method of describing the physical relationship of one thing to another—the use of the term "superior" for example, when it seems to the layperson one really means "top." One doesn't have to be an anatomist, however, to envision how "top" might be confusing. For example, picture a can of sardines sitting on the kitchen counter. If it is right side up—that is, if the flat side of the can with the writing on it is up—no fool could mistake the top of the can. If you flip it over, however, the "top" is at the bottom. If it were very important that one always know which side of the sardine can was which, one would say that the "superior" side of the can is the one with the writing on it, and it is the superior side regardless of the can's orientation in space. Anatomists and, thus, surgeons (since anatomists make most of the rules regarding names of structures) describe the various parts of the human body as though the body were always standing up straight, no matter what position the body might be in during surgery. The superior surface of the cerebrum is what's on top when we're standing at attention; it's still the superior surface if we're standing on our heads. In the same vein, "posterior" means behind something, and "anterior" would be in front of something. (Anatomy teachers tell their students to think of antlers as being the anteriormost aspect of a deer.) The opposite, in space, of "superior" is "inferior."

The only way to catch a neuroanatomist flat-footed is to ask a very general, very simple question—or, as a neuroanatomist might say with a measure of disdain, "a gross" (meaning "one which takes no account of minutiae") anatomical question.

The first question one asks about Peter Jannetta's work is, "Where is the cerebellopontine angle?" This is a gross anatomical question.

Imagine the brain as half a cantaloupe, with the cut side up and the rind side down. Imagine a banana placed with one end in the soft center of the cantaloupe, where the seeds are, but at the back of the center ("posterior to") rather than at the center of the center. The curve of the banana follows the curve of the cantaloupe, as opposed to opposing the curve; it implies the completion of the sphere, rather than the beginning of a figure eight. The banana represents the brain stem (anatomically, it would narrow and become the spinal cord); the cantaloupe is the cerebrum. Behind the banana—"posterior" to the banana—place half an orange, which is the cerebellum. The portion of the cantaloupe directly beneath (but, anatomically, "superior to," of course) the orange represents the occipital lobes of the cerebrum. Neuroanatomy can be no simpler than this.

Now place a plum anterior to the banana as it enters the cantaloupe. This is the pons, which is primarily white matter, or connective tissue (as opposed to the more familiar gray matter, of which most of the cerebrum is composed), and which contains neural connections between the cerebrum and the cerebellum. Place all of this in a fruit bowl just larger than the cantaloupe, but deeper—the bowl is the skull—and one is now looking, schematically, at the brain from its inferior aspect, or from the underside. The area bounded by the plum, the part of the banana that emerges from the cantaloupe, and the half an orange is the cerebellopontine angle.

In the fruit bowl, as within the skull, the cerebellopontine angle is not very large. But within it are structures that regulate three important groups of activity: the cerebellum controls the coordination of many of our voluntary movements (placing the cantaloupe within the bowl without dislodging the banana or the plum is a function of movements controlled by the cerebellum); the brain stem is the center of involuntary control of heartbeat, respiration, blood pressure, as well as the beginning of the spinal cord, through which neural impulses are transmitted to most of the body; and arising from the underside of the brain, along the brain stem, are the cranial nerves, which are concerned most prominently with what nonneuroanatomists call the "senses"—sight, hearing, taste, smell, and, to a degree, touch (primarily of the face).

Moving from the schematic to the real and imagining, rather than fruit, the actual structures of the brain, one sees an important principle of anatomical construction at work: the more important a structure is, the better hidden within the skull. To reach the cerebellopontine angle, one must bore a hole through the skull, cut through the tough and fibrous sac that encases the brain within the skull, and move the cerebellum. It is the body's version of a vault within an interior room behind a series of doors, one of which is made of bone. A neurosurgeon doesn't stray into the cerebellopontine angle, but only enters for the most compelling of reasons—a tumor, an aneurysm, or, in Peter Jannetta's case, to relieve cranial-nerve compression.

The cranial nerves are at once so integrated with how we are able to function as human beings and at the same time so hidden from our consciousness that it is no wonder that most people live their lives blissfully unaware of their existence. If one's cranial nerves are working properly, one cannot help but take them for granted. The activities for which they are pathways (nerves are, finally, pathways) are either completely ingrained, so that we do not think of them, or passive, so that we do not think of them unless something is wrong.

Take, for example, a toothache. Anyone who has had a toothache is aware that what makes a tooth ache is decay of the hard part of the tooth, which leaves the nerve of the tooth less protected than it should be. So the tooth hurts, alerting the owner that something is wrong. The nerves in the teeth are but branches of nerves that are branches of one of the cranial nerves—the fifth, or trigeminal, nerve, which arises within the cerebellopontine angle. This is one of the reasons that Stanley Risk went to a dentist, who pulled a tooth, and an oral surgeon, who did a root canal. Toothache, after all, is probably the most common cause of facial pain; and, in a sense, the symptoms of trigeminal neuralgia are similar to the symptoms of toothache, only much more intense. It is not unusual for neurosurgeons to see people with trigeminal neuralgia sporting new sets of dentures, having had a likely cause of pain completely eliminated before searching for a less likely cause.

An example of ingrained cranial-nerve function might be the work of the oculomotor (or third) nerve, which controls the movements of the eye through its branches to a group of tiny muscles, in conjunction with branches of the trochlear (or fourth) nerve and the abducens (or sixth) nerve. While movement of the eyes may be unconscious, it is not necessarily involuntary: when one looks up from reading a book, one moves one's eyes; when one rolls the eyes in exasperation, one is depending on one's cranial nerves.

As a group, the cranial nerves are twelve pairs, one set on each side of the brain stem, and, for the most part, dividing their duties along the midline of the body. There are a great

many more than twelve mnemonic devices invented to remember their names and the order in which they arise, ranging from the nonsensical to the bawdy. A Midwestern, mid-
dle-class version might be something on the order of "On Old
Olympus' Towering Top, A French And German Viewed
Some Hops," or (I) olfactory, (II) optic, (III) oculomotor,
(IV) trochlear, (V) trigeminal, (VI) abducens, (VII) facial,
(VIII) auditory, (IX) glossopharyngeal, (X) vagus, (XI) spinal accessory, and (XII) hypoglossal.

Not all of the cranial nerves arise within the cerebellopontine angle, and it is important to note here that the cerebellopontine angle is not a rigidly defined area, but amorphous,
given that one of its boundaries—the cerebellum—is moved
by the surgeon in order to gain access and given that we are all
constructed differently within the skull as we are outside it.
But access to the cerebellopontine angle generally means access to the origins of the fourth through tenth cranial nerves,
depending on the retraction of the cerebellum, and access is
gained by entering the skull about one fingerwidth toward
midline of the mastoid eminence, which is the bony knot directly behind the ear.

The final bits of neuroanatomy necessary at this point for
visualizing where Peter Jannetta works and under what conditions involve the blood vessels that wind their way along the
underside of the brain. The cerebral arteries, as a group, are
well understood schematically: the circle of Willis lies in the
center, just anterior to the pons, and is not really anything
itself, but rather the name for the circle of a dozen or so pairs
of arteries that feed other parts of the brain. The largest artery,
and an unpaired one, coming from the circle of Willis is the
basilar, which runs along the underside of the pons and
branches off into the vertebral arteries, the spinal arteries, and
the inferior cerebellar arteries, of which there are two pairs,

anterior and posterior. The anterior inferior cerebellar arteries, which everyone calls AICA (and pronounces "eye-ka"), and the posterior inferior cerebellar arteries (PICA, pronounced "pie-ka") and *their* branches, run over, under, and among the origins of the cranial nerves that arise within the cerebellopontine angle. For the most part, they provide blood to the underside (the "inferior" side) of the cerebellum and cause little trouble. But if AICA or PICA or one of their branches happens to cross one of the cranial nerves in a particular place, one has the ingredients for vascular compression.

The Three Princes of Serendip were not neurosurgeons; they were fairy-tale princes when what we now call Sri Lanka was the island of Serendip. The writer Horace Walpole coined the term "serendipity" in a 1754 letter to his good friend Horace Mann, to "describe the faculty of making happy discoveries by accident," which these three princes possessed.

Peter Jannetta was visited by these princes late one night in the anatomy lab, where he was working on those dissections for the dental students. Dr. Robert W. Rand, a neurosurgeon at UCLA, had the idea of preparing the dissections ("dissection" as a noun is a peculiarly medical term for describing the results of dissecting something) of the cranial nerves and broadcasting them via closed-circuit television, under magnification, to the dental students. "I was working in the lab on a dissection of the right trigeminal nerve," Jannetta recalls, "and I noticed something that I hadn't noticed before. The trigeminal nerve is generally described as emerging in two bundles, sensory and motor—the portio major and the portio minor. I found what seemed to be a third bundle, between the other two and, when I traced it back, discovered that it was made up of branches from both the motor and sensory roots.

It seemed to me that if we sectioned the portio major, but left these other branches, we'd get rid of the pain but keep light touch perception."

Jannetta discussed this the next day with Dr. Rand, who remembered that Walter Dandy had made a similar observation back in the 1920s or 1930s. Jannetta dug Dandy's articles out, reviewed them, found that Dandy had named this third bundle the "accessory sensory fascicles," and had stated that light touch could be preserved if these branches were preserved and the portio major alone were cut. If this were true, why didn't anyone else know about it?

For one thing, Dandy had made his observations via operations within the cerebellopontine angle, supported only by line drawings he had done (Dandy practiced long before the advent of the surgical microscope and worked, as described above, in an environment less than open to his ideas). Thus, his reports of the accessory fascicles that Jannetta found were dismissed in much the way his reports of selective sectioning of the trigeminal nerve were. Jannetta also read, in those anatomical reports of Dandy's, of "anomalous" blood vessels in the area around the root of the trigeminal nerve.

Jannetta went back to the cadaver lab and did a long series of dissections, followed by a series of cadaver "operations" on the trigeminal nerve using what is anatomically described as a "transtentorial" approach. The tentorium cerebelli is a part of the dura mater—the tough, fibrous outermost covering of the brain within the skull. The tentorium forms a tent, or covering, over the cerebellum, beneath the occipital lobes of the cerebrum (on our fruit bowl, it would be between the inferior posterior surface of the cantaloupe and the superior surface of the orange). To operate "transtentorially," the skull is opened at the temporal fossa (just behind the ear), the temporal lobe of the brain is retracted, which exposes the tentorium, the tentorium is cut through, and the cerebellum is slightly retracted.

From this vantage point, one can reach the trigeminal nerve as it emerges from the pons, and, if one can use the surgical microscope, one can clearly see it.

In 1966, the surgical microscope was itself the subject of controversy—or, perhaps more accurately, a certain measure of disdain—among neurosurgeons. It had been available for several years, and some neurosurgeons were using it (Jannetta had used one at Penn, during a National Institutes of Health Fellowship in Academic Surgery, to dissect the vestibular system in the cat and to place monitoring electrodes in the spinal cord); but its reception was similar to the reception of most innovations in neurosurgery—a cool one, at best. The generation of neurosurgeons who preceded Jannetta, which included many of his teachers, had learned their neuroanatomy without it, had learned their surgical technique without it, had learned all the procedures they knew without it; thus, many of them didn't think they needed it. In fact, the microscope that Jannetta was using at UCLA was one that Dr. Rand had purchased with his own money—the department hadn't yet seen a need for one.

The advantage of the microscope seems simple and obvious—now. The trigeminal nerve as it emerges is certainly visible to the naked eye, as are many of the cerebral arteries that course around it. What Dandy had seen without the benefit of the microscope (Jannetta hypothesizes that one of Dandy's unrecognized gifts was extraordinary eyesight), and what Jannetta saw with the microscope, were those "accessory fascicles"—in essence, a third branch of the trigeminal nerve, where historically only two had been seen. Pick up a neuroanatomy textbook printed, say, in the 1950s, and you will see the trigeminal nerve depicted as having two branches at the root: portio major and portio minor; pick up a new textbook, and you will see the "portio intermedius." Preserve the portio intermedius when sectioning the portio major, and you preserve light-touch perception—the brush of a cobweb across the cheek—while eliminating the pain of trigeminal neuralgia. Do this while approaching the trigeminal nerve through the tentorium, and you are in essence improving the classic operation for trigeminal neuralgia, because the transtentorial approach allows visualization of the roots more clearly than the subtemporal approach of the Spiller-Frazier technique, without the necessity of operating within the cerebellopontine angle, which was still, in 1966, considered far too risky to do if other options existed.

In February 1966, Jannetta performed his first transtentorial microsurgical procedure for trigeminal neuralgia. He did it not at UCLA, but at Harbor General Hospital, in Torrance, where Dr. John Alksne, one of the first neurosurgeons to recognize the advantages of the surgical microscope, was Chief of Neurosurgery; Rand and Jannetta brought Rand's microscope with them in the car to use during the procedure. The patient was a fifty-one-year-old man with a twenty-one-year history of right-sided trigeminal neuralgia; he had been treated over the years with alcohol injections and medication, but had had nothing but temporary relief. When Alksne admitted him to Harbor General, the man had attacks of pain up to ten times an hour, each lasting for about twenty seconds.

At operation, Jannetta, with Alksne assisting and Rand observing, exposed the trigeminal nerve and saw a loop of artery compressing it, an artery held in place by the spiderweblike connective tissue called pia arachnoid. The pressure of the artery was such that the diameter of the nerve was decreased by half. "That's the cause of the tic," Jannetta said quietly. It was what he still refers to as one of the three "serendipitous observations" that form the basis of the principle of vascular compression and microvascular decompression.

Jannetta was able to free the artery by cutting away the pia arachnoid and then went ahead and selectively sectioned the portio-major root of the nerve. The patient awoke free of pain, with mild diminished sensitivity to pain on the lower half of the right side of his face—the result of the sectioning of the nerve. He is still free of pain.

The third visit by the Three Princes of Serendip (the first had been in the anatomy lab, when Jannetta first saw the intermediate branch of the trigeminal nerve) came in May 1966. Between February and May, he had operated on several patients for trigeminal neuralgia, using the microscope via the transtentorial approach to selectively section the nerve, as he did on that first patient at Harbor General. In late May, in the outpatient clinic at UCLA, Jannetta saw a patient with hemifacial spasm—spasms of the muscles controlled by the facial, or seventh, cranial nerve. Because the facial nerve is only a motor nerve (as opposed to the motor and sensory functions of the trigeminal nerve), the condition is painless but, in its classical state, pulls the muscles of the face into contraction. Treatment for hemifacial spasm classically had been similar to treatments for trigeminal neuralgia—involving some form of trauma to the facial nerve. Unhappily, many sufferers of hemifacial spasm are thought to have a "nervous-habit spasm" and are sent for psychiatric help.

This patient, a forty-one-year-old man, was unable to work because the spasm of the muscles closed his left eye. What Jannetta suddenly saw as he sat across from the man was, in Jannetta's words, "trigeminal neuralgia in a motor nerve." And Jannetta said to the patient, "The spasm is caused by an artery pressing on the nerve that moves the muscles of your face on the left side. We can treat the spasm by operating and moving the artery away from the nerve."

The man responded by asking, "When can you do it?"

Jannetta would have done it that afternoon. The mechanism of vascular compression now all fit together: his observation of what Dandy saw at the roots of the trigeminal nerve;

Dandy's description of the "anomalous" blood vessels; the February operation in which the blood vessel was compressing the trigeminal nerve; and now a man with hemifacial spasm. The February operation suggested that a blood vessel might be involved in trigeminal neuralgia. Seeing a man with hemifacial spasm suddenly suggested that what might be the culprit in one condition might well be the culprit in others. "The light bulb," says Jannetta, "went on."

Jannetta operated on the man on June 2, 1966, at UCLA. Because he was looking for arterial compression of the seventh nerve, he entered the skull suboccipitally—beneath the left occipital lobe of the brain. Jannetta would be operating within the cerebellopontine angle and, moreover, would be working in the area where the eighth, or auditory, nerve emerges. And the auditory nerve is notoriously fragile—stretching it during retraction of the cerebellum generally means loss of hearing on that side.

Jannetta found no artery compressing the facial nerve, although he spent a good deal of time looking. Instead, he found a very small vein, just the kind of blood vessel that a neurosurgeon—even a very good neurosurgeon—would be unlikely to see without the microscope. Veins differ from arteries in a textbook-sized number of ways, but the significant differences are simple. Arteries supply oxygen and nutrient-rich blood to specific parts of specific organs; interrupt an artery's work, and you interrupt the flow of oxygen and nutrients. Within the brain, this has a common clinical name: stroke. Also, blood coursing through arteries is pumped by the heart. The arterial system is a closed system, like the cooling system of an automobile. A cut artery, like a cut radiator hose, means that the fluid within the system will keep pumping from the cut. Neurosurgeons have tremendous respect for all of the structures within the skull, but few structures garner more than AICA and PICA. These arteries are very small—

perhaps a quarter of an inch in diameter—have a number of even smaller branches, are extremely difficult to sew closed when accidentally cut, and supply blood to the inferior side of the cerebellum.

Veins, on the other hand, are somewhat disposable. Since they only return "used" blood into the venous system, sealing off a vein does not seal off blood from something vital. Also, the venous system is not pressurized the way the arterial system is—blood from small cranial veins doesn't spurt, but drips. Finally, if a small vein is closed, the blood that used to pass through it simply backs up and passes through other small veins on its way to larger veins and eventually to the heart, where it is pumped into the lungs. Small veins are dispensable, and Jannetta dispensed with this one, "coagulating" it—sealing it off—with electric current and then cutting it in half with a scalpel.

When Jannetta divided the vein, the facial nerve moved slightly, released from the compression of the vein. The operation was finished, the wound closed, the patient sent to the recovery room. He awoke with mild hemifacial spasm, which dissappeared the next day. It never returned.

The final step, as far as Jannetta thought he was concerned, would have to be actual decompression of a blood vessel—moving away an artery and keeping it away, and seeing if the symptoms went away as well. He operated on five more patients with trigeminal neuralgia in the spring and summer of 1966, upon all of which he performed the selective sectioning of the sensory root of the nerve, but in all of which he also was now looking for vascular compression, which he found. In all of the cases, the nerve was compressed by very small arteries, so small as to be almost invisible to the naked eye. By dissecting away the pia arachnoid, the arterial branches could be freed.

Jannetta now had data from several series of operations, each of which in its own way supported the theory. First, he had a series of operations on cadavers, none of which showed vascular compression of the trigeminal nerve. Second, he had made observations during operations within the cerebello-pontine angle undertaken for other reasons such as tumors or aneurysms, again with no evidence of vascular compression. Then he had the six patients with trigeminal neuralgia, in which he was able to find compression of the nerve. Finally, he had the experience with the operation for hemifacial spasm, in which releasing the artery had relieved the symptoms. What was left was obvious: an operation on a patient with trigeminal neuralgia but with the goal of decompressing the nerve, not sectioning it.

This, however, would be a big step—perhaps too big. Even if there were no other way of testing the theory, to test it by performing a major brain operation on a patient and then not doing what had been clinically demonstrated as the most efficacious treatment in favor of a theory that was already causing rumblings among established neurosurgeons was risky. Experimentation—and, objectively, this was what Jannetta was doing—is generally not introduced so quickly into clinical medicine. But what Jannetta was trying to prove did not seem to be provable any other way—lab animals, for example, don't tend to have trigeminal neuralgia and, at any rate, would be difficult to assess for relief of pain. If Jannetta were trying to demonstrate the efficacy of, say, a new medication for high blood pressure, a clinical trial where some patients took the medication for a short period and some didn't would be appropriate; after all, if it didn't work, those who had been taking it could then take something else. In this case, however, the patient would be asked to undergo dangerous surgery a second time.

It is difficult to grasp all of the conflicting desires that might affect a physician in Jannetta's position: the desire to demonstrate the truth of a theory; the desire to find a better way of treating a disorder; the desire for one's patients to do well. The short description of what transpired is that Jannetta, with Dr. Rand assisting, on August 8, 1966, performed microvascular decompression for relief of trigeminal neuralgia on a private patient of Dr. Rand's at UCLA Hospital and that the operation was a success. To best understand the implications of what transpired, though, and to understand the reaction to what transpired, it is instructive to understand exactly what it is that Peter Jannetta does.

2

Getting the Show on the Road

It is 7:03 A.M., and Madeline Cooper, already drowsy from a sedative, waits in the "bullpen" of the operating suites at Presbyterian-University Hospital. Next to her are four other patients, each lying on a hospital gurney. Some are covered with light cotton blankets because the bullpen area is cold. Across the aisle, the operating-room shift supervisors sit behind a counter heaped with folders containing X rays, boxes of surgical masks and shoe covers, and the all-important operating-room schedule. Madeline is scheduled for 7:30 A.M. in Operating Room 8; her procedure is listed as "Rt. RMC MVD Vth Nerve," which translates to a right-side retromastoid craniectomy for microvascular decompression of the trigeminal, or fifth, cranial nerve. It also lists the anesthesia (general), the anesthesiologist (Khalouf), and the surgeon—Peter J. Jannetta.

In 1981, Madeline was eating lunch with her sister in a Philadelphia restaurant when she felt a "jab" in her lower right jaw. "I thought, 'uh-oh, I broke a tooth,'" she recalls after the operation. "I went to the dentist the next day, and he started working on my teeth. The more work he did, the worse the pain got. He did a root canal on my third visit, but that didn't help either; the pain would get worse and worse. When it started, I tell you, it was like being electrocuted—there is just no way to describe that kind of pain."

People with trigeminal neuralgia go to great lengths to try and find words to describe the pain: "lightning bolt," "electric shock," "being burned with a hot wire." Because the pain is often set off by certain movements or touching "trigger points" on the face, sufferers become extremely cautious and, often, withdrawn. For Madeline, who works as a counselor for emotionally disturbed children and has three children herself, being withdrawn was a price she could not pay. "After I was diagnosed, I went to a neurologist and said, 'What can we do about this?' He said, 'Well, there's medication.' In four years, I took every medication and every combination of medication there is for this. I started out on one hundred milligrams a day of Tegretol and worked up to one thousand three hundred fifty milligrams a day, and the pain just got worse. Every night when I'd lie down in bed I'd think, 'Well, it can't get any worse,' but it did. It went on and on and on."

One of the side effects of Tegretol in large doses is drowsiness and lethargy; 1,350 milligrams of Tegretol left Madeline unable to do much more than sleep. "I'd take my medication and drop right off to sleep; when I'd wake up, the pain would be back, and I would wait to take more medicine; then, of course, I'd fall right back asleep. It was like living in a dream world."

Unable to work, unable to function, Madeline sought a second opinion. She visited a neurosurgeon in Philadelphia who told her about Jannetta and microvascular decompression. "At that point, surgery wasn't an 'option,' it was a necessity. I said to the Philadelphia doctor, 'I'm just going to say my prayers and go.' So he called Pittsburgh right then, when I was sitting in his office, and we set the date."

In the weeks before her clinic appointment with Jannetta, a new fear emerged. "I wasn't afraid of the surgery, I wasn't afraid of dying. What I feared most was that he would say, 'I'm sorry, I can't help you,' " says Madeline. "When he examined me and said, 'I think we can do something for you,' it was like a whole new world opening up in front of my eyes. I said to him, 'Well, I'm ready,' and he just smiled and said, 'Well, I am, too.' "

So now Madeline, covered with a light cotton blanket, lays on her gurney, waiting to be moved into Operating Room 8. At 7:20, Jannetta breezes in through the automatic doors and checks in at the OR desk before going over to Madeline and squeezing her hand. "We're going to get started here in a minute," he says to her, and Madeline replies, "I'm ready." Jannetta laughs. "I'm ready, too," he says and returns to the desk for a scrub suit before heading down the corridor to the surgeons's dressing room.

An orderly appears to wheel Madeline past the OR desk and around the corner to Room 8. The OR is already a bustle of activity. Nurse Lisa Hawkins, Chief of Neurosurgical Nursing, is inventorying and arranging rows of surgical instruments while explaining some of the intricacies to a new nurse on the service (at Presby, all new operating-room nurses rotate through each of the surgical services as part of their orientation). While the new nurse, Roxanne, will nominally be the "scrub," or sterile, nurse for Madeline's operation, she will be shadowed by Lisa Hawkins. After three years in Presby's operating rooms and hundreds of operations with Jannetta, Hawkins knows how to anticipate him; and during the course of Madeline's surgery, she will prompt Roxanne when the new nurse needs prompting, alternately nod or shake her head when Roxanne looks at her before handing Dr. Jannetta an instrument, and confer with Roxanne in whispers during lulls in the procedure, explaining to her how "to be invisible but always there," which is what a scrub nurse aspires to be.

Hawkins and Jannetta see eye to eye on how an operating room should be run. "*Everything* is always ready, and *every* operation is exactly the same," Hawkins says. "Jannetta is *so* fast, and he is so involved, that everything has to be ready, and everything has to be perfect. When I walk into the OR, I expect to be able to look at the wall shelves, the instrument tray, the worktable, and see everything exactly where it's supposed to be. Or someone hears about it."

This morning, as Madeline Cooper is being positioned on the operating table, Jannetta comes in wearing a blue surgical scrub suit, a green paper OR hat, and a green paper surgical mask held against his face by his right hand; he is checking on the preparation before scrubbing. "Do we have the lines in yet?" he asks the anesthesiology resident. He asks it jocularly; it is clear that the anesthesiologist's monitoring lines are not connected yet. He is simply anxious to get started. A voice comes from behind Madeline, who is now lying on her left side on the operating table, in the "lateral decubitus position"—her back is curved, her arms are out in front of her, and her knees are drawn up halfway to her chest.

"No, not yet—five more minutes," says the voice.

"Okay," says Jannetta, "I'm going to Twelve"—OR 12, where the other "first" patient of the day is being readied— "to see how they're doing there, and I'll be back in five minutes." He scans the room and spots Hawkins, who is talking to the new scrub nurse. "Lisa Lovely, how are we today?"

He is already halfway across the room to the door before she replies, a standard "Good morning, Doctor."

"When things are going well, it's 'Lisa Lovely'; when they're not, it's Li*SAA*, *c'mon*," she says.

The patient arranged to her satisfaction, the anesthesiology resident commences the administration of the anesthetic.

Neurosurgical cases are challenging to manage for the anesthesiologist for several reasons. First, only inhalation anesthetics are used, because neurosurgeons want their patients to
come out of anesthesia as soon as possible after the end of the
operation. Anesthetics that are administered intravenously
are more predictable in their effect but "paralyze" the patient
for long periods postoperatively. Thus, any possible complication—a blood clot, pressure on the breathing and circula-
tion control centers in the brain stem—would not necessarily
become apparent until long after there would be time to do
anything about it. "The neurosurgeons want to be able to talk
to the patient on the way to the recovery room," says one
anesthesiologist with only mild exaggeration. If the effects of
anesthesia linger too long after the operation, the neurosurgeon can't ask the patient questions, can't ask the patient to
move an arm or leg, can't be told about severe headaches
which might indicate that something's wrong in time to go
back in to the skull and fix it. Hence, the use of inhalation
anesthesia, which means that throughout the two or three
hours of surgery, the anesthesiologist will walk a tightrope
between anesthesia that is so deep that the patient's respiration
and blood pressure fall too low, and anesthesia that is too
shallow. Throughout Madeline's operation, the anesthesiologist is in constant motion, watching her monitors, checking
the level of gases in Madeline's blood, pinching Madeline's
fingernails to see how long it takes for the tissue beneath them
to turn from white to pink. She seems to pay not the slightest
bit of attention to what is happening on the other side of the
table. But let Jannetta ask "How's the pressure?" and the response is immediate: "Fine, one-twenty" or "Okay, one hundred." Like a television producer, the anesthesiologist follows
the course of the operation by watching her monitors.

While Madeline is being stabilized on the anesthesia, Dr.
Eric Altschuler, the resident who will assist Jannetta today,

methodically scrubs his hands in the scrub room adjacent to OR 8. Altschuler is a second-year resident who went to medical school at the University of Arizona, and his rotation through the hospitals of the University Health Center of Pittsburgh will last seven years, including his first-year internship. Madeline's operation today will be one of three in which he will be assisting this morning.

In years past, one often heard of a "neurosurgeon's personality"—someone who had the nerve and the confidence to take what the medical community often thought of as unacceptable risks. In the last twenty years, however, neurosurgery has changed as much as it had in its first seventy-five; with better anesthesia, a better understanding of the response of the brain's delicate tissues to the touch of an instrument, new diagnostic tools such as CT scanning, better monitoring, and the operating microscope, brain surgery no longer has unacceptability high mortality and its practitioners no longer are automatically thought of as reckless. Altschuler, with his wire-rimmed glasses and boyish grin, might be an accountant or a psychology major, except that they seldom begin the day by opening the skull of a client and peering inside.

While Altschuler scrubs, the circulating nurse, Mary, whose job it is to fetch instruments for the scrub nurse and keep a count of the materials used in the operation, begins to drape the operating microscope with sterile plastic. The surgical microscope might serve as a paradigm for what contemporary neurosurgery has become: high-tech, polished, versatile. It rolls quietly on casters, balanced with a counterweight the size of a watermelon, and contains not just the optical system that allows the surgeon to see, but a duplicate set of eyepieces—the teaching scope—that allows a second person to see exactly what the surgeon does. Generally, the attending surgeon will watch the resident's work through this until the resident reaches the limit of his experience; then they switch places, and the attending surgeon operates while the resident watches and learns. The process is accretive; no resident suddenly performs an operation from start to finish, but rather does a little bit more each time.

"I remember vividly the first time I did a case all the way through," says Dr. Mark Dias, a senior resident on the neurosurgical service. "I was going right along, just concentrating on what I was going to do next, and I realized that I was doing it without anyone telling me what to do. The attending was just sitting there very quietly at the side microscope, not saying anything, and I thought, 'That was it; I'm there.' It's an eerie feeling the first time to recognize that you've just done an entire operation without any help."

Dr. Don Marion, another senior neurosurgical resident, agrees. "Most of what you're thinking when you're operating is that 'It's important not to make any mistakes; I'm not going to do anything that I'm not absolutely sure about.' But gradually, you're sure of more and more; all the things you're worrying about are coming later and later in the procedure, and eventually you're thinking of the operation as a whole, not only as a series of steps. Then you're getting close."

For Altschuler, who is now rinsing the soap from his hands and arms, doing an entire operation—particularly a retromastoid craniectomy—is in the future. Today, he will prepare the skin, make the incision, control the surface bleeding, and open the skull. In a few months, he will open the dura mater—the smooth covering over the brain itself. In six months or a year, he will be perceptibly further along; the year after that, further along still. Eventually, he will take his turn in the rotation as chief resident and pick the cases that he will see all the way through. But this morning, he is learning to open and close.

Mary, the circulating nurse, finishes draping the scope; it now looks as though it has been poorly gift-wrapped in clear cellophane. She checks to make sure that the controls of the microscope, which look like bicycle handgrips, are covered properly and then stretches two foot pedals across the operating-room floor so that Roxanne, at Jannetta's request, can activate the 35-millimeter camera to take still photographs and the color videotape camera, which will record the view of the operation through the microscope.

Against one wall of the operating room, a video monitor sits on a cart. For those in the operating room who don't rank a look through the teaching eyepieces, it will be their only view of what is happening during the operation.

While the anesthesiologist has been been putting Madeline to sleep, her head has been placed in a three-point fixation head holder, which will keep her head perfectly still during the operation. Her right shoulder is taped down across her body, and she is also taped, across the hips, to the operating table so that the table may be tilted during the operation. When she was placed on the operating table, her head was at its foot so that Jannetta's knees would have room underneath the table when he sat on the stool he uses when he operates. And she is draped, and draped, and draped. First, a large green cloth drape covers her shoulders; to it is stapled a smaller drape across her head; then another layer is placed over this. All that is visible from the surgeon's side of the table now is the right side of the back of her head. The hair behind her ear is shaved away, and the skin is scrubbed with antiseptic and drenched again. Before antibiotics, if a patient got an infection, the patient died. Meningitis, an infection of the meninges that surround the brain and spinal cord, meant almost certain death, because the "blood-brain barrier" prevents the body's immune system from fighting off an infection inside the dural sac. Much of modern neurosurgery has developed around ways of preventing infection from occurring.

Altschuler backs into the room, hands held out in front in

the position known to most Americans as what a surgeon looks like just before operating. Roxanne hands him a sterile towel, and he dries his hands. Next comes the gowning, a practiced pirouette during which he steps into the sleeves of a green cloth surgical gown and the circulating nurse ties him in. Next come the gloves; one, then the other is held open, and he reaches down as though he is going to grab something off the floor. The gloves snap up around the cuff of the gown, and Altschuler is ready to enter the field.

First, he stretches a sheet of sterile Pliofilm across the shaved area behind Madeline's right ear. Next, he paints a line approximately five and a half centimeters long just behind (the "retro" in "retromastoid") Madeline's mastoid eminence, which is the bony protuberance one can feel behind each ear. Another sheet of Pliofilm is applied over the ink.

Jannetta comes in again. He has peered in through the window several times already. "Is this the same case?" he asks.

"Same case," says Altschuler, without turning around. One of the first things a resident on the neurosurgical service learns is that Jannetta likes things to move at a brisk clip, and his asking if this is the same case is Jannetta's way of making light of his impatience.

"They're just getting started in Twelve," says Dr. Jannetta. "I'm going to scrub here first. Are we ready to go, Lisa?"

"Ready to go," says Lisa Hawkins. She is helping Dr. Aage Møller string the lines for his auditory nerve monitoring equipment across Madeline's shoulder. During the course of Madeline's operation, Møller will monitor the performance of the eighth, or auditory, cranial nerve. Because the cerebellopontine angle is such a small place, the cerebellum must be retracted—moved back—in order for Jannetta to see and reach the trigeminal nerve. Moving the cerebellum, however, can stretch the auditory nerve. Stretch more than the slightest bit, and its function may be impaired.

But the cerebellum must be moved; there is no other way into the cerebellopontine angle that provides the exposure necessary for microvascular decompression. The solution hit upon by Drs. Møller and Jannetta is monitoring the patient's hearing on that side during the operation. Once the dura is opened, a tiny electrode will be attached to Madeline's auditory nerve, and short bursts of sound will be delivered into her ear through an earphone. The difference between the picture on Møller's oscilloscope of the sound going in and the sound coming out is described as the "latency." A latency, or delay, of 0.5 milliseconds is the benchmark; if the delay stays in that range, Madeline's hearing will not likely be affected. But if the cerebellum is moved in such a way as to increase the latency, Jannetta knows that he is doing something wrong to the eighth nerve, and he can change the position of the retractor. All through the operation, Jannetta will call out, "How we doing, Aage?" and Møller will reply with the latency range.

Jannetta enters the scrub room and methodically begins to wash his hands. As he does so, he also begins to hum, or rather starts humming again; on the days he operates, Jannetta's humming, punctuated by occasional snatches of lyrics, is commonplace. "I remember the shock I experienced when we first began recording the operations on videotape," he recalls as he scrubs. "I settled down to watch that first tape, and there was this humming in the background. 'Who the hell is humming?' I thought. It was apparently the same person who was cursing, because the humming would stop when the cursing began. I had always thought I was under perfect control in the operating room, and yet here was this foul-mouthed *crabby* jerk cursing under his breath—and occasionally cursing over it—and just being the kind of bastard I was always pleased that I wasn't. It was absolutely unconscious. I had no idea I sounded that way; and, of course, because of the way

I sounded, no one dared tell me. It really opened my eyes, and I resolved then and there I was going to clean up my act, because I *hated* surgeons who couldn't control themselves in the OR." He laughs. "I *think* I've cleaned up my act, anyway."

The scrubbing ritual lasts for about five minutes. Each time that Jannetta leaves the OR and returns, he will repeat it, so that when he is bouncing back and forth between cases, he may scrub five or six times for one pair of operations. He seldom is able to use more than two rooms at a time, but that isn't necessarily because he doesn't want to. Operating-room time is one of the most precious commodities in a hospital, and most surgeons wish for more time, more rooms. As for a schedule that puts him in two operating rooms at once, Jannetta maintains that it allows for two things: adequate training for the residents, and efficient use of his time. "It's a waste of everybody's time to do it any other way," Jannetta has said. "We've done thousands of operations with this system—literally thousands—with good results, so we must be doing something right."

A typical question asked by patients is: "Will you do the surgery?" Generations of Americans have for several reasons a generalized fear of the resident doctor. One reason often cited is that they are "only" students—they aren't really doctors, are they? Another reason has to do with the capitalist's desire to get his money's worth—if I'm paying Dr. Smith to do the operation, I want *him* to do the operation, not somebody else. A third reason is television: the antics of the residents on a show such as "St. Elsewhere" raise the viewer's consciousness in a particularly brutal and unenlightening way.

Physicians, particularly residents, scoff at these notions. "How do these people think surgeons like Jannetta came to do the things that they do?" asks Dias. "There may be—*may* be—a slightly higher risk in being operated on by a resident instead of the attending, but the truth is that the supervision and the guidance is there, and you're taught to recognize your limits. You don't learn neurosurgery by being turned loose in the OR. But you don't learn it just by watching someone else do it either."

If a patient balks at the idea of a resident participating, even after Jannetta's patient explanation of how things will go, Jannetta raises the suggestion that the patient might be happier having the surgery performed elsewhere. "I tell them I have to be free to do things the way I think they ought to be done, and I think that having the resident assist is the way things ought to be done," says Jannetta. "I tell them that this is the way that I learned, and that it's going to be the way that the residents here learn."

Sometimes, however, patients automatically assume that Jannetta will be doing their operations from incision to suture, and are disconcerted to find out otherwise. "One time I went in to visit two ladies who were both scheduled for seven-thirty procedures with Jannetta and who happened to be roommates—this was the evening before surgery," says Dias. "They had been talking to each other, and they both knew they were scheduled for the same time. And when I asked if they had any questions, one said, 'Well, how is he going to operate on both of us at once?' So I explained how it worked, how there was a resident assisting on each case, and how Jannetta went back and forth between the two cases. They were a little apprehensive, so we talked about it for quite a while; by the time I left, they had both decided that it was okay if Jannetta did it that way. But whose OR would I be in? They had decided that they both wanted me, and wondered if I could go back and forth, too." Dias laughs. "Most of the time, the question of residents comes up as a manifestation of the patient's preop anxiety; I've never heard of a patient who took Jannetta up on his offer to arrange for the surgery at another hospital."

When he can reserve the time in the operating room, Jannetta likes to do five or six cases on his OR days, which are generally Tuesdays and Wednesdays. If he misses one of these days because he's out of town, he might operate on a Monday or a Friday—"A week without surgery is a week without fun," he says as he backs into OR 8 and takes the towel from Lisa Hawkins. He is gowned and gloved in seconds. Unlike Altschuler, he wears a disposable green paper gown with a belt that wraps around his waist before being tied. It hangs just to his knees. "Okay, Doctor, let's get this show on the road," he says in between snatches of lyrics from the old song "Lazybones."

"Okay to start?" asks Altschuler.

The anesthesiologist waits a moment and replies, "Whenever."

Altschuler takes the scalpel from Roxanne and elegantly makes his incision. It is 8:23 A.M. when Madeline's operation actually begins.

It is generally believed that the first surgical operation for the treatment of *tic douloureux*—trigeminal neuralgia—was carried out in the mid-1700s. A case report by the French surgeon Nicholas André in 1756 detailed the exposure of the intraorbital branch of the nerve and its destruction with a caustic liquid. André, of course, did not open the skull, but instead dealt only with the branches of the nerve within the skin. Since then, the trigeminal nerve has been burned, cut, stretched, injected with alcohol, and otherwise abused. Jannetta's technique is less traumatic for the nerve but potentially more dangerous for the patient, because the cerebellopontine angle is an unforgiving place to operate. Risks include dangers from the anesthesia, the chance of infection, the possibility of a blood clot, trauma to the brain stem and the cerebellum, the loss of hearing. The surgical microscope has removed some of the danger, and the availability of specialized instruments and intraoperative monitoring also have helped. But one does not enter the cerebellopontine angle without a compelling reason for doing so, and one does not enter without extreme care.

For Madeline Cooper, much of that care has begun long before Altschuler made his incision. There are the monitors; there is the trained team of professionals who make the operation as safe as possible. But, ultimately, her prognosis is in the hands of Jannetta. She made the decision to have the surgery in the hopes that it will free her from the pain. She also hopes that she will fare better than many of the thousands who suffered before her when neurosurgery was in its infancy. They are her predecessors, too.

"Bipolar," Altschuler says softly, almost apologetically, and Roxanne hands him the bipolar coagulators, a device that is the third and fourth hands of a surgeon. Looking like a pair of electric tweezers, the bipolars use low voltage current to seal up the blood vessels that were severed when Altschuler cut through Madeline's scalp. It makes a buzzing sound. Roxanne alternately provides irrigation with sterile water and suction as Altschuler methodically works his way around the wound. Next, the muscles and fascia that lie under the skin are opened, and a self-retaining scalp retractor is used to spread the incision wide and hold it open.

"Periosteal," says Altschuler, and he begins to pull back the periosteum, the tough covering over the skull. Jannetta is humming but looking over the resident's shoulder. "What's all that blood doing there?" he asks, and Altschuler is handed the coagulators again. Irrigation, suction, coagulation, and then the periosteal elevator. At 8:59, the field is clear, the bone of the skull is exposed cleanly, and Roxanne hands Altschuler

69

a pneumatic drill powered by compressed nitrogen with which he opens a hole in Madeline's skull.

The drilling lasts only for a few seconds; a pressure sensor in the bit stops the drill automatically when it touches the dura. The hole is relatively small—much less than an inch in diameter at this stage—and Altschuler will use rongeur forceps—a pair of biting pliers—to clip away the bone until the opening is 2 × 2.5 centimeters (about the size of a quarter). As Altschuler inserts the jaws of the rongeur into the burr hole, Jannetta steps around him and watches the wound closely; Jannetta is still singing softly under his breath. *Snip.* The first sliver of bone is bitten away. (The bone chips will be saved to pack back into the wound after the operation so that the patient will have no "soft spot" in the skull.) *Snip.* Another sliver. "Get your point up," says Jannetta, and Altschuler changes the angle at which he holds the rongeur but apparently not to Jannetta's satisfaction, because Jannetta sharply repeats, *"Up, up, up."* Altschuler changes the orientation again, but before he can squeeze the handle, Jannetta deftly reaches in and pulls the handle of the rongeur down, which raises the point up. "C'mon, this is *up*. Raise the damn thing *up*," he says. Jannetta lets go, and Altschuler holds the rongeur exactly in the position Jannetta left it in. "You don't want it poking down into the dura, do you," he says—a statement. *Snip.*

Fifteen minutes later, the opening in the skull is satisfactory to both Drs. Jannetta and Altschuler. It is a rectangular hole that still looks very small. Bone wax is applied around the edges of the hole in the skull. Since the skull is not solid, some of it being made up of sinuses—holes—and some being fibrous tissue and fluid, the putty-like wax is used to fill these openings in the edge of the bone so that the sinuses don't leak.

Now the dura is opened. The dura mater is a tough, fibrous tissue that covers the outside surfaces of the brain; it is watertight and impervious, the brain's last defense. Fossil skulls have been found that bear the marks of craniectomy—prehistoric man's ritual trephining of the skull to let the demons out, perhaps—and some of the skulls show that the bone had healed, indicating that the patient had lived for some time after the operation. But they did not open the dura, because infection would have killed the patient long before the bone had begun to knit.

Altschuler steps back now, and Jannetta steps in; Altschuler will not open the dura today. Jannetta makes a swift, delicate curved incision in the dura, and in a matter of seconds has stitched it back with sutures so that it forms a flap, out of his way. *"Lazybones, sleeping in the sun, how you gonna get your day's work done?"* Jannetta sings as he places the Jannetta self-retaining pillar and post retractor into the wound. He designed the retractor out of the parts of two more complicated brain retractors, and the manufacturer, V. Muller, markets the retractor as the "Jannetta Posterior Fossa Retractor Set" along with Jannetta microforceps, Jannetta angular dissectors, Jannetta alligator grasping forceps, and even the Jannetta sterilizing and storage rack to keep them in—four pages worth in the V. Muller *Surgical Armamentarium,* among instruments designed by Mayo and Yasargil and Cushing and Apfelbaum. In medicine, as in tennis, endorsements count.

The self-retaining retractor solves one of the primary problems in operations in the cerebellopontine angle—gentle and precise retraction of the cerebellum. No matter how gently the tissue of the brain is touched, bruising results; as bruising is minimized, so are morbidity and mortality. The Jannetta retractor has adjustable posts and clamps that allow the blades—the parts that actually hold the cerebellum back out of the way to expose the cranial nerves—to be adjusted in small increments, and to be reoriented easily in order to improve the exposure or to relieve stress on the auditory nerve.

"Never get your day's work done, lyin' in the noonday sun," sings Jannetta softly as he adjusts the retractor. "Okay, let's have the scope over," he says, and the circulating nurse begins to wrestle the microscope over toward the operating table. It is almost a draw: the microscope is not only taller than Mary, but outweighs her by at least a factor of two. Slowly it moves toward the table. Jannetta waits with his back to the scope for what seems to be sufficient time, then turns around and asks, "Why do we always have the smallest person in the room push the microscope around?"

No one answers, but three other people in the operating room, including Dr. Møller, spring forward to help her move the microscope. With the added propulsion, it threatens for a moment to roll right over Jannetta. "Stop, stop, stop, stop," he says. "Okay, stool in, glasses off."

There are three stools in the operating room, the nearest raised to a height convenient for an observer using the teaching scope. The circulating nurse begins to spin the seat to lower it. Jannetta glances at her, looking as though he would be drumming his fingers on the operating table if he weren't scrubbed. He points to another stool. "Here—here's one that's already low, honey," he says. Mary gives up on the stool she had been working on and wheels over the lower one. She reaches up to take off his half-glasses and slides the stool in behind him. He sits and says immediately, "Wet stool. Am I sitting in water?"

"It's just cold," says Hawkins, and she snatches a drape off a stack and crouches behind him. "Lift up," she says.

"Too late," says Jannetta. He rocks back and forth on the stool. One of its legs is sitting on top of an electrical cord. "Don't we have one that's not so wobbly?"

Mary and Hawkins both reach down for the cord. "Up," says Hawkins, Jannetta rises slightly, and she jerks the cord out from under the leg of the stool. At last he's settled. Lisa says something to the circulating nurse, who nods.

"All right, let's have your famous forceps now," he says to Roxanne. It is 9:29 A.M. when the preliminaries are finally finished and the operation begins in earnest.

For some reason, perhaps an atavistic belief in safety in numbers, the number of people on a surgical team is often of interest to those curious about what happens in the operating room. Some patients take both pride and encouragement at the presence of visitors, particularly if the visitors are from a foreign country. One of Jannetta's patients, a man from Michigan operated on for relief of vertigo, kept a careful census of the visitors to Dr. Jannetta's operating room and their country of origin. "On the day he operated on me, there were two visitors from England and one from Holland," says Barry Carlson. "And, of course, there was Dr. Sen, who is here on a fellowship. He's originally from India."

When told that in the previous week—the day of Madeline Cooper's operation—there were two visitors from Sweden and one from Italy, Barry's grin grows wider. "He must be doing something right to have all these people coming to watch him work. Just think, a man that people come to watch from all over the world is *my* doctor!"

For Chief Nurse Lisa Hawkins, the visitors can sometimes be a travail; Madeline Cooper's operating room does seem crowded. For one thing, her own presence is in a sense unusual; she is there to help Roxanne, when there usually would be only one scrub nurse. There is also Dr. Møller and his two technicians; they tend to stay over near Møller's monitors and, thus, do not really add to the crowding, except when they come over to watch the video monitor. There is also a resident from the neurology service. The time is long past at the University of Pittsburgh when neurosurgeons and neurologists had little to do with each other; residents from

73

neurosurgery regularly rotate through neurology, and vice versa. Also watching Madeline's operation is a third-year medical student, a member of the hospital's Public Relations Department, a visiting writer, the two surgeons from Sweden who have stopped off en route to California to visit with Møller and see Peter Jannetta work, and a visiting surgeon from Italy who is spending a week at Presbyterian-University Hospital with Jannetta. This is in addition to the circulating nurse and the anesthesiology resident. "Who *are* all these people?" Lisa Hawkins asks at one point. Jannetta usually introduces the visitors, but today, either because the presence of the Swedish visitors was a surprise or because he thought Møller had already done so, he has not. The room does seem crowded.

Jannetta begins the dissection of the pia arachnoid, the spiderweblike connective tissue that lines the cerebellopontine angle. He is using the microscope now, and Altschuler perches on a high stool and peers into the teaching scope. Across the room, the visitors crowd around the video monitor and watch as the arachnoid is clipped away. The difference between the image on the video monitor and the image in the microscope is one of dimension and resolution; after watching the operation on the monitor, the view through the teaching scope is startling—most prominent is the clarity of the depth of field. On the monitor, one sees only in two dimensions, as if one were watching "St. Elsewhere." Through the scope, one sees all the different layers clearly and in proportion. The view most closely resembles that of a Victorian stereoscopic postcard viewer, except that the colors are brilliant: red and white and gray and the silver of the instruments as Jannetta inserts them into the cerebellopontine angle.

"All right, let's roll the tape, Roxy," says Jannetta.

And Roxanne steps on the foot pedal that activates the videotape camera and replies, "Tape on."

"Dr. Altschuler, why don't you tell us about Mrs. Cooper?" asks Jannetta as he adjusts the retractor to allow better exposure of the underside of the brain.

"Mrs. Cooper is a fifty-five-year-old special-education teacher from Philadelphia," begins Altschuler, "who first experienced symptoms of TGN in nineteen eighty-one. She thought it was a toothache. After extractions and a root canal, she was diagnosed as having trigeminal neuralgia and was placed on Tegretol, which was only partially successful. She has labile hypertension and pain in Vee-one and Vee-two."

"Labile hypertension" is high blood pressure that is not constant—Madeline Cooper's blood pressure is not always high; "Vee-one" (V_1) and "Vee-two" (V_2) refer to regions of her face where the pain occurs.

"And does she have trigger points?" asks Jannetta.

"Multiple trigger points," says Altschuler. "She stated that chewing food, face washing, and even a light breeze on the face would cause an episode."

"We're right over Eight here," says Jannetta. "We usually start a bit lower. I'm about to put the electrode in, Aage," and he feeds the tiny monitoring electrode wire into the cerebellopontine angle.

"Okay, Peter," says Møller. "We're ready when you are."

Jannetta pushes the electrode in with a pair of microforceps and touches it against Madeline's eighth nerve. On the monitor, the electrode is a wispy, threadlike snake; the auditory nerve is grayish and runs across the top of the image on the screen.

"Electrode's on," calls Jannetta.

"Okay, Peter," says Møller.

Now on Møller's monitor, two jagged lines appear, one on the upper half of the oscilloscope and one on the lower. Møller and the technicians peer at it with interest. "About a one-half millisecond delay, Peter," Møller calls. The upper jagged line indicates the sound going into the auditory nerve through the earphone in Madeline's ear, the sound waves being converted into electrical impulses; the lower line is what the impulse looks like when it passes the electrode that Jannetta has attached to her eighth nerve inside the cerebello-pontine angle. Ideally, the two images would be almost the same. When one of the technicians turns a dial, he superimposes the second wave over the first. If the images were identical, there would be no "latency," or delay, at all. This would violate the laws of physics, because there is no perfect conductor of electricity—there will always be a slight difference between the two images. For the rest of the operation, Dr. Møller will continuously monitor the function of the auditory nerve; a small computer stores the data on floppy disks so that at any time in the future he may review Madeline's eighth nerve function at any point in the operation. Six or seven years ago, the neurosurgeon had only dexterity and intuition to use in the effort to avoid hearing loss in a patient undergoing microvascular decompression: Møller's monitors are the equivalent of performing a hearing test continuously throughout the operation. Hearing loss, once the most common complication of procedures in the cerebellopontine angle, is now relatively rare.

"Tilt the table toward me, please," says Jannetta.

The circulating nurse goes to the head of the table and says, "Tilting the table now." She presses a lever, and the table is tilted electrically toward Jannetta.

"Stop," he says.

In order to find the blood vessel he expects to find compressing Madeline's trigeminal nerve, Jannetta does two things. First, he changes the position of the retractor that holds her cerebellum away from the origins of the cranial nerves. Second, he tilts the table to change the perspective of the microscope. And he gently, delicately, explores the cerebellopontine angle with the use of microsurgical hooks and forceps.

"Forty-five hook," he says, and Roxanne hands him a microsurgical tool that tapers to a point and ends in a 45-degree angle. With it, he lifts away a strand of arachnoid.

"Forceps." The microforceps are long and elegant, and angle down 45 degrees between the handle and the blade so that the surgeon may see what he is reaching for instead of seeing his fingers. "Surgical skill" may sound redundant; most neurosurgeons are amazingly dextrous (it is difficult to be a neurosurgeon without being so). But are there differences in skill—*tangible* differences in skill? Lisa Hawkins has a story she likes to tell about Peter Jannetta and his hands. "Once he was doing a procedure, and he asked for the microforceps. As soon as he had them in his hand, he said, 'These don't feel right, Lisa.' So I took them back, and I looked at them, and they looked fine—they felt all right to *me*. So I handed them back, and right away he said, 'Nope, there's something wrong here.' So I took them and *really* looked at them closely. And down at the tip there was the tiniest crack imaginable—just a thin, thin line. You couldn't see it unless you were looking for it, and even then it was hard. He could tell it, though—immediately. And it wasn't because he saw it. It was just because they didn't feel the way they were supposed to feel."

"Tilt the table away from me a little, please," says Jannetta.

"Tilting the table."

"Stop."

Jannetta moves the retractor. "Okay, there we are, there's a vein running right through the nerve. Can you see it on the screen?" he asks.

On the video monitor, the vein looks like a tiny dark line

running parallel to the trigeminal nerve where the nerve emerges from the brain stem. Jannetta lifts at it with a probe. "How we doin', Aage?" he asks.

"Still about a half-millisecond delay."

"Forty-five hook." A pause. "Ninety hook." A pause. "Forty-five hook."

To observe Jannetta when he operates is to observe a man hunched on a small stool, staring into a microscope. His arms rarely move except to withdraw an instrument and receive another one. Some operations take three hours, and in that time he may not move from the stool or the microscope, but sits patiently exploring. "I'm looking around the other side here, now, but this is exactly what we expected to find," he says. "It's right where it's supposed to be."

Patiently, he probes and probes, trying to mobilize the vein away from the nerve. If the offending blood vessel were an artery, his task would be to mobilize it away so that shreds of Teflon could be interposed between the blood vessel and the nerve. Since this is a vein, he must move it into such a position that he can coagulate it with the bipolar coagulator and divide it in two—veins are dispensable, arteries are not. If the vein is broken before it is coagulated, blood would obscure the field and he would be trying to coagulate two separate pieces of a bleeding vessel. To coagulate it, though, it must be in a position so as not to damage a branch of the nerve with the heat of the bipolars. And all of this is accomplished through an opening in the dura the size of a quarter.

"Okay, how about a forty-five hook and a big hook in the same hand?" This is a new one for Roxanne, but she deftly slips the two instruments into his hand like chopsticks.

"Nope," says Jannetta almost immediately. He was hoping to tease the vein off the nerve using the two hooks as a sort of primitive pair of forceps, but he cannot get near the vein and see what he is doing at the same time. He pulls the instruments out and holds them toward the scrub nurse, his eyes still glued to the microscope.

Roxanne takes the right-angled hook—the "big hook." But because Jannetta had the forty-five hook in his hand already, should she take it, too? She hesitates for a moment—only a moment—and then Jannetta's voice booms. *"Take them both, damnit, c'mon. C'mon, Lisa, teach her!."*

Roxanne takes the offending instrument as Lisa Hawkins, who was across the room at the time, moves quickly toward her. But there is nothing for her to do. Jannetta is humming again.

"Tilt the table away."

"Tilting the table."

"Stop."

"Let me have a probe. Have we got the Apfelbaum bipolars here?"

The Apfelbaum bipolar microcoagulators have a forty-five-degree bend in the tip; one pair tilts up, and the other pair tilts down. And they are not on Roxanne's tray. "Noo," says Hawkins, and she begins to move through the group of people huddled around the monitor toward the door.

"That's all right," says Jannetta. But she is already gone and reappears in seconds with a drape-wrapped oblong package. She opens back the drape and holds it toward Roxanne, who opens it the rest of the way and exposes a tray of instruments, including the Apfelbaum coagulators. The circulating nurse changes the wires on the coagulator's power source to the Apfelbaums. "They're ready," says Roxanne.

No response. Humming. On the monitor, the probe runs up and down along the vein; with only a two-dimensional perspective, it is difficult to see exactly what the problem is. Because of this, Altschuler at the teaching scope has been displaced by a string of interested onlookers—first the visitor from Italy, then the Swedish surgeons, then the neurology

79

resident. It is 9:59 A.M., and Dr. Don Marion, senior resident in neurosurgery who has begun the case in OR 12, is probably waiting for Jannetta. The next case in OR 8, Madeline's room, is scheduled for 10:30, but Jannetta does not seem rushed. He patiently probes the vein that runs along Madeline's trigeminal nerve.

The view through the teaching scope reveals the problem in three dimensions: the vein is running *in* among the nerve branches near the root of the trigeminal nerve. Jannetta has been trying to mobilize it away from the nerve branches so that he may coagulate it. Five minutes later, he does. "Okay, let's have the Apfelbaums on one," he says. "One" is the setting on the coagulator. The lower the number, the less current and, hence, the less heat produced at the tip of the coagulators as they complete the circuit and seal the vein.

"Bipolars on one," says the circulating nurse.

"Bipolars on," says Jannetta. The on/off switch is controlled by Roxanne with a foot pedal. There is a hum. "Off," says Jannetta.

"On." The hum.

"Off."

"On. There's something wrong with these. What's it set on?" he asks.

"One," say three people simultaneously.

And then the circulating nurse says, "Do you want it on two?"

"*No,*" says Jannetta. "On. There we go." He has coagulated the vein that has been causing Madeline Cooper's trigeminal neuralgia for the past five years, just like that.

The rest of the operation moves swiftly. The vein is divided—cut—across where the bipolars have sealed it, and Jannetta moves the retractor one more time. "I'm just taking a quick look around here—make sure I haven't missed anything," he says. "Everything okay, Aage?"

"Fine, Peter."

"Okay, I'd like Valsalva in a minute here, please," Jannetta says to the anesthesiologist. The Valsalva maneuver, initiated by the anesthesiologist, strains the circulatory system in such a way as to allow the surgeon to check for possible bleeding.

"Okay," says the anesthesiologist.

And Jannetta says, "Now is fine."

"Valsalva, one-thousand-one, one-thousand-two, one-thousand-three."

"Again," says Jannetta.

"One-thousand-one, one-thousand-two, one-thousand-three."

Satisfied, Jannetta now removes the electrode from the auditory nerve and then eases the retractor blade away from the cerebellum. "Okay. Call upstairs, and tell them everything is fine," Jannetta says, and the circulating nurse reaches for the wall phone. This is one of Jannetta's rules: you always call upstairs and tell the family that everything is fine.

The screen on the video monitor blurs as he stitches the dura mater closed. The microscope comes away, and Dr. Altschuler steps in to finish closing. It is 10:20 A.M. when Jannetta tears off his gown and gloves, and takes a quick look around the room. "Hey, a couple more of these and you're gonna be a *star*, Roxy," he says to Roxanne. "Okay?"

She nods.

"Got the lines in the next one?" Jannetta asks in a loud voice.

And someone says, "Yes, he's right out there in the hall." It is a joke. It will probably be 11:30 before the next patient is ready in OR 8.

"Okay, thank you everybody, thank you," Jannetta says. "I'm going to twelve now."

And he moves quickly out of the room, humming "Lazybones."

Altschuler carefully packs in the bone chips saved from the opening of the skull and begins the stitching of the soft tissues. At 10:45, he finishes with the scalp, and Madeline Cooper is whisked to the Postanesthesia Recovery Room, where she will be monitored as she awakens from the anesthesia. From there, she will spend the night in Presby's Unit 84, the Neurosurgical Continuous Care Unit. She will stay six nights in the hospital and, one week after her surgery, will return to her home in Philadelphia, pain-free for the first time in nearly five years.

3

A Little Bit of Fuzz

When one watches the smoothly functioning world of microvascular decompression in the 1980s, it is difficult to imagine that any part of that world might be tinged with uncertainty. At Presbyterian-University Hospital, the program resembles nothing so much as a medium-sized manufacturing concern, where patients come in, are evaluated, scheduled, tested, operated on, observed, tested again, and sent away—a dozen or so a week, forty or forty-five weeks each year. Similarly, around this assembly line for the treatment of cranial-nerve disorders has grown a network of cottage industries—the residency program, the Center for Clinical Neurophysiology, the technicians and nurses and physicians' assistants who manage the patients and the specialized equipment, the clinical coordinators and administrators who try and assure a semblance of order in the scheduling, treatment, follow-up, and billing procedures. The business of microvascular decompression runs like a well-managed production facility, and those who work in it and run it have no more doubt about the efficacy of—and the demand for—their product than does Toyota or General

Foods. It seems a long time ago to some of them that anyone was uncertain about the efficacy; and to the rest, such as those who have joined the firm in the last ten years or so, there hasn't been any uncertainty.

Or, perhaps, any day-to-day uncertainty. Everyone affiliated with the Department of Neurosurgery at Presby (and a large number who aren't affiliated) knows that the chief has been surrounded by controversy for a long time. But they tend to think about it in the abstract, the way that people who work for Ted Turner are never surprised when the boss is in the news; such knowledge seems part of the territory.

In terms of how changes in the field of medicine come about, however, it wasn't so long ago that Peter Jannetta was out there on his own, so to speak, without the forces of a large and successful institution behind him. In 1966, when all that would be microvascular decompression was new, Jannetta experienced firsthand the responsibility that comes with having a new idea.

The most difficult part of re-creating what it was like is a result of it having been such a short time ago by medical standards. Jannetta's old chief at UCLA only retired in 1986; his cohort, Robert W. Rand, with whom Jannetta co-wrote his first paper on microvascular decompression, is still practicing at UCLA; W. J. Gardner, the Cleveland Clinic neurosurgeon who performed the first decompressions of the trigeminal nerve, although he didn't use the surgical operating microscope, retired in the 1960s. (Jannetta has in fact reoperated on several of Gardner's patients—at the time Gardner was working, a bit of Gelfoam, which is absorbable, wound in between the blood vessel and the nerve was the most satisfactory implant material available. But as this Gelfoam was slowly reabsorbed, the condition recurred, and those early patients sought out the theoretical heir.) In terms of the history of medicine, it all happened yesterday.

Jannetta's theory, based on the three-part observation of the anatomical relationship of blood vessels and cranial nerves in cadavers, the one hemifacial-spasm case where decompression of the nerve resulted in alleviation of the symptoms, and a dozen cases in which he performed partial sectioning of the trigeminal nerve while observing similar compression was, unhappily for him, tailor-made to upset his profession. Part of the upset had to do with Jannetta's age and rank; part had to do with his use of the surgical microscope; part had to do with the profession's relationship to new ideas; and, finally, part had to do with Jannetta's own unawareness of these things. It sounds naïve, but he really just wanted to practice surgery, and he thought he had a good idea. To him, it was natural to let people know about it.

In this way, Jannetta was one of his own enemies—not the worst, but one of them; he had always been. The very method by which he had ended up in a neurosurgical residency program in the first place made him stand out. He had entered a general surgical residency after medical school, rather than moving directly into subspecialty training. He chose neurosurgery not out of any long-standing desire to be a neurosurgeon, but because he had a meeting with his professors at Penn and they all kicked around the possibilities. Several of those he trusted thought that neurosurgery had great potential in terms of growth and research, so that was what he picked. The general-surgery residency was unusual (now, would-be surgeons enter the specialty of their choice directly from medical school); too, general surgery is a different world from neurosurgery. But the general-surgery residency allowed Jannetta to stay at Penn, which at the time he wanted to do. The payoff was when Penn was selected as one of the sites for a new kind of fellowship training, a program sponsored by the National Institutes of Health for subspecialty training in surgery. Jannetta's mentors in the program there—principally Dr. Brooke Roberts of the Department of Surgery and Dr. Sol Erulkar of the Department of Pharmacology—decided Jannetta would be their fellow. All that remained was to choose the area of specialization.

Unlike most people who end up being neurosurgeons, Jannetta had no strong or abiding passion for the field. (A more typical would-be neurosurgeon is Dr. Mark Dias, who knew by age eight he would be a surgeon and by high school that he would work exclusively with the brain.) In fact, Jannetta was leaning toward cardiac surgery, a particularly prominent field at Penn in the late 1950's. Neurosurgery, by contrast, was not a high-profile specialty at Penn, and the specialty as a whole still had a somewhat checkered reputation. Because neurosurgery is such a clinically oriented field—that is, because the vast majority of the progress comes only from operations on patients—the influence of the practitioners, rather than that of the theoreticians or the lab researchers, is pervasive. The neurosurgeons at the height of the profession in the 1950s were by and large men who had trained in the 1920s and 1930s. There were neurosurgeons practicing in the 1950s who had trained under Harvey Cushing or his colleagues—the internal-medicine equivalent of training under someone who had studied with Pasteur. The NIH Fellowship Program in Academic Surgery was intended to begin regularizing the training of students in surgical specialties by giving them training in the laboratory—and to try to keep promising surgeons within the academy.

So Jannetta spent fifteen months as a fellow in Sol Erulkar's Neurophysiology Laboratory, working on experiments on the spinal cords of cats. It was here that he learned the value of basic research to the surgeon, which led him to institute the one year of basic science research for residents at Pitt much later in his career.

It was also in the lab at Penn that Jannetta first got to use an operating microscope, and, as Sol Erulkar recalls, Jannetta was captivated. "Peter was very, very taken with the microscope," he says. "At the time, we were working on intracellular monitoring of single nerve cells in the spinal cord, which required a very delicate dissection. Early on, Peter perfected the use of the microscope, got used to seeing things under high resolution, which, of course, later was of much importance in his work at UCLA."

What Jannetta also developed at Penn was, says Erulkar, the ability to take advantage of a certain kind of freedom. "The timing was right for someone like Peter to happen," he says. "The milieu in medical research, the atmosphere, at that time was such that a researcher could be creative. It was possible to work a bit more at the edges of a specialty. I'm not sure that something like that could happen today."

It helped that Jannetta was an independent thinker, someone who "liked to get to the bottom of things," as Dr. Brooke Roberts describes it. "He never was one to simply accept the common wisdom. In general, it's the younger ones in the profession who tend to have the open minds and the older generation who tests them, and Peter certainly was tested."

Roberts remembers discussing Jannetta's cranial-nerve compression work at the height of this testing, when many of the established physicians in the field were calling it a hoax. "He was sort of matter-of-fact about it. I remember him saying, 'It fits the facts; it makes sense,' and I told him that if he was right, he'd be *proven* right. I think he was a bit astonished at some of the resistance."

The resistance to Jannetta's work was primarily focused on three points: first, that the theory itself was wrong—that a blood vessel pressing on a cranial nerve could not be the cause of something like trigeminal neuralgia and that trigeminal neuralgia could not be relieved by putting in a "little bit of fuzz," as one critic referred to the felt Jannetta uses to decompress the blood vessel; second, that Jannetta ought not to be messing around like that anyway, since acceptable treatments, many involving less medical risk, were already available; and, third, that what Jannetta was talking about was exactly what Walter Dandy and others had already "discovered" and Jannetta was fraudulent in suggesting that he had found anything new. This last line of defense still haunts Jannetta. He is scrupulously careful always to make reference to the work of Dandy and Gardner when he points out the distinctions between his work and theirs—that cranial-nerve compression is significant only when it occurs at the root entry zone of the nerve, not farther along the nerve, and that Gardner was limited by not using the operating microscope. But one of the first criticisms of Jannetta's theory was that "he hadn't done the reading"—hadn't examined the work of his predecessors with sufficient throroughness—and that he needed at least to finish his residency before claiming to make far-reaching discoveries.

As Jannetta came to understand later, these reactions might have been—and perhaps should have been—expected. At the time, however, he was puzzled and more than a bit frustrated. Interestingly, at about the time that Jannetta was first talking to people about microvascular decompression and encountering resistance to the idea, a young physicist was encountering similar resistance to work of his own—a long essay not about physics, but about the way scientific revolutions happen. When Jannetta read *The Structure of Scientific Revolutions* by Thomas Kuhn, he came to understand something about science and scientists, and about settling in for the long haul.

Kuhn wrote about how scientific communities react to major change, and about how new ideas within a community become assimilated or don't. He would understand the reaction to Jannetta's work by the neurosurgical community as Jannetta finally came to understand it. The three most common reactions that Jannetta encountered—that the work was a hoax, that the work was unnecessary, and that the work was derivative—fit perfectly with Kuhn's schematic about how scientific communities can behave. The first point, that the theory was incorrect, is in retrospect the most predictable. The world of neurosurgery is a hierarchical and political one (as most scientific communities are), with set ideas and common understandings—what Kuhn calls "paradigms." The paradigm about trigeminal neuralgia in the mid-1960s was something like "The only way to treat the trigeminal nerve is to partially destroy it." And while methods varied, all accepted treatments for TGN were based on this paradigm. Jannetta's was not. Hence, the neurosurgical world could be expected to react strongly and adversely to a theory that threatened one of its paradigms. Accepting such a theory would mean acknowledging that something the community had accepted was in fact wrong.

The second point, that Jannetta's work was unnecessary because acceptable treatments already existed, also fit a paradigm of the neurosurgical world, one that might be paraphrased as "The procedures that are the least risky are the best; risky procedures must provide great benefits." This paradigm still holds to some degree within the profession. For every patient with trigeminal neuralgia who chooses surgery for microvascular decompression, there are perhaps twenty who choose, or are counseled to choose, less interventional therapy—for example, rhizotomy. It is unlikely that everyone with trigeminal neuralgia or hemifacial spasm will eventually be treated through surgery, because as the profession of neurosurgery has matured, it has also become more cautious—rightfully so, in many cases. (For example, one of what Jannetta calls "his many false starts" involved treatment of patients with a condition called "carotid cavernous sinus fistula"—an abnormal passage between the internal carotid artery and one of the large venous sinuses within the brain. The treatment consisted of having a cardiac surgeon stop the patient's heart and put the patient on a heart/lung machine, which allowed Jannetta to control bleeding and blood loss while he closed the passageway. While this could be said to have worked, the risks turned out to outweigh the advantages—setting a broken leg might be easier for the doctor, and work just as well, if the patient were under general anesthesia, but no one recommends this.) The profession as a whole has grown to ask not "Can I do that?" but "Should I do that?" If Jannetta's theory was well accepted by his peers, as has gradually happened, this paradigm would be re-evaluated—that is, if everyone agreed that the results were excellent, an examination of the risks and the benefits could be made somewhat objectively. But because his theory contradicted the paradigm about risk, many thought it was foolish even to consider performing microvascular decompression.

The third point is common to new work in any organized community of investigators. One of the first things that a casual reader of a medical journal (or a journal of literary criticism or political science or horticulture) notices are the footnotes—columns and columns of footnotes. Footnotes are one way of paying homage to one's predecessors, of demonstrating that one has done one's homework, and of suggesting the historical framework of the work being reported. Traditional novels rarely have footnotes, because a traditional novelist is assumed to be presenting a completely individual creative work. The work of academic physicians, as highly individual and creative as it may be, is seldom based on one individual's work. For one thing, it is impossible to operate on a patient's brain alone; for another, almost everything imaginable has been thought about or tried in one fashion or another. Jannetta's after-the-fact search of the literature turned up not only Dandy's articles, but Gardner's and several isolated case reports by others as well. It is reasonable to suggest that the reason that no one ever followed up, that the theory of cranial-nerve compression never caught on before Jannetta *made* it catch on, had to do with a paradigm that members of all scientific communities are familiar with, one that might be stated: "If this idea were any good, we would already know about it." Jannetta was seen by some as claiming to have found a definitive answer to a vexing question, when all he was really doing was what Dandy and others before Jannetta had tried. And if it were effective, it would have caught on before.

Two more factors at least contributed to the initial reception of Jannetta's work and both reinforce Kuhn's theories about how science changes. The first factor was Jannetta's use of the operating microscope. The neurosurgical establishment—"the grand old men" of the profession—were not as entranced as Jannetta was with the microscope. Until the early 1970s, neurosurgical techniques were primarily gross techniques, as they were when Cushing and Dandy were practicing. A common measure of a surgeon's skill was how good his eyesight was. (There are stories—perhaps apocryphal—about surgeons who would *remove* their eyeglasses when they entered the operating room: they might need them to read the footnotes in a medical journal, but their eyes were still good enough to do brain surgery.) Thus, neurosurgical programs were slow to acquire microscopes, and residents were slow to learn to use them—the senior members of the departments sometimes never learned to use them at all. It is perhaps understandable that there would be some discomfort on the part of the establishment at watching their profession begin to pass them by.

Today, nothing has changed so dramatically. All residency programs in neurosurgery require their students to become proficient at microsurgery; no hospital does very much neurosurgery at all without the microscope. At one time, it appeared as though microsurgery would even become a subspecialty in itself, but its benefits were so wide-ranging that it became completely assimilated into the profession. By 1978, the microscope was such a standard piece of equipment in the neurosurgical armamentarium that M. Gazi Yasargil, the great Swiss neurosurgeon (and a now grand old man himself), gave the Olivekrona Lecture, which is arguably the highest honor in the profession, on microsurgical techniques for the removal of acoustic tumors. Following Yasargil in quick succession were other surgeons reporting on microsurgery: Dr. Leonard Malis of New York's Mount Sinai on microsurgical techniques for parasellar tumors in 1979; Dr. Charles Wilson of the University of California at San Francisco on pituitary microsurgery in 1982; and, in 1983, Peter Jannetta on microvascular decompression of the cranial nerves. Gone are the days when neurosurgeons will load a microscope into the backseat of a car to take it to another hospital, as Peter Jannetta and Robert Rand once did at UCLA. Microsurgery had become a paradigm of its own.

The second factor has changed with time, as might be expected. It has to do with Jannetta's age and rank. If the grand old men of a scientific community determine that community's paradigms, then the time comes when there is a changing of the guard. It was an important moment for Jannetta when he realized that his job was not so much to convince the grand old men as much as it was to work slowly and steadily, and wait for a new generation—his generation—to itself become the grand old men. Then, if the theory held, it would become part of the accepted base of knowledge and information within the profession.

"It takes twenty years for anything new to really catch on," Jannetta once said, "not because it takes that long to convince the establishment, but because it takes that long for there to be a changeover to people who have grown up with the new idea as being accepted."

As Jannetta became a grand old man, he found that his work was being accepted more and more—the Olivekrona Lecture being an excellent example of just how accepted. Jannetta now has the attention of the neurosurgical world. And although many still disagree with him, some vehemently, he is not usually dismissed as a lunatic or a crackpot, as he had been before. How much of this is due to his dues-paying and how much is due to his self-acknowledged mellowing is not easy to assess, perhaps because one has a great deal to do with the other.

In 1966, though, Jannetta hadn't thought about any of this. He felt that he had made an interesting and potentially important observation, and he wanted to share that observation. His enthusiasm and confidence quickly got him branded as brash. And, according to himself and those who were close to him at the time, he was in fact a very angry young man.

He was angry in part because he couldn't understand the reception his ideas received. Shortly after he and Rand had reported on the first microvascular-decompression operation at a local neurosurgical-society meeting, Jannetta was invited to attend an exclusive conference in Los Angeles of some of the world's most prominent experts on trigeminal neuralgia. He asked for permission to go, which was not granted, the reason given being that Jannetta was Chief Resident and thus responsible for the neurosurgical service. Jannetta arranged with a colleague to cover the service, but permission was still not forthcoming—and the colleague got the chewing-out of his life for interfering. One of the reasons for this had to do with the concept of vascular compression. Another had to do with what Jannetta calls "the concept of a young smartass finding the cause of trigeminal neuralgia. I was two things that didn't fit into the establishment," he says. "The first was that I was brash, and the second was that I was intuitive. I thought I had done something good, and I admit I wanted the credit for it. What I found was that the reaction was not to steal a new idea, but, rather, to try and squelch it. They reacted the way that they did for a very simple reason: it was too much for them to bear."

The "they" to whom Jannetta refers are by and large nameless. "They" were at that time the most respected neurosurgeons in the world. As a group, they could find no place within the paradigms of their work for such an unusual concept; as individuals, they found many ways of expressing this. "Oh, those early meetings!" Jannetta recalls, laughing now— but not then. "I was ridiculed. Not in the formal sessions—I was usually greeted with a sort of stony silence. But outside in the halls, one surgeon to another, they were laughing at me and they were calling me a liar. I tried to keep it all in perspective. My perspective was, 'Ask tough questions.' I honestly believe that no one wanted to know if I were right or wrong more than I did, but that's a hard perspective to present when you're being treated with derision."

It was hard on Jannetta. Those close to him at that time talk primarily of two things: his almost obsessional energy for operating and reporting his results, and the deep depressions that would occasionally overtake him. Sol Erulkar remembers Jannetta returning to Penn to give a lecture and the reception Jannetta received. "The Penn neurosurgeons gave him a very tough time. He stayed very calm and cool during the question-and-answer period, but it was clear that he wasn't being welcomed back with open arms. The hardest thing for people to accept was that some of the techniques were radical. But he handled the criticisms very well, I think; he had a great deal of perseverance, he didn't give up. He seldom got angry at the people who were criticizing him, but I think it also made him feel very much alone—it made part of him into a very private person."

Dr. Leonard Miller, a general surgeon who did his surgical residency at Penn with Jannetta and stayed on to become Professor of Surgery there, also remembers that lecture. "The audience here made no bones about it—they thought it was all just so much bunk. But Peter weathered it. It's an intensely competitive field, and there is tremendous professional pressure. But Peter learned early on how to stay in there and take it."

He had to. In 1966, he completed his residency and left UCLA to make what also may be seen as a rather brash move: the assumption of the Chairmanship of the Section of Neurosurgery within the Department of Surgery at Louisiana State University's School of Medicine in New Orleans. In the context of traditional career moves in academic medicine, Jannetta was taking a chance, because the division of neurosurgery at LSU was well off the beaten path of the neurosurgical establishment. In one sense, Jannetta was again challenging the professional paradigms. To move from Chief Resident to Associate Professor and Chairman—even of a small program—was unheard of. Neurosurgeons were supposed to move up through the ranks: instructor here, assistant professor there, a move to a bigger school, to a bigger hospital, to a more prestigious program. Jannetta had found a small pond in which to be a big fish, perhaps, but also a place where one might vanish without a trace, because neurosurgery at LSU was not a high-profile specialty. Dr. Richard Paddison, the Chief of Neurology at LSU who recruited Jannetta for the chairmanship, had been there since 1954, and he knew very well what Jannetta was up against. "It had been an uphill battle all the way along to establish programs in the neurosciences," Paddison says, "because there was a great deal of resistance from the chief of surgery. We had a string of candidates for the neurosurgery position who were not satisfactory to the chief, and then along came PJ. PJ went to the Dean of the medical school and said, in essence, that nothing was going to happen without a good program in neurosurgery."

The Dean agreed with Jannetta's perspective and his plan, and Jannetta had his chance. "It helped a great deal that PJ is as charming as he is," says Paddison, "because he's a good organizer, a good thinker. And he broke down a lot of barriers there—built a real fine residency program, recruited a lot of fine people—made them glad he was there. And that was not easy."

It also gave Jannetta a chance to pursue his theory. Operating at the Charity Hospital in New Orleans, Jannetta treated several series of patients with both hemifacial spasm and trigeminal neuralgia, and reported on them in medical journals. By 1967, he felt that he had the foundation of the theory of vascular compression clear in his mind, and the results in these early patients seemed to bear this out. But the work was still considered highly controversial.

By this time, Jannetta was aware of some of the reasons why: he had a sense of what Dandy had been up against and why Dandy's theories had never caught on. Dandy, involved in political infighting with the establishment as represented by Harvey Cushing, was unable to influence enough of the rest of the neurosurgical world to examine his work, to try and replicate it, to try and see what it was that he was doing. Dandy challenged the profession, and Dandy lost.

Dr. Rosa Pinkus, the Department of Neurosurgery's ethicist, was trained as a historian, and, in a fascinating look backward, she examined the scientific, political, and social worlds of neurosurgery at the time of Walter Dandy and Harvey Cushing as it pertained to trigeminal neuralgia. In a paper in the medical journal *Neurosurgery*, she looked at the underlying "values" (a term from Thomas Kuhn) and found that while Dandy's technique and observations were adopted by a small number of neurosurgeons, the political, personal, and technological issues overrode this and stifled any further testing of Dandy's innovative hypothesis. "Dandy's . . . few heirs had not the political stature to keep his work in a favorable light," she concludes and notes further that "the developing profession of neurosurgery strove during the years 1920 to 1945 to unite around a single set of rules. . . . An apparent side effect of adopting these common rules for the treatment of [trigeminal neuralgia] was an attempt to exclude Dandy's perspectives from the mainstream of thought and activity. . . . This response . . . is not unusual given the tenuous nature of the 'neurosurgical group' in the 1920s and 1930s."

Finally, she refers—obliquely—to Peter Jannetta (her article was published in 1984): "[Dandy] documented and published his findings in spite of the political setbacks brought about by so doing. He provided a comprehensive written history of ideas for neurosurgeons to reexamine and to test at a later time when the profession, firmly established, could withstand and survive the internal strife that resulted as his innovative observations were applied, altered and verified in the clinic."

Jannetta didn't want to be a Walter Dandy. He wanted the scientific community at least to address his ideas, to test them, to challenge them. So he put his ideas out there—in journal articles, in papers given at neurosurgical and neurological-society meetings, at lectures such as the one at Penn. The payoff was that his ideas were being talked about. The price was, according to Paddison, "that Peter was seen as beating the drum a little too hard. Skepticism in the face of something new is not unusual, and Peter was seen as being a little bit too enthusiastic. He didn't always feel that he was getting the recognition that he should, but you have to remember what a shock something like his theory—and ol' Peter *himself*—was to a sort of hidebound profession at that time. Some still don't think he has been quite critical enough. If he has any sins, it's because he believes in what he's doing."

In public and in print, Jannetta was infinitely patient with his critics. In private, there were periods of great difficulty. "It's sort of hard to think about now," he recalls years later, "because I've tried to put all that behind me. But of course it was difficult. I paid a certain price for being out there and for being sure about what I was doing. You're a lightning rod, and in my case I was a lightning rod for everything."

"Everything" refers in part to other specialties besides neurosurgery: neurology, oral biology, otolaryngology, and, lately, as a result of his work on "idiopathic" hypertension (that is, hypertension of no known cause), cardiology, nephrology, internal medicine. Medicine, as it has grown increasingly specialized, has also unavoidably become increasingly "turf conscious." If neurologists don't like wide-ranging "cures" upsetting and redefining the range of their specialty, one can imagine what a disparate field like cardiology makes of a man who claims to be curing hypertension through brain surgery. In many ways, 1987 is much like 1967 for Jannetta. He publishes his reports; he gives papers at meetings; and then he endures. The hypertension work is an extension of the general theory of cranial-nerve compression. Jannetta believes that vascular compression on a portion of the brain stem that controls blood pressure causes some cases of high blood pressure, and he has begun to demonstrate that microvascular decompression can alleviate the cause—and the symptoms. The difference in the way that this theory is being received by the medical community, as compared to the way Jannetta's original observations about trigeminal neuralgia were received, is not one of degree—there are lots of people who are calling it—well—"bunk." Instead, the difference is one of climate, because in the intervening twenty years, other neurosurgeons—many of them trained by Jannetta, some of them former Pitt residents—have applied Jannetta's theories, tested them, verified them. In doing so, these neurosurgeons, just like Jannetta, are going over the same ground that Pinkus suggests Walter Dandy established sixty years ago, even though the work did not catch on at the time. Neurovascular compression as the cause of some syndromes is now relatively well accepted within the profession, and this makes it almost certain that any new ideas from Jannetta will be given a fair hearing. In the years since 1966, Peter Jannetta has managed to add a paradigm to his profession. Simply stated: "Neurovascular compression can cause cranial-nerve disorders, and microvascular decompression can cure them." Walter Dandy may have understood principally the same thing, but only Peter Jannetta managed to get the rest of the profession to believe it.

4

The Medicine Man

At 7:29 A.M., Peter Jannetta strides through the doors of the operating suite and heads for the desk where the operating-room shift supervisors keep track of who should be where in Presbyterian-University Hospital's fifteen operating rooms. "Good morning, I'm here," he says.

One of the supervisors smiles and says, "Good morning, Doctor," handing him a blue scrub suit.

He does an about-face and heads down the hall to the surgeons' dressing room. It is Wednesday, and there are only three cases scheduled for him, which is a light operating day. He has done six cases a day many times and would like to do six cases a day more often, but meshing his schedule with the schedules of his patients does not always work out. And, at any rate, there is plenty to do today: before leaving the hospital, he will have performed the three operations, spoken with the patients' families, dictated operating-room notes, dictated his own notes, dictated letters to the referring physicians, visited three patients in the Neurosurgical Continuous Care Unit, visited seven patients on the Neurosurgical Patient Unit, attended three one-hour clinical conferences, visited the patients he has operated on in the Recovery Room, signed a stack of patient charts in the Medical Records Department, answered a stack of mail, arranged for a rental car, and taken a twenty minute nap.

And because it is such a light day, he will stop and play squash for an hour or so on the way home.

"You know what someone once said about me?" he asks as he changes into his scrub suit and ties his iodine-stained, beaten-up-looking "OR shoes"—once-white athletic shoes that saw plenty of duty on a squash court before seeing plenty of duty in an operating room. "That the world would be a better place if I didn't have so much energy." He laughs as he slams his locker and heads out the door. "And I'm not so sure that isn't right."

How much of his energy is due to his nature ("I'm long-term patient, but short-term impatient") and how much is due to being an important cog in a very large and complex health-care machine is not always clear. As Chairman of the Department of Neurological Surgery at the University of Pittsburgh School of Medicine, he has many demands on his time that are not strictly related to performing surgical operations. When he came to Pitt in 1971, the department had part-time academic neurosurgeons only—a faltering residency program, no neurosurgical research program, and no one remotely like Peter Jannetta. Now, the department employs more than one hundred people, including twenty full-time faculty members, twenty part-time faculty members, a dozen residents in training, an ethicist, a fiscal manager (the department is organized as a professional corporation), and approximately $1 million a year in funded research. As a whole, the department treats about 4,000 inpatients and 5,000 outpatients each year, consults on 4,500 more, and performs more than 2,000 surgical operations. To do this, faculty members must be recruited, candidates for residency must be interviewed, grant proposals and journal articles must be written, committees must be convened and served on. Jannetta's is really three jobs: surgeon, administrator, teacher. "And if you don't have energy for everything, you don't get to spend it on the things that are really important to you," says Jannetta, "like surgery, like research, like patients." So the days are full.

This day begins with surgery. Scheduled for 7:30 A.M. are two cases. First, in Room 12, is Xavier Williams, who suffers from hemifacial spasm. Xavier has undergone an unsuccessful microvascular decompression earlier in the year—at "another hospital," in the parlance of professionally courteous physicians. Peter Jannetta is one of the few surgeons in the world who reoperate on patients who have neurovascular-compression disorders. Also scheduled for 7:30 is Janice Slater, who has suffered for five years from disabling positional vertigo. Her operation will be in Room 8. At 10:30, Ellen Goldberg, the wife of a New York physician, will undergo microvascular decompression for relief of her trigeminal neuralgia, in Room 12.

While waiting for the anesthesiologist in each room to minister to the patients—inserting lines for monitoring blood chemistry, administering and stabilizing the patients on the inhalation anesthetics that are used for brain operations, attaching blood-pressure and heart-rate monitors—Jannetta stalks around the halls and passageways of the operating-room complex, peering into the windows of "his" two operating rooms and waiting for the hospital's dietary service to deliver the five-gallon insulated container of coffee to the surgeon's lounge. He is very impatient when waiting for a patient to be readied, and he is very impatient when waiting for the coffee to arrive. The image of the neurosurgeon who religiously eschews coffee in fear of unsteady hands and frazzled nerves is shattered as Jannetta makes a beeline for the coffee pot in the surgeons' lounge moments after it has been delivered.

Throughout the course of the day, he will consume perhaps twenty-five cups—in the surgeons' lounge, in the doctor's dining room, in the clinical conferences, in his office. Before his surgical cases, he drinks coffee; between his surgical cases, he drinks coffee; after his surgical cases, he drinks coffee; in between clinical conferences, he pops into the Department of Neurological Surgery office on the fourth floor of Scaife Hall to get coffee, because the coffee there is better than the coffee provided for the clinical conferences. When he doesn't have a plastic-foam cup filled with coffee, he has either just finished one or is on his way to get one—or he is operating on someone's brain. And he looks amazed when he's asked if all that coffee doesn't bother him. "Apparently not," he replied once.

Tying on a paper surgical mask and covering his head with a matching cap, Jannetta walks to OR 8, where neurosurgical resident Mark Dias is preparing to begin Janice Slater's operation, microvascular decompression of the auditory, or eighth cranial, nerve on the right side, to relieve her vertigo and disequilibrium. Dias, who will shortly finish his rotation at Presbyterian-University Hospital and move to Children's Hospital, is a veteran of many operations in the cerebellopontine angle. He will do the initial exploration while Jannetta tackles the tricky reoperation in OR 12.

"Same case?" Jannetta asks.

And Dias replies without looking up, "Yep, same case."

Dias is already gowned and gloved. He is moments from starting the case. "Don't get into any trouble," Jannetta says as he leaves the room. But it is not an admonishment—it is a way of saying "Good luck."

Moving rapidly down the hall to Room 12, Jannetta plans the logistics of the two cases with Aage Møller. Like Jannetta, Møller is for all practical purposes in two places at once this morning. Although Møller has a technician in each room to watch the monitors, when Jannetta is ready to do the actual decompression of the nerve, it is Møller who is staring at the oscilloscope, and it is Møller whose voice rings out if it appears, electrophysiologically, that Jannetta is doing something he shouldn't. All morning, Møller acts like the governor on Jannetta's engine, slowing things down with a word.

In OR 12, the resident, Eric Altschuler, is preparing the back of Xavier Williams's skull. The patient, already under anesthesia, is a big man "with big muscles," says Jannetta. "Sometimes these are the toughest cases—you don't know what you're going to find in the way of scar tissue."

"Good morning, everybody," says Jannetta.

And there is a chorus of "Good mornings" muffled by surgical masks.

He enters the scrub room and begins scrubbing for the first time today. He stands over the sink, using a disposable pre-soaped brush on his fingers, hands, and forearms. This is a routine that approaches ritual. It is hard sometimes to separate routine from ritual, because Jannetta's activity is so routine. There is a way in which all operations in the cerebellopontine angle are supposed to proceed, and Jannetta proceeds with the confidence of a man who is the center of a tiny universe. No one wants to be the one who slows things up, because that is an excellent way to get run over.

After rinsing, he backs into the OR, dries his hands on a sterile towel, and announces, "Let's get this show on the road."

He is gowned and gloved, and approaches Xavier Williams. Altschuler has already seen to the shaving and scrubbing of the scalp, down to the painting of an "X" just behind Xavier's ear. For some cases, Altschuler will open the skin, but for this case, he stands aside, hands up and ready for Jannetta to begin. Reoperations can be difficult, because the healing tissues from the first operation sometimes form a tough, unyielding mass beneath the scalp that is richly revascularized—filled, that is, with tiny, newly grown blood vessels. When Jannetta opens the skull, he will find that scar tissue has formed within the cerebellopontine angle as well, making it difficult to proceed. But now, as he makes his incision and begins coagulating the blood vessels, the immediate inconvenience is the amount of scarring underneath Xavier's scalp. "This is something," says Jannetta at one point. "Big, muscular men tend to form big, muscular scars, and," Jannetta nods toward Xavier Williams's considerable presence on the operating table, "this is a big, muscular man."

It is interesting to see Jannetta doing much of the opening work, because it is tough and inelegant—much prying and poking and scraping. The periosteum, which is the fibrous covering that adheres tightly to bone, seems to have been glued on with particularly efficiency—it only comes away under the most aggressive scraping with the periosteal elevator. A carpenter would call the periosteal elevator a chisel. This instrument is, with the possible exception of the mallet, the most unneurosurgical-looking tool.

Hemifacial spasm, like trigeminal neuralgia, is not a new affliction, and of the cranial-nerve disorders treated through microvascular decompression, it is one of the few that have an outwardly visible appearance. It generally begins in middle age with the intermittent twitching of one of the tiny muscles responsible for moving the eyeball—the inferior orbicularis oculi. The twitching gradually becomes more persistent; it begins to spread. Sufferers generally seek treatment only after the twitching affects all of the muscles that control facial expression. There are two trademarks of hemifacial spasm: the clinician notices the grimace and involuntary closing of the eye on the affected side; the casual observer probably first notes the oversized sunglasses invariably worn by sufferers in an effort to conceal the twitch.

In a chapter on hemifacial spasm for the medical textbook *Current Controversies in Neurosurgery* (which more than one neurosurgeon familiar with Jannetta's work has described as the most likely place to find a chapter by Peter Jannetta), Jannetta describes in little more than a paragraph the reasons why people like Xavier Williams end up on an operating table:

> Patients are often thought to have a habit spasm or "tic" and many are sent for psychiatric evaluation and care. . . . [They] come to operation for cosmetic reasons, as their social lives and business activities are gradually eroded. Since this is not a lethal condition, surgery must be safe as well as effective. Over the years, a number of articles have appeared concerning the cause and treatment of this distressing affliction. The etiology has remained obscure; the treatment has generally consisted of varying degrees of destruction of the facial nerve.

The etiology, according to Jannetta, no longer remains obscure, as he reopens the old hole in Xavier's skull. "What we're going to find here is microvascular decompression nowhere near the cause of the problem"—the scrub nurse hands him the rongeur forceps, with which he will snip away bits of bone and enlarge the opening enough to work through—"because that's what we almost always find when we reoperate. Isn't it, Aage?"

Aage Møller, whose role during this operation will be to monitor, through the use of a cunningly designed electrode attached to the side of Xavier's face, the spasm of the facial muscles—electromyography—responds promptly, "That's right, Peter."

Translated, what Jannetta expects to find when he finds Xavier's facial nerve is that the surgeon who preceded him into Xavier's cerebellopontine angle found a blood vessel compressing the facial nerve all right, but not a blood vessel compressing the facial nerve where the roots of the nerve emerge from the brain stem. And it is here at the root exit zone where the magic happens. Decompression—the insertion of those tiny bits of Teflon felt between the nerve and the blood vessel—farther out on the nerve won't cure the spasm, or at least won't cure the spasm forever.

Again, some neurophysiology is in order. The cranial nerves as originally designed and installed are not intended to be manipulated. An analogy might be the wiring inside a clock. Electricity enters through a reasonably stout cord, but once inside the cabinet, the wiring becomes less stout. The wires that power the bulb that lights the face are not stout at all, nor are they insulated to the degree that the power cord is, which, in turn, is not insulated to the degree that it would be if it were designed to be outdoors and exposed to the elements. Nerve tissue, which is never meant in nature to be exposed to the elements (think of a cavity in a tooth—a severe toothache is the result of the decomposition of the enamel and dentin of the tooth, which brings the elements a lot closer to the nerve than one likes), thus is not well insulated, which causes it to respond dramatically when disturbed.

And unless the neurosurgeon is extremely careful, and in fact is operating with a very high priority of *not* disturbing the nerve, the nerve will be touched by surgical instruments, it will be stretched slightly, it will be bumped. In the parlance of the neurosurgeon, the nerve will be traumatized, and trauma affects one cranial nerve differently than another. If the auditory nerve is traumatized, irreversible deafness is usually the result; the auditory nerve is so fragile it cannot bear more than the gentlest manipulation under any circumstances. In the case of hemifacial spasm, however, the facial nerve responds in an unusual way: traumatizing the facial nerve almost invariably relieves the spasm.

A controversy within a controversy now emerges. How does Jannetta or any neurosurgeon know that the spasm disappears because an offending blood vessel has been held away from the nerve and not just because he or she traumatized the nerve during the operation? Traumatizing the nerve, after all, has a long history: a German neurologist named Bernhard had violently stretched the facial nerve of a hemifacial-spasm sufferer in 1884; not only did the spasm go away, the facial muscles were paralyzed. As function returned, however, so did the spasm. Other neurosurgeons in the intervening years have deliberately manipulated and traumatized to lesser degrees, with varying degrees of success.

Xavier Williams is, in a sense, the embodiment of Jannetta's answer: relief of symptoms through trauma of the facial nerve is relatively short-lived, whereas relief of symptoms by microvascular decompression is virtually permanent. In the larger framework of the theory of cranial-nerve compression, this fits—the hypothesis is proved by the negative, by the fact that the spasm doesn't recur.

The methodical side of Jannetta—the scientist's side—has taken this a step further. In his first operation for hemifacial spasm, performed in 1966, the expected blood vessel was exceedingly small and very difficult to find. Mild trauma to the nerve was not particularly an issue, but finding the expected blood vessel was. The vessel was found and decompressed, and the patient has remained spasm-free. Mindful of the trauma issue, however, the second patient's case was handled differently: the facial nerve was deliberately *not* touched during the operation. The patient awoke from the anesthesia with severe hemifacial spasm, an event that had an unsettling effect on Jannetta. But something interesting happened. Over the following month, the spasm gradually faded away and has been absent now for twenty years. Here is how Jannetta accounted for it in a case report in 1976:

Direct trauma to the facial nerve may have been held responsible for the improvement if it had been present immediately post-operatively, but the fact that the patient awoke with spasm that gradually abated, not to return, strongly suggests that the facial nerve . . . at the brain stem is the area where vascular compression . . . causes hemifacial spasm. . . . Relief of compression without trauma to the nerve is followed by gradual return of facial function to normal.

Finally, though, there is an alternative hypothesis favored by several neurologists, one of which suggests that the Teflon implant causes *continual* mild trauma to the nerve and thus keeps the spasm at bay. In the immediate circumstance, Xavier Williams would appear to be disproving this hypothesis, too, because his hemifacial spasm went away but eight months later is back. And everyone in the operating room knows that it is back, because the electrode attached to his temple sends data to Dr. Møller's monitor, a monitor that expresses the data in two ways. The method of most interest to Dr. Møller is a graphic representation on an oscilloscope, where the spasm appears as a jagged line. The second method might smack of the tiniest bit of showmanship: the spasm is reproduced as sound—an intermittent popping sound—for all to hear.

While microvascular decompression as treatment for trigeminal neuralgia started it all for Jannetta, it is hemifacial spasm that regularly makes believers out of skeptics because of what Dr. Dias refers to as "hard electrophysiologic data"— the jagged line on the screen and, now, the popping sound from the speaker. Trigeminal neuralgia, remember, is pain, and pain is invisible to the outside observer. So is the dizziness of disabling positional vertigo. To assess improvement in any of these conditions, one must rely upon the patient for the data, because no one else can feel it.

It is typical for the residents who pass through the program at Pitt to be skeptical early on in their residencies of the miracles seemingly wrought by Peter Jannetta for all the usual reasons, such as "It's too simple."

"He is *so* sure of himself."

"When we finally learn all there is to know about neurophysiology, *then* maybe—*maybe*—we'll know."

"He's a medicine man."

"Watch him with the patients. They love him so much, they would deny that the sun was shining if he said he had made it dark."

"People can make themselves believe what they want to believe."

"How could a tiny blood vessel be in just the right place every time?"

"It's an act of faith."

"It's psychological, like hypnosis."

"It's pretty hard to believe."

"It's subjective, totally and completely subjective."

But hemifacial spasm now can be *seen.* Charisma can't make it disappear, nor can faith. Dias was one of the grand skeptics. "We all experience the skepticism, to some degree, for a couple of reasons. First, the theory is unexpected; it's a unique way of looking at disease. Second, because of the rotation through the residency program, where you never get to follow-up on the patients you operate on or see operated on, you learn to be a cynic. To be a believer, you have to see the operation, and then you have to see the patient eighteen months later. And eighteen months after the operation, you're at some other hospital, with a whole different series of cases. It's an interesting problem with residency.

"I remember very clearly when I first began to suspect that Jannetta was up to something. It was a hemifacial-spasm case. I was at the teaching scope watching PJ do the dissection, and

I saw him, very clearly, isolate a blood vessel and lift it off the facial nerve. And at the instant he did so, Aage said, 'The spasm is gone.' I looked up. There was no way that PJ could see Aage, and there was no way that Aage could see what PJ was doing—Aage was glued to his screen, he had his back to us. Then, PJ let the vessel back down onto the nerve, and Aage said immediately, 'The spasm is back.' PJ lifted the blood vessel again, and Aage says, 'It's gone again.' I was elated and annoyed at the same time. I had just seen the whole framework laid out before me. Remove the cause, and the symptoms disappear. And I had just seen the symptoms dissappear. Something like that goes a long way toward altering your perception of microvascular decompression."

In Xavier Williams's case, however, that outcome is still much in doubt, because the scar tissue is so intractable. In a textbook dissection, the layers open up and fold away as though seen in an animated cartoon: the skin is white; the muscle is red; the skull is bone; the dura gray; the pia arachnoid a dewy spiderweb white; the cranial nerves taupe; the blood vessels maroon. In this case, everything is the consistency and color of gristle, and the procedure is not going well. Jannetta normally hums during an operation; it is not unusual for him to sing, to joke, to talk to the resident and the scrub nurse. This is not an operation to joke through, because it is almost nine o'clock, and he has not even opened the dura.

An operating room in which a neurosurgeon is working within the patient's skull is unlike most others. Once the cranium has been opened, things generally quiet down for all concerned except the surgeon always, the resident often, and the anesthesiologist usually. The surgeon is working through a very small opening, using very slight movements. And if he or she is satisfied with the position of the patient and the instrument in hand, long periods may pass where it might seem that a group of gowned and masked men and women are watching someone fix a watch. At most, the animation at times like this is a quiet shuffling, as though the others in the room are in fact waiting their chance, and the less patient ones betray a slight wish that the surgeon would hurry things up. But while "fast" is an adjective invariably applied to a neurosurgeon of Jannetta's talents, it does not mean that things move quickly. During Xavier Williams's operation, there is a full complement of personnel, minus some of the visitors and the extra scrub nurse who were present during Madeline Cooper's operation. It is Altschuler who seems most absorbed by the slow and tedious work of coagulating the blood vessels that pervade the scar tissue in Xavier's wound. He stands at Jannetta's shoulder and, at Jannetta's instruction, operates a suction device to clear the field of blood. The saline solution that the scrub nurse is squirting in helps Jannetta see where the bleeding is coming from, so that the cut vessels may be sealed shut with the bipolar coagulators, which are like tweezers, and the monopolar coagulator, which is in essence an electric needle.

At the other end of the interest and involvement spectrum, the circulating nurse, whose job is to gather and count used sponges, fold soiled drapes, answer the phone (she is not sterile), and check off the use of instruments on the operative-notes checklist, sits on a metal stool and waits, her foot tapping against a counter in syncopation with the sound of the patient's hemifacial spasm. The others wait expectantly.

It is not hard to visualize what Jannetta is trying to do as he works his way through the scar tissue. Imagine a stack of construction paper soaked with Elmer's glue and left to dry until it is grayish-clear—not brittle, but tough and pliable. Imagine that all of the sheets are white, but that a sheet near the center is the one sheet that mustn't be torn. That sheet is the dura, and in this case it looks pretty much like everything else, except that it cannot be bulldozed through. To make the image more accurate, imagine that as each sheet had been put down and covered with glue, a tangled pinch of sewing thread had been tossed in as well, and that every time a thread is cut, you have to stop and seal each of the cut ends. The scrub nurse for this operation is Jean Stelnak, who is superb in the handling of the instruments and the irrigation of the field.

As Jannetta approaches the dura, he switches instruments. Instead of the coagulators, he asks for and receives a pair of long-handled tweezers and hands the monopolar coagulator to Dr. Altschuler. "Hold it against them," Jannetta says somewhat shortly. He is thinking of Room 8, where Mark Dias is doing the exploration; he is thinking of the 10:30 A.M. case; he is thinking of the afternoon clinical conferences, which he hates to miss because he believes that it is important for him to be there; but mostly he is thinking of getting through the scar tissue and finding whatever it was that the surgeon at the other hospital missed.

Altschuler's first attempt to do what Jannetta has asked does not go well. What Jannetta wants to do is use the forceps—the tweezers—to grasp the blood vessels and have the resident hold the point of the coagulator on the hinge of the forceps so that the current runs through them to the tips and seals off the vessels. It is a simple concept if clearly explained—the other residents know how to do it, and in fact learned it just this way. But Altschuler at first holds the coagulator against the rubber-coated grips of the forceps, which succeeds in scorching the grips but does not send the current down to where Jannetta wants it.

So Jannetta must look up. "Hold it against the metal, the *metal*—up *here*," he says even more sharply. Then immediately his voice is at once apologetic and explanatory. "You need to hold the point on the metal, Doctor, not on the plastic, so we can close these off."

With some trepidation, Jannetta finally opens the dura. Inside, the geography of the cerebellopontine angle is featureless, a map of whitish tissue: everything is stuck to everything else, which means that Jannetta will be at his most circumspect. Anatomical relations within the brain are not static. Things are not in the same place in everyone, for one thing. Also, the position of the head during the operation and the amount of retraction applied to the cerebellum change the orientation of the cranial nerves to each other and to the brain stem. Scar tissue such as Xavier's also distorts anatomical relationships. So until Jannetta knows where something is, he has to operate under the assumption that something he does not want to disturb—the auditory nerve, for example, or the anterior inferior cerebellar artery, which runs under the sixth cranial nerve (the abducens) and over the seventh and eighth (the facial and auditory nerves, respectively)—is lurking out of sight but within harm's way. Compounding the difficulty in this case is a nick in the dural sinus, which is a large vein just inside the dura. The dural sinuses are collecting points for the drainage of venous blood from the brain, and now the one at the bottom of Jannetta's operative field is leaking blood just fast enough to be annoying; irrigation and suction are necessary every twenty seconds or so to allow him to see what he is doing.

Jannetta probes patiently, patiently, using a blunt dissector, which is analogous to a butter knife—bladelike but dull—and a blunt-tipped probe. He begins to hum. In the background, the audio representation of Xavier's spasm continues to pop rhythmically, and at 9:30 Jannetta stops his probing long enough to say to Aage, "Would you turn that down, *please?*" Aage does so immediately. Though Jannetta begins humming again, it has been an uncharacteristic, curious interlude and mirrors the frustration that Jannetta is experiencing. It is as though the spasm were challenging him to find it in a game of cerebellopontine hide-and-seek.

At the other side of the table, the anesthesiology resident is having her own quiet frustrations with trying to keep the patient stable. Her situation is not helped by the memory of a confrontation with Jannetta two weeks earlier over the management of a patient during an operation. This case is taking a long time; and, with some patients, the longer the operation, the harder they are to balance because of a combination of the patient's size, metabolic rate, and particular response to the blend of gases keeping him or her unconscious. Xavier, although Jannetta doesn't know it at this moment, is having some problems. His blood pressure and heart rate are swinging like a pendulum during the operation. When blood pressure drops, the anesthesiologist has two choices: decrease the anesthesia or increase circulatory volume—the amount of fluid in the circulatory system—by adding sterile saline through an intravenous line. The resident is now doing both and is also placing a quiet call to Dr. Fred Khalouf, the anesthesiologist of record, who is in some other operating room dealing with some other difficult-to-manage patient. Fred Khalouf's mornings are often like this. He may be in charge, formally or informally, of half a dozen cases at a time. And he walks or trots through the halls of the OR suite, going from room to room, always cool and upbeat but resembling some days an old variety-show performer who is spinning dinner plates atop bamboo sticks, only the sticks are in five or six different rooms. In phone consultation with Khalouf, the resident makes some adjustments but still does not look happy.

Neither does Jannetta. He is clearly frustrated with the scar tissue. Open and shut operations, while not the rule, are not the exception either. Many patients who have undergone microvascular-decompression operations are out of the room in two and a half hours, and the pace of the operation is geared to that theoretical ideal. This is not an ideal case; things are still at an impasse. Jannetta carefully inserts the retractor; the retractor paddles will hold back Xavier's cerebellum so that access may be gained to the cranial nerves. In this case, retraction at this point is minimal. Jannetta needs to move the cerebellum to find out where he is, but he doesn't want to move the cerebellum until he has some idea of where he is. "I don't know where I am," he says conversationally. "There's no room at the inn here at all." He readjusts the retractor again and again.

Imagine pressing into that stack of construction paper with a butter knife, trying to move it so that you can expose a live electric wire that is somewhere underneath. You have to move the paper to find the wire, but you don't want to plunge in willy-nilly because you don't want to touch the wire—you'd get an electric shock. Jannetta must be supremely gentle. He won't get an electric shock if he retracts the cerebellum too much but, instead, could stretch the auditory nerve, which would cause Xavier to lose his hearing on one side, or could bump the medulla, which could stop Xavier's heart or breathing. There is never a rush to adjust the retractor.

"Let's bring the scope in," he says, and the circulating nurse wheels the Contraves binocular operating microscope over to the table. "Lights off, glasses off," Jannetta says next, and the room lights dim as the nurse lifts Jannetta's half-glasses off his nose and places them carefully on the ledge of the window separating the OR from the scrub room. Jannetta readjusts himself on his stool, hoping that the high-resolution microscope will allow him to find something familiar. The venous sinus still leaks slowly, and he stretches a small cotton pad over the base of the operative site to soak up the oozing blood. "I don't know what's going on," says Jannetta after a few minutes of desultory probing. "I don't know where I am." His voice, though soft, is edged with frustration. He pulls his instruments out and sits up straight. "I'm going over to Eight for a while. I've got to think about this. Let's go get some coffee, Aage."

And he stands up, strips off his gloves and paper gown in one swift, practiced motion, picks up his glasses from the window ledge, and stalks out of the room, saying to Altschuler as he leaves, "Don't get into any trouble." Aage Møller follows after a hurried consultation with his technicians.

Instead of going straight to OR 8, where Mark Dias is working on Janice Slater, Jannetta enters the surgeon's lounge and draws a plastic-foam cup of coffee before sprawling in one of the vinyl lounge chairs of a style found in physicians' waiting rooms across the United States—low and wide, they are never particularly comfortable, but they are sturdy. He lights a Pall Mall and stares at the ceiling. Aage comes in, sits down across from Jannetta, and stares at the ceiling. Behind them, two anesthesiologists talk about sports cars.

"I don't know," Jannetta begins. "I don't know if I'm getting anywhere. We may want to look a bit lower." This would involve changing the angle of the table and probing even more blindly than before. "I expect that what I am finding is tentorium, but I can't really tell at this point."

The tentorium cerebelli is the extension of the dura that separates the two largest structures of the brain, the cerebellum and the cerebrum, from each other. If it is indeed tentorium that Jannetta is finding at the upper end of the operative wound, then he is in all probability too high to find the cranial nerves. The tentorium opens to provide passage of the cerebral peduncles, which wrap around the innermost aspects of the brain stem approximately at the level of the third and fourth cranial nerves. Jannetta is looking for the seventh nerve. However, if he is *not* finding the tentorium and is indeed where he thinks he is supposed to be, moving lower along the base of the brain will take him very quickly into an area where he doesn't want at all to be, because the ninth, tenth, and eleventh cranial nerves, for example, arise very close to the medulla oblongata, which controls respiration, heart rate, and blood pressure. He will be very, very careful when he moves down this low.

"He should have come here first, eh?" says Møller with a laugh. Aage Møller is probably the most matter-of-fact believer in Jannetta's work in the entire university, perhaps in the entire universe. Møller keeps the records, for one thing—the audio tapes and computer disks that store the electrophysiological data of hundreds of operations in the cerebellopontine angle. When compiling data for articles to submit to medical journals or papers to present at medical conferences, he can review the progress of each operation by watching the screen of an oscilloscope. Since Møller has seen Jannetta cure the problems that he (Møller) has spent his professional career studying, Jannetta must be doing something very right.

Jannetta inhales a third of his cigarette and shakes his head. "These guys . . . some of these guys who don't know what they're doing are the same guys who say that the operation doesn't work. They won't come here and spend the time to learn to do it right. But that doesn't stop some of them from trying."

The case of neurosurgeons—and surgeons in general—reading or hearing about a procedure and then trying it themselves is a two-edged scalpel. The key word of contemporary medicine is "reproducibility," which means that if surgeon A does a procedure and alleviates a problem, surgeon B, by doing what surgeon A says he did, should be able to get the same results. Reproducibility is crucial to acceptance by the medical community of a new surgical technique, a new medication, a new regimen of treatment for a disease. If it works in

Pittsburgh, it should work in Omaha or Phoenix or Paris. If it doesn't work in these places, then the medical community gets suspicious of what's going on in Pittsburgh.

On the other hand, all new regimens of treatment are not equal, because reproducibility of results is necessarily related to reproducibility of technique. The gold standard of objective validation of results is the randomized double-blind trial in which, say, 100 people with high blood pressure are given a vial of pills to take three times a day. Half get a new blood-pressure medication, half get sugar pills or "placebos." No one—not the doctors running the study, not the patients, not the drug company—knows which subjects are getting the medication and which are getting the placebo, because the vials of pills have been assigned randomly by a computer and the labels on the bottle have no name—only a code number that corresponds to a sealed list, also generated by the computer.

The blood pressure of the subjects is checked regularly, and any improvements and side effects are noted. At the end of the study, the code is opened and the physicians judge the efficacy of the medication by looking at which subjects received the medication and what their progress was as compared to those who received the placebo. If the 50 who received the new drug had lower blood pressure during the trial, the medication would appear to have some benefit. The group that received the placebo (the "control" group) will likely not have benefited, because nothing special was done for them. The double-blind study has the obvious benefit of easily reproducible technique—anyone can do it, and can do it in pretty much the same way as the initial study was done. It is through such studies that so-called "miracle" drugs, such as laetrile, have been shown, to the medical establishment's satisfaction, to have no benefits.

Surgery, though, is different, because reproducibility of

technique is never guaranteed. Surgeons differ in skill, dexterity, training, background, experience, and all of these play a part in a successful operation. Most of these are very difficult to document, as are even more amorphous characteristics such as personality and adherence to beliefs and the harboring of prejudices. If you can invent a surgical technique that is safer, faster, less complicated, more efficacious, or easier to do, you will likely get the procedure named after you and gradually see it become standard technique—if the procedure catches on, which may be a big if.

Few problems that lend themselves to neurosurgical management can be addressed in a double-blind study. If a neurosurgeon finds an operable tumor, he operates to remove it, using a combination of training, experience, and good judgment. If he removes it using an approach that differs from what is strictly standard, he may report it in a medical journal, hoping to hear from other neurosurgeons who may have tried something similar, to share his new knowledge with other neurosurgeons who may have patients that would benefit from the new approach, and to establish that he has done something different and may likely be doing it again when the opportunity arises. If the new approach worked well, he may try it again should the situation arise in another patient. It is through this process that a "series" of patients is accumulated. It would not do to operate on a patient in any fashion other than what is medically indicated when the condition is a tumor or an aneurysm or an arteriovenous malformation. There is no control group of patients for these conditions either, no objective way of comparing one operation to another, because every patient and every tumor is different.

Over a period of time, the surgeon with a new technique may begin to be sent patients by other surgeons who think that the new way might be most appropriate for the patient, and that the colleague that has been reporting on these cases in the *Journal of Neurosurgery* is perhaps the best one for the job. So the series of patients gets larger and larger, the residents at the institution where the surgeon practices and teaches learn the new technique as a matter of course, finish their residencies, and go on to do the technique at their own institutions, teaching it to residents themselves and reporting the results as their mentor did.

But if the new technique seems an excellent way to treat a common problem or a problem for which there have been no excellent solutions in the past, other surgeons may begin to try the technique, based on their readings in the literature, their attendence at presentations at conferences, and their own generally sophisticated skill, knowledge, and experience. In many situations, this is sufficient. A thoracic surgeon tries a new method of suturing that has been reported to heal faster and leave less of a scar. If he finds that his results are as satisfactory as the inventor of the method reported, he may report it himself, which validates the initial report and reproduces the results. If his experience with the new method is a failure, he may still choose to report it as so, he may try it again, he may forget about it completely, but his initial experience does not absolutely negate the originator's claims. Time, after all, will tell.

But what if the originator's claims seem extraordinarily extravagant? And what if the originator also posits that the technique is only successful if it is done "properly" when the meaning of "properly" is not easily described in a case report? This is the situation Jannetta has found himself in over these last few years with microvascular decompression in general, and the situation he now finds himself in as he stubs out his Pall Mall in an ashtray and refills his coffee cup. Xavier Williams was first treated surgically for hemifacial spasm at another university medical center, a center whose name is synonymous with medical excellence. The surgery was performed by a neurosurgeon with a sterling reputation in his field. Jannetta, sitting on a vinyl chair in the surgeons' lounge at Presbyterian-University Hospital, has a strong suspicion that the operation was not done—well—properly. The other neurosurgeon had read Jannetta's papers, had heard Jannetta at conferences, and had seen, undoubtedly, the reports of other neurosurgeons performing MVD. So he operated on Xavier and got a poor result, which he likely will report. It is not an oversimplification to say that microvascular decompression is not easy, that it must be done correctly, and that it requires consummate skill and patience—Jannetta himself has gotten some poor results. What is difficult to say is that, in essence, you had better have Peter Jannetta teach you the procedure—either in a visit to Pittsburgh or by inviting him to your institution—or you are not going to be able to reproduce his results. This is difficult because there are few procedures where this is true.

"What happens most often is a good neurosurgeon reads the literature and says, 'I can try that,' because he's done dozens and dozens of operations in the posterior fossa, he's had lots of patients with trigeminal neuralgia and hemifacial spasm—we all have—and it doesn't sound any more difficult than a lot of other operations. But what he doesn't do is take me up on the standing invitation," Jannetta says, and Møller nods vigorously.

The "standing invitation" is just that: an open invitation to come to Presby for a few days, see some cases through the teaching microscope, talk to some patients before and after the procedure—learn to do it firsthand. Lots of neurosurgeons do make the visit or invite Jannetta to their institutions. Others don't.

"My favorite was the surgeon who came here who told us that his chief had told him he had to stay until he saw the spasm go away," Møller says, laughing. "He said, 'No offense, but I can't go back until the spasm is gone.' And he didn't—until *it* did."

Jannetta shakes his head. "Let's see how Dr. Dias is doing," he says. He throws his coffee cup in the wastebasket and heads out of the lounge toward OR 8, where cynic-turned-believer Mark Dias is exploring the cerebellopontine angle of Janice Slater, hoping to leave her vertigo in the operating room.

5

Tough Cases

Mark Dias, M.D., did his undergraduate work at the University of California—Davis before medical school at The Johns Hopkins University, followed by residency in neurosurgery at the University of Pittsburgh. The operation he is performing on Janice Slater—microvascular decompression of the eighth, or auditory nerve, to try and cure her disabling vertigo ("disabling positional vertigo" is the name that Jannetta and Møller have given this particular set of symptoms, or DPV in the acronymic shorthand of the medical community)—falls almost exactly at the midpoint of his residency training. In one month, he will cross the driveway of Presbyterian-University Hospital to the adjacent Children's Hospital of Pittsburgh, where he will continue to work in very tight spaces: on tumors, lipomas with spinal-cord involvement, intracranial aneurysms—all in children. The next year will be spent mostly in the laboratory—a Jannetta-instituted requirement states that all residents spend a year doing basic research—before he returns to Presby for his turn as chief resident.

This morning, things are going well. In mannerism and

deportment, Dias is the classic combination of California cool and old-Eastern-establishment-medical-school confidence; his operating room is a quiet, orderly place.

Jannetta, humming, scrubs briskly in the adjacent scrub room. Dias knows that Jannetta is there. Another resident might back off slightly, waiting for the master, and a year earlier, Dias most certainly would have. But in the step-by-step accruing of experience that is the biggest part of the resident system, Dias is one year older and wiser; he continues working to isolate the branch of the anterior inferior cerebellar artery (AICA) that is pressing on Janice's auditory nerve. Here the dissection is artistic—no blood in the field, structures clearly delineated from one another even on the video screen; through the teaching scope, the view is breathtaking. One can see where the branch of AICA has gently, over the years, worn a slight groove in the soft, buff-colored nerve.

Jannetta backs in and steps into the gown held up by the circulating nurse. "Same case, huh?" he asks. Dias's response is barely audible—he is deep into his work. Jannetta peers into the teaching scope. "Well, we can see the problem here, can't we?" he asks. "Is the tape rolling?"

The tape is indeed rolling, and Dias—reluctantly—deftly removes the instruments he is using and backs away.

"Why don't you tell us about Janice Slater?" Jannetta asks as he situates himself on the metal stool.

"Janice Slater is a forty-three-year-old woman who presented with a five-year history of disequilibrium and vertigo," begins Dias. "The symptoms began suddenly in nineteen eighty-one, disappeared, then reappeared intermittently every two to three weeks, gradually worsening to multiple episodes each day. Electrophysiological testing has been alternately positive on both sides, but there's clear evidence of pathology here on the right side."

As Dias recites the history, Jannetta works quickly with a

blunt hook to move the vessel from the nerve. Or, rather, it seems quickly as compared to the slow and messy progress in Room 12 earlier in the morning. Dias stopped at exactly the limit of his expertise—perhaps a bit further, as he is supposed to. He doubtless could have gone ahead and lifted the vessel himself, put in the bits of felt, closed dura, packed bone chips, closed scalp—he has done so before. But this case is an eighth-nerve case, and the compression is a particularly tortuous branch of AICA. The eighth nerve can be as fragile as wet Kleenex, and a tortuous branch of AICA is not something that a resident wants to cut, because AICA arises from the basilar artery, which supplies the upper brain stem with blood and itself supplies the pons. Stretch or traumatize the eighth nerve, and Janice Slater will be deaf in her right ear; cut AICA, and she has a very good chance of dying.

So it is left for Jannetta to tease the artery away from the nerve gracefully. On the video monitor, where the tip of the instrument is lost in the murky resolution, the branch of the blood vessel at once seems to levitate away from the nerve. "How we doing?" Jannetta asks—one of Møller's monitors is attached to the eighth nerve.

And Møller replies, "Only about a quarter of a millisecond, Peter." In other words, Jannetta is doing just fine.

"What's been her clinical history?" asks Jannetta and, con-versationally, asks the scrub nurse—it is Lisa Hawkins again—for "three pieces of felt, one medium and two small." Hawkins tears off a piece of felt about the size of a pencil eraser from a pad of Teflon about the size of a Band-Aid, and then expertly separates it into two pieces, one of which she rolls between her thumb and forefinger until it looks like a miniature cigar—half a dozen medium pieces would be about the volume of a raisin. She puts the piece in the jaws of a pair of microforceps and places the forceps into Jannetta's hand. As he works, she rolls the two small pieces to finish the order, and lets them rest on the tip of one finger.

Dias is reciting, for the benefit of the video sound track, some of the high—or low—points of Janice's visits to most of the neurologists, psychiatrists, neurosurgeons, and chiropractors on the eastern seaboard. One acupuncturist is also thrown in. Jannetta shakes his head. "Now here is a lady with classic, classic symptoms who saw who knows how many doctors with no relief, and how many of them kept telling her the same things?" No one, of course, answers, because no one knows the answer better than Peter Jannetta. Janice Slater had been to see specialists in four states, beginning within weeks of her first episode of vertigo. The first diagnosis had been an "oversympathetic nervous system," which is another way of saying that something is wrong but the doctor can't put his finger on it. Next, an ear specialist said that nothing was wrong and sent her to a neurologist, who said that something was wrong all right, but that there was nothing anyone could do. He prescribed Valium. Then Janice went to a famous neurologist, who concurred. He prescribed Inderal. Next came a chiropractor, two more neurologists, the acupuncturist, then two psychiatrists. One said she suffered from agorophobia—a fear of the marketplace, he described it. The other, diagnosing along similar lines, said it was a deep-rooted depression about her mother. Through all this, Janice experienced the most profound vertigo. But she kept looking, making a string of appointments using an assumed name, because most of the specialists in her relatively small home state had heard about her by now and were somewhat loath to see her. No one likes to be reminded of the limitations of a profession in such a dramatic way.

Janice finally heard about Peter Jannetta, but from an unlikely source—the *National Enquirer*, in a story about a woman who was cured of unexplained vertigo by a brain operation. A doctor she knew said that Jannetta was most likely a quack, but Janice got one of the neurologists—one of the early ones who knew her by her real name—to make the referral. Then came the trip to Pittsburgh for Thursday-morning clinic, the examination by Jannetta, and the words from him that she works into conversation every chance she gets now that she is postoperative and cured: " 'I think I can help you,' he said. *Five* years, and he says it as simple as that."

Dias, with appropriate operating-room demeanor, glosses over some of this history. Besides, Jannetta has worked in the medium roll of Teflon and one of the small ones; interspersed between the vessel and the nerve, the felt looks like a pair of pillows propping up the tiny branch of AICA. He won't use the third piece after all. It looks like Janice Slater is vertigo-free. "That should do it," Jannetta says, "but I'm going to take another look around and make sure I haven't missed anything."

This is another Jannetta rule: you always look around to make sure you haven't missed another vessel pressing against the nerve. He adjusts the retractor slightly, probes with a blunt hook—gently, gently—and pronounces, "Okay, I'm done. Nice work, Dr. Dias." Jannetta rises, tears off his gown and gloves, shouts a general "Thank you" to everyone in the room, and heads for the door. He pauses, and turns to the anesthesiologist. "Have you got the lines in the next one?" And then Jannetta is gone to the lounge for a quick cup of coffee and a cigarette before tackling Xavier Williams, who, although he doesn't know it, is one of those rare patients whose condition requires a bit of time for reflection and thus has now been waiting forty-five minutes for Jannetta to return.

Each day of Peter Jannetta's week has an outline to it, a framework of routine built around one or two major events. Mondays begin with paperwork at home, paperwork being

the writing of journal articles or books chapters or, less ap-
pealingly, department paperwork. Monday afternoons are
office days, made up of committee meetings, department business meetings—which he despises—correspondence. Tuesday is a surgery day, as is Wednesday, which is also the day of
the weekly clinical conferences: neuropathology at 1:30, clinical neurosciences at 2:30, and neurosurgery residents at 3:30.
Thursday morning is clinic, Thursday afternoon is catchall
time—interviews with residents, catching up on mail, going
to the tailor or the barber. Friday is another half day of work
at home, Saturday morning is the complications conference,
Sunday is paperwork and writing time.

When things are going according to the routine, Jannetta is
out of the OR on Wednesdays in time to talk with the families
of the patients on whom he has just finished operating, eat a
quick lunch, and dictate notes before heading to the weekly
conferences. The weekly conferences are important to Jannetta for several reasons. First, he is the chairman of one of the
major departments involved (the others being neurology and
neuropathology), and he finds it worthwhile to be there as a
symbol of sorts. Second, the neurologists and the the neurology residents are there, and the days are long gone—at least at
Pitt—where the two departments are in open warfare with
each other. Neurologists and neurosurgeons need each other,
Jannetta believes, and they need to know that he believes that
the clinical conferences are important. Finally, he is a teacher,
and the best teachers are always, at some level, students, too.
He likes to know what is going on.

But it is after ten o'clock when he crushes his empty foam
cup and heads back up the hall toward Room 12, where Xavier
Williams has not gone away. Dr. Altschuler is sitting at the
microscope, padding up the blood that oozes from the nick in
the venous sinus. He rises as Jannetta backs into the room,
hands dripping from the third scrubbing of the day. Jannetta

is gowned and gloved, his glasses are removed and set on the ledge, and the lights go down. "Okay," he says. "Let's see what we've got here."

The probing begins as before, following an adjustment of the table. It is rotated toward him, which will allow, he hopes, better access. The retractor is readjusted again as well, and then the quiet probing. Everyone in the room has readjusted, too, to a state of readiness and an anticipated wait, when Jannetta gleefully blurts out, "Ta-da! A nerve!" He has found something—finally.

What he has found is the eleventh, or spinal accessory, nerve. This is not what he was looking for in the specific sense, but, in the general sense, he has found a landmark. It is the feeling one has when, groping in the dark front hall, the hand touches the newel post of the stair railing: suddenly, one knows where everything else is, too.

The eleventh nerve is very low, emerging from along the medulla oblongata, but a neurosurgeon who knows where eleven is knows where everything else is—or knows how to find it. Jannetta moves a blunt probe along the course of the accessory nerve, sees the vagus, or tenth, nerve, briskly dissects away the scar tissue, which is but a minor annoyance now that he knows where he is, adjusts the retractor slightly, checks with Møller, and adjusts the retractor again to expose, wound in among the delicate pia arachnoid, the facial nerve emerging from the pons. Jannetta is absolutely gleeful. "This is virgin territory, here," he says. "Nobody has operated down here before."

What he means is that his earlier suspicions have been confirmed: in Xavier's initial operation at the other hospital, the neurosurgeon found a vessel against the facial nerve all right, but it was not compressing the nerve at the point of emergence, which Jannetta knows is what causes hemifacial spasm. Somewhere along the course of the facial nerve, there is likely a little pad of Teflon, during the insertion of which the facial nerve was traumatized enough to give Xavier the temporary relief he experienced before the return of the symptoms.

Jannetta begins to hum. Altschuler stares motionless through the teaching scope. The others in the room watch the progress on the video monitor, where, finally, there is something to see: on the monitor, the nerve is hard to distinguish from the surrounding connective tissue, but the blood vessels stand out in deep red, AICA snaking across this screen, too.

Jannetta works with microscissors and forceps on the pia arachnoid. "Can you see what I'm doing on the screen?" he asks, and there is a chorus of muffled "yeses." Almost everyone—except Møller, who is watching his oscilloscope—is turned to watch the screen, when a curious thing happens: the operative field, which is in fact the innermost recesses of Xavier Williams's skull but which is generally referred to as the operative field, begins to blur because it is moving. The operative field is moving because the patient is moving, and the patient is moving because the anesthesiology resident has finally lost the game of cat and mouse she has been playing all morning with Xavier Williams. Xavier Williams is waking up.

It is difficult to analyze the various actions and inactions that occur in the next five seconds. Jannetta, having been in the most advantageous position to see his patient begin to move, has stopped the movement of his instruments and extracted them. The anesthesiologist is, somewhat unusually it seems, making a phone call. Jean Stelnak, the scrub nurse, has moved half a step closer to the patient as though to comfort him, though she will touch him only upon instruction. Jannetta, holding his instruments in front of him, says, his voice dripping with perfect disgust, "You let him wake up, didn't you?" It is a rhetorical question.

Xavier has stopped moving. As reconstructed later, he really only moved twice: one movement, a sort of rolling motion, as though he wanted to sleep on his back; and the other, a sort of shrugging motion of the shoulders. By then, the anesthesiologist had turned a valve and quieted him down. But all is not well.

"I want Fred Khalouf in here," Jannetta orders bluntly.

And the resident responds quietly, "I've already called him," which explains, in retrospect, the phone call at what seemed the moment of highest drama. She does not look over the patient toward Jannetta; she is very busy watching Xavier's vital signs. But one senses that if she had absolutely nothing to do, she would find something to prevent her from peering over the operating table at one very angry neurosurgeon.

Jannetta leans back on his stool. At moments like this, wearing sterile gloves inhibits the typical body language of frustration. Jannetta rises from the stool and turns his back on the operating table. One stained track shoe taps on the linoleum floor.

A minute later, Fred Khalouf, the anesthesiologist in charge, breezes in, cheerfully calling out, "How we doing today, Peter?" It would be most surprising to hear Jannetta answer. The casual greeting is Khalouf's way of saying, "It's okay." He is over with the resident immediately, talking briefly with her as he hangs a bag of saline on an IV stand and opens the valve on it wide. Xavier's blood pressure is low, probably from the dose of anesthetic he got in the effort to quiet him down. Khalouf confers again with the resident and then calls across to Jannetta, who is studiously not looking over at the two anesthesiologists. "Everything okay, Peter?"

Jannetta turns slowly, "This can't go on, Fred," he says.

"Everything is gonna be all right here in a minute, Peter," Khalouf replies. He sounds jovial and relaxed. Behind his mask he is grinning his grin, trying to calm everyone down.

Jannetta turns away again. He will not speak sharply to Khalouf, with whom he is a very good and close colleague, but that doesn't mean he has to watch Khalouf and his ministrations. Instead, he looks up at the ceiling, around at the circulating nurse, who sits very still indeed, up at the ceiling again, and finally at Altschuler. Altschuler shrugs. Khalouf pulls over a tall metal stool, clambers onto it, kneeling, and begins squeezing the plastic IV bag between his hands with all his might, pumping it into Xavier Williams in an effort to get him stable again. All the while, he is talking softly with the resident, who does not look him in the eye.

"You'll be all set in a minute, Peter," Khalouf says, and Jannetta turns around again and approaches the table as Khalouf comes down off the stool.

Jannetta situates himself on his stool, but he still has not looked over at the anesthesiologists. He peers into the microscope as Altschuler steps in next to him. "Now, where were we?" Jannetta asks of no one in particular, but the scrub nurse hands him the microforceps, which was what he had had when the patient began moving.

"Everything should be fine now, Peter," says Khalouf, edging out of the room. Jannetta looks up for a moment and then back down into the microscope. Order has returned, but there is still a great deal of tension in the room. It is 10:45 A.M., but compressed into this morning have been enough difficulties and annoyances to last a week, and there is still this operation to finish and one more to go. No one is humming now.

Jannetta begins to dissect the pia arachnoid again, exposing the facial nerve. No blood vessel is immediately apparent, so the retraction is changed slightly, the table is tilted, then tilted back, and Jannetta probes.

Cranial-nerve decompression surgery resembles no other operation in that the drama is sustained and continuous—like a play by Chekhov; unless something unusual—such as the patient waking up—occurs, the offending vessel is found and is isolated from the nerve, and the surgeon leaves through a side door. This is the case, finally, with Xavier Williams. "Here we go," Jannetta says quietly, and everyone looks at the monitor. There is a thin red line at a forty-five–degree angle across the root exit zone of the facial nerve, just at the top of the field. It is a tiny vein, and Jannetta is sure that this is causing Xavier's hemifacial spasm. "Here we go, here we go," Jannetta repeats. "There isn't much to it, is there?" He is referring to the minute diameter of the vessel. "I'm going to lift it off the nerve now, Aage," he calls, and Møller and his technicians stare at their monitor.

Jannetta works a probe under the vessel, but the spasm continues sending a jagged line across the screen of the oscilloscope. "Nothing yet, Peter," says Møller.

"We'll just wait a bit. This just has to be it," Jannetta replies. "There's nothing else around here."

He calls for the microcoagulators and coagulates and divides the vein, more properly described because of its size as a venule.

"I'm sure we got it," Jannetta says.

But Møller replies, "No real change, Peter."

"I'll look around some more, but that should have been it," says Jannetta. He probes along the perimeter of the nerve but finds nothing. "Anything?"

Møller says no, nothing really. It might be slightly decreased, but the spasm is still there.

Jannetta is unperturbed. "We'll wait." And he leans back on his stool and waits.

With another patient waiting in OR 8, with the time of the clinical conferences rapidly approaching, with the apparent precarious state of the patient's anesthesia, it might seem to be a curious thing to do—this waiting. But from Jannetta's point of view, it makes sense. Hemifacial spasm is not always an on/off condition. Remember the second patient ever on whom Jannetta operated for HFS: the symptoms were dramatically present immediately postoperatively but gradually abated over a period of weeks. Jannetta is not going to wait weeks, of course, but sometimes it is instructive to wait and see if the spasm begins to abate after decompression.

But this morning Jannetta does not wait long ("long-term patient, but short-term impatient"). Instead, he asks for a blunt probe and says to Møller, "I think I'll beat up on the nerve a bit." And deftly he does just that, delicately running the tip of the probe against the nerve in an effort to diminish the spasm through deliberate traumatization of the nerve, which often in intractable long-term cases such as Xavier's, relieves the spasm in the short term until the expected permanent effect gradually arrives. "I'm looking around again, but he's gonna be okay," Jannetta says. The spasm is still prominent on the oscilloscope, but Jannetta is, to his mind, done: remove the cause and the symptoms disappear, and Jannetta has removed the cause—again, to his mind. Møller is also convinced, pointing to the monitor and talking to his technicians in low tones as Jannetta begins to close.

Closing the wound is to some degree the resident's job, depending on the level of his or her expertise. The scar that Xavier Williams will live with above one ear will be from stitchwork done by Eric Altschuler, but Jannetta will close the dura himself this morning, mostly because the wound is so inelegant from scar tissue. And it is here that the final dramatic moment of Xavier Williams's long bout with hemifacial spasm occurs—not counting the drama of the disappearing spasm: as Jannetta patiently stitches the dura, standing over the table, his half-glasses back on and the microscope pushed out of the way, a fountain of dark red venous blood suddenly erupts, spurting six inches out of the wound before cascading over Jannetta's gown, scrub pants, white socks, and already-mottled track shoes. Xavier's blood pressure has come back up with a vengeance, forcing blood out of the nick in the venous sinus. Such a blood loss, late in the operation and from a vein, is not particularly dangerous, just spectacular to watch for the two or three seconds it flourishes. Jannetta stares at it for those two or three seconds and then pokes a finger into the wound and presses on the cut in the sinus. The blood stops spurting like water through a dike and slows to a dribble. He doesn't even look over at the anesthesiologist, because he knows he doesn't have to. The scrub nurse passes over three small cotton pads and prepares to irrigate and suction the wound.

By the time that the nick in the sinus has been sutured and the dura closed, it is after eleven o'clock. Jannetta steps back from the table and says ceremoniously, "Dr. Altschuler." Altschuler steps in to pack in the bone chips and finish closing as Jannetta tears off the paper gown and his gloves, and calls to Møller, "I'm going over to Eight. Why don't we get some lunch?"

"In a minute, Peter," Møller replies. He is busy with his computer.

So Jannetta turns back to the OR staff, calls "Thank you, everybody," and stalks out of the room. He is out the door so fast that the chorus of muffled "Thank yous" reverberate off the door as it swings shut.

6

Interim Reports

One of the most awkward, banal, and, finally, inaccurate analogies of the twentieth century is the comparison of the computer to the human brain. The workings of the brain, beyond a most general designation as an "information processor," have little in common with any machine that a human being can make. A slightly more accurate comparison, however, might be between a neurosurgeon and the method of time sharing used by large computers. If your computer is too big for the demands you place on it, its inner workings are idle for what are to the computer vast amounts of time. A computer is well suited for its uses when it is required to be doing something almost all of the time it is in use. In computer usage, this is called "efficient." If one has such a computer, one asks it to be working on tasks for an amount of time just under what would overwhelm it. A contemporary neurosurgeon does almost the same thing, although, unlike the computer, the neurosurgeon's work load is, to a great degree, self-imposed. The "neurosurgical personality" used to describe surgeons who could bear up under the stress of 50-percent mortality in their patients; the new neurosurgical personality describes surgeons who have moved beyond the usual motivators of efficiency—money, curiosity, guilt, self-examination—to a psychological perspective where efficiency is an end in itself. It is not that these neurosurgeons don't know how to have fun, but rather that they don't consider having fun except when they have already done everything else that they can do. Part of this perspective is learned by being around other neurosurgeons who act this way; part of it may be that something attracts a certain kind of personality to the practice of neurosurgery. At the upper end of an efficiency curve are the neurosurgeons who are always doing what they are supposed to be doing, even if they didn't know they were supposed to be doing it until moments before they had to begin doing it. If something unexpected makes a window in the psychological schedule, a good neurosurgeon has a dozen competing activities with which to fill that window.

Peter Jannetta stands outside the swinging doors of OR 12, where he has just finished with Xavier Williams, and thinks for a moment about how to use the time he has before the third patient of the day is ready. If he were a computer, little lights would be flashing as he examined the possibilities. He could visit the families of the two patients operated on so far, but that would mean a second trip up to the patient unit when he finished the third case. He could do his rendition of rounds by dashing through the rooms of those patients on whom he operated the previous week, all of whom are ready today or tomorrow to be discharged. He could see the patients in the Intensive Care Unit—those he operated on yesterday—but they are all up on the eighth floor, too. He could dictate notes; he could sign charts; he could go back to his office and deal with *that* subset of problems; he could change his bloody scrub suit and have lunch. It is a bit too early for his nap.

The decision only takes a moment, and then, decision made, Jannetta goes off in search of someone to tell. He stops at the OR desk, waits politely until one of the nurses behind the desk finishes a phone call, and then tells her, "I'm going to change out of these." He gestures at his scrub shirt and pants, covered with blood from the nick in Xavier Williams's venous sinus. "Go and sign some charts, stop back here, and have lunch. We're still in Eight, you know. Call the office for me?"

The nurse says fine and hands him a new scrub suit before calling Jannetta's office and telling Jannetta's secretary/aide-de-camp/administrative assistant/right-hand person, Patty Caldwell, Jannetta's whereabouts for the next hour or so. One of Patty's hardest jobs is knowing where Jannetta is at any given time, because, in the course of any given day, she is asked that question on fifty or a hundred occasions. Jannetta tends to be better than many in telling someone where he is, will be, or is supposed to be; he is better than most in actually being there. In certain hospitals—and in all hospitals portrayed on television—people need to know where the chief is because he is, or tries to be, in charge of everything, the man to call when a trauma case comes in, the man to call when one of the junior men gets in trouble, the man who rushes in and takes charge. Jannetta has consciously, over the years, designed the program at Pitt quite differently. Each of the hospitals—Presby, Montefiore, Children's, and the Veterans Administration—has its own chief, and each informal subspecialty—vascular cases such as aneurysms, tumors, malignant tumors, spinal work, trauma, stereotaxis—has its own informal chief as well. As for his own cases, Jannetta seeks to be instantly available for the residents who are opening for him on any given day. He is rarely called in for anyone else's case, because the neurosurgeons he has assembled have been assembled, in large part, because they don't need to call the chief.

That he isn't expecting to be summoned into a strange operating room at any given moment doesn't mean, however, that he has any fewer demands on his time. It simply means that the demands take a different form than they would in a more hierarchical department. Furthermore, asking for the chief is in many cases a reflex on the part of most petitioners. For many things, such as university administrative duties, no one but the chief will do anyway. But for many others, Jannetta delegates. He delegates a great portion of his professional working life to his factotum, Patty Caldwell; he delegates other portions, *in toto,* to Ellen Scott and Carol Schuit, the department's administrators; when he went on a sabbatical in 1985, he delegated the chiefdom to Dr. Paul Nelson, who retained that role at Presby when Jannetta returned. And on the medical side, he delegates a little bit of everything to everybody, telling callers with bad backs to see Nelson, callers with cranial-based tumors to see Dr. Laligam Sekhar, callers with malignancies to see Dr. Robert Selker, and so on. After the severest winnowing possible, he is usually left with a day's work at five or six o'clock, which isn't bad for a department chairman. If he didn't delegate, he might never get to play squash or the banjo.

He is detoured almost immediately from changing his scrub suit by two things, one an unanticipated delight and the other a necessary task. The delight takes the form of a kitchen worker hoisting a fresh cauldron of coffee onto the counter in the surgeon's lounge. Although Jannetta doesn't know it, an orthopedic surgeon had raised hell about the coffee running out by mid-morning, and the kitchen had responded by sending over a fresh ten gallons just as Jannetta was passing through the lounge. His face lights up, he smiles, he chats politely with the kitchen worker. He is first in line. With the coffee, he suddenly has time for a cigarette.

As he stretches out in a chair, Fred Khalouf comes in.

"Peter, Peter, Peter," Khalouf says, smiling and sitting down next to Jannetta.

"I don't want to hear about it, Fred," Jannetta says, shaking his head.

"We've got some rough spots," Khalouf continues, still smiling.

Khalouf has what is called a "therapuetic personality": no matter how pressed he is, he makes one feel as though the most important thing on earth is the conversation he is having right now, and that the conversation will, in short order, not only solve whatever immediate problems may or may not exist, but all other problems, too. It is impossible to be cross with someone as genial and anxious to please as Fred Khalouf, a situation he uses to good advantage a dozen times a day.

"These are tough tough cases," he reminds Jannetta, "and it takes a really light hand to make them happen. Those inhalation anesthetics . . ."

He doesn't finish the sentence. Neurosurgeons and anesthesiologists know all about inhalation anesthetics. Anesthesiologists take every opportunity they can to remind neurosurgeons that one of the prices the surgeon pays for light anesthesia is that sometimes it is a little too light. Neurosurgeons then remind anesthesiologists that if neurosurgeons let anesthesiologists have their way, the patients would be out for days. And the anesthesiologists cluck sympathetically and remind the surgeons that these are tough, tough cases.

"I can't be screwing around in there," Jannetta says, unmollified. "We could have killed that guy."

Khalouf nods. "I know, I know, Peter. We're working on it. Okay?" The smile.

Jannetta nods grudgingly. "Just fix it. All right?"

Khalouf slaps Jannetta's knee and stands up. "We will, we will. We'll get it all squared away. I promise."

Khalouf breezes out of the lounge, and Jannetta stubs out his Pall Mall and stands up. He likes Fred Khalouf, knows Khalouf does good work, but he *hates* it when things are screwed up. The sensation of feeling Xavier Williams move as Jannetta poked around near his brain stem with a metal probe hasn't left him yet. It is the kind of thing that neurosurgeons despise, because, beyond the obvious and immediate danger to the patient, it reminds the neurosurgeon of all the things that can go wrong, of all of the things over which the neurosurgeon finally has no control.

"Controlling personalities" is something that neurosurgeons hear of almost as much as they hear of "neurosurgical personalities," but the labels only serve to remind them of just how much is in fact *out* of their control. One can't control the anatomy, and one can't control the physiology; so one has to control oneself and the operating room. Because of this, most neurosurgeons snort at the whole debate about "personality" and surgical specialities—the argument that a certain type of person is drawn to neurosurgery is most often answered with an argument about confusing cause with effect. It is evocative to consider that perhaps neurosurgeons and their infamous "personalities" are made in the operating room, where absolute autocracy is one's best hedge against someone else screwing up your patient. As polite or surly as a neurosurgeon may be, he knows above all else that he couldn't be doing what he is doing if he didn't know exactly what the hell he *was* doing, and letting anything impinge on that is a sure way of giving someone or something the opportunity to mess up an operation. "Rehab[ilitation] wards were designed for pretty good neurosurgeons" is an adage quoted in one form or another by neurosurgical residents all the time. What the residents learn in addition to their craft is the stark difference between fallible and infallible. The whole idea of neurosurgery has come to depend on having the only possibility for error rest within the surgeon, and having him not make any errors. Having a patient wake up puts an even keener edge on already scalpel-sharp days.

After Jannetta changes his scrub suit, he puts on a freshly starched white lab coat, knee-length with "Peter J. Jannetta, M.D., Neurological Surgery" sewn in blue script across the left breast pocket, and walks briskly down to the first floor and enters Medical Records. He zips past half a dozen clerks, saying "Good morning" to each "Good morning, Doctor," and reaches a small desk stacked with patient records. Each patient, past and present, at Presbyterian-University Hospital has a manila file folder with color-coded tabs on the edge stored here. Contained within the record are all of the paraphernalia of modern record keeping: lab reports, progress notes, medication notes, admission notes, discharge notes, preoperative reports, operative reports, postoperative reports, visits on rounds, visits by consultants, visits by social service, by nursing, by dietary. The theory is that the sum and total of the patient's hospital experience is contained in objective detail within the medical record, and the information therein belongs, in essence, to the patient, although the record itself belongs to the hospital. A hospital patient leaves behind him or her a paper trail, and, technically, no admission is finished until the paperwork is done. The stack of charts before Jannetta represents two months worth of his patients. Each chart has a cover sheet that lists the patient's name, number and dates of hospitalization, the admission diagnosis, and the discharge diagnosis. And each cover sheet needs to be signed by Peter J. Jannetta, M.D., himself, in person, in ink, and with no abbreviations, no initials, no illegible scrawls. Patty Caldwell can sign his correspondence, his paycheck, and his memos, but charts need to be signed by the attending physician. And no clever rubber-stamp fascimiles, either. He takes out a Pall Mall and a pen, lights one, brandishes the other, and sets to work.

As he signs his name, he gives an "uh-huh," as though this is the final step in the treatment—which, in a sense, it is. For patients covered by Medicare, Medicaid, or most private insurance plans, the hospital can't be paid until the chart is signed. Patient Accounting would thus prefer that each chart is signed on the day of discharge. Most physicians would choose to come in once a year or perhaps every other year and sign them all at once; Medical Records plays the heavy and tries to get the physicians to come in on a fairly regular basis.

It is not onerous work—Jannetta zips through the charts with a practiced hand, finishing in about twenty minutes—but it is not neurosurgery, either, and he moves as though he can't wait to get out of there. From Medical Records, he climbs a flight of stairs, ducks down a hall, and enters Dining Room II, which is where hospital physicians can eat a quick lunch. The food is the same as is served in the hospital's main dining hall, but it is quieter and secluded. Presby's main cafeteria is, for all practical purposes, open to the public, and doctors, often accused of being aloof and hard to find, do spend a great deal of their time with the public. Dining Room II is a hideaway.

Jannetta fills his tray—baked fish, roasted potatoes, green beans, a salad, coffee—and sits down with Aage and Margareta Møller. Both, like Jannetta, wear lab coats over scrub suits. Aage is telling Margareta about Xavier Williams.

Margareta Møller, M.D. and Ph.D. (in neurophysiology), performs much of the neurological testing for Jannetta's patients with acoustic disorders, such as Jannetta's other first patient this morning, Janice Slater, whose disabling positional vertigo Jannetta is certain he has cured. Specialized neurological testing at Presby is a small industry of its own primarily because of the dramatic improvement and sophistication of current physiological testing techniques, but also because Jannetta wants—and needs—electrophysiological data on patients with cranial-nerve disorders to support his contention that something physiological (as contrasted to, say, the purely psychological) is wrong with the patients in the first place and that microvascular decompression makes what is wrong right again in the second. In Janice Slater's case, a test of the electrical activity of her auditory nerves suggested a definite pathology on the right side, manifested as a latency in the evoked potentials similar to what Aage Møller monitors intraoperatively when he is watching a patient's auditory nerve. Auditory evoked potentials are well understood as diagnostic tests for conditions such as acoustic-nerve tumors—the presence of the tumor alters the electrophysiological performance of the nerve. But Janice Slater had no tumor—the CT scans and other confirmatory tests were negative—which left Jannetta fairly sure that what she had was vascular compression of the auditory nerve.

Interestingly, several of the evoked potential tests on Janice Slater were positive for the left side as well, so Margareta Møller is interested in finding out what Jannetta found at operation. "I don't know if she's got a problem on the left side or not," he tells her (he has had two patients where the compression was truly bilateral—both the right and left nerves were compressed, necessitating two operations). "But we definitely had a problem on the right side, and we definitely took care of it. She's going to be fine." A classic Jannetta Statement of Fact. Margareta Møller nods and smiles, then quips about one of Janice Slater's many diagnoses—the one about an "oversympathetic nervous system." "The left side was sympathizing with the right, no?" and they all laugh.

Jannetta would like to linger over another cup of coffee, but he has one more patient in the OR, and it is almost noon. "I'm going back down, Aage," he says as he stands and stretches.

"Be right with you, Peter," Møller replies, but by the time he finishes the last syllable of "Peter," Jannetta is already halfway out the door.

He moves down a back hallway, past dietary carts full of the detritus of patients' meals, through an unmarked doorway, doubles back, and enters another unmarked door, which puts him just off the surgeon's lounge. A stranger could follow him a dozen times and still not pick up the route, but Jannetta is emphatically at home in the warrens and passageways of Presby's second floor. In the locker room, he hangs up his white coat and heads for the OR, picking up a new paper mask en route. In Room 12, the scene is much as it was when he left an hour ago, only Xavier Williams has been replaced on the operating table by Ellen Goldberg, who has trigeminal neuralgia. She is already asleep, and Dr. Altschuler is meticulously dabbing up a bit of blood from the opening he has made in her skull. The timing is perfect. Since it is three minutes after twelve, Jannetta says, "Good afternoon, everyone," as he passes into the scrub room to wash his hands for the sixth time. When he comes out, Aage Møller is at his monitor, Jean Stelnak is standing next to Altschuler, and the circulating nurse helps Jannetta step into his gown. "Tra-la-la," he says as he spins through three-quarters of a pirouette so that the gown's paper belt can be tied around his waist; the tension of the first operation in OR 12 is gone, replaced with Jannetta at his most businesslike.

Gloves on, he steps up to Ellen Goldberg's head, accepts a scalpel from Jean Stelnak, and opens the dura. This is textbook surgery. The dura is sewn back with a few stitches, the retractor's first placement can't be improved upon, and, within a very few minutes, the microscope is in, Jannetta is on his stool, and he is looking for the cause of what he jocularly refers to as "the trouble."

Ellen Goldberg is luckier than many sufferers of trigeminal neuralgia. First, she lives in New York City. Doctors and nondoctors alike will tell you that if you have something unusual, it's better to have it in a big city than a small town—there are more doctors willing to take a crack at discovering what is causing the trouble, and you're less likely to end up using pseudonyms, as Janice Slater did, as you pursue a diagnosis and a cure.

Second, Ellen's husband is a physician himself. Jannetta always refers to him as "an enlightened physician" when discussing Ellen, because he was not only open-minded enough to pursue alternative diagnoses, he was also open-minded enough to have faith in the diagnosis—and the proposed treatment—that he found most plausible: trigeminal neuralgia treated by microvascular decompression.

Still, it wasn't easy for Ellen to find her way to Pittsburgh. She started out with a dentist, who didn't diagnose trigeminal neuralgia. In addition to the spasms of pain common to most sufferers, she had a constant dull ache in her jaw as well and thus was sent to a temporomandibular-joint specialist. From there, she went to a neurologist, who diagnosed TGN and prescribed Tegretol, which didn't work. Then she went to a relaxation therapist, another neurologist, two oral surgeons, an ear, nose, and throat specialist, and an acupuncturist ("And no 'professional courtesy' from acupuncturists," Dr. Goldberg told Jannetta). From there, with the pain coming more and more frequently, Ellen and her husband went to a medical center in the East to see an eminent neurologist who prescribed Dilantin, and a neurosurgeon who didn't think she was a good candidate for rhizotomy. Then, their son mentioned his mother's problem to an acquaintance in the Department of Anesthesiology at Montefiore Medical Center, New York City, and the acquaintance mentioned Dr. Ronald Apfelbaum, a neurosurgeon there who was a former colleague of

Jannetta's. Apfelbaum suggested microvascular decompression and asked if they were willing to go to Pittsburgh. At this point, Ellen Goldberg would have gone to the moon.

Her trigeminal neuralgia first manifested itself almost three years previously, when she bit down on a sticky cough drop. For the next thirty-three months, her life changed so dramatically that she was afraid that she would go mad.

"I'm sure that everybody talks about the pain," she says, after the operation, "but there is really no way to talk about the pain. It's a . . . *presence,* as though you're really two people, one a prisoner and one a torturer—you're a prisoner of the pain. I couldn't do anything that normal people do: I couldn't brush my teeth, couldn't put on lipstick, couldn't talk. For a year, I don't think I said more than a dozen words, because as soon as I opened my mouth, the pain would be there. I would carry a note pad and a pen, and my husband and I would have these conversations. He would talk, I would write." She laughs, something else she didn't do for nearly three years. "It was so *frustrating.* We didn't have an argument the whole time, because I couldn't keep up my end. I would write in big letters, 'I'M SHOUTING AT YOU!!' on the note pad.

"Oh, and the telephone. We had to have a second line put in, because I'd answer and all I could say was 'Hm.' So we had another phone put in just for my husband, so he could talk and I wouldn't have to." She laughs again. "When I get home, I am going to run up the world's largest phone bill—phone phone phone phone phone! I may *never* shut up!"

The cause of Ellen Goldberg's trigeminal neuralgia is easy for Jannetta to find. In the relatively short history of microvascular decompression, the small branch of the anterior inferior cerebellar artery—AICA—that is pressing against the root of her right trigeminal nerve fits the definition of "classical." "Look at this one, Aage," Jannetta calls, and Møller comes over, watches the monitor for a moment, and then steps up to the teaching scope when Altschuler steps aside.

"So there it is," says Møller.

"There it is," says Jannetta. "Say, is the tape on?"

The tape isn't on. Jannetta has been moving briskly, and no one thought to roll the videotape. Jean Stelnak does so now, and Jannetta zips through the narration himself. "This is a forty-five-year old woman—the wife of an enlightened New York City physician—with right-sided trigeminal neuralgia. There was an abrupt onset of symptoms . . . three years, Dr. Altschuler? . . . three years before operation. In the last year or so, she had thirty to forty episodes per day of forty- to sixty-seconds duration. What we see here is a branch of AICA that is wound against the root entry zone of Five, and we're about to lift the artery away from the nerve. Let's have some small pieces of felt—two or three—while I take a quick look around and see if there's anything else here."

Jean Stelnak has the felt ready on the microforceps, and when Jannetta is ready, he deftly interposes first one, then another, in between AICA and the nerve. He snakes out the electrode that has been monitoring the patient's eighth nerve and, backing away slightly, deftly begins to close the dura. He also begins to hum. "You can call upstairs and tell them that we found the trouble and we fixed it, and that I'll be up in a bit," he says, and he backs away from the table. "Doctor?"

Altschuler steps in to close the skull and the scalp, and Jannetta calls out his "Thank you, everyone" as the door of the operating room swings shut behind him. In stark contrast to Xavier Williams's long morning, Ellen Goldberg has had not quite fifty minutes with Peter J. Jannetta, something that she says she plans to tell anyone who will listen, along with three years worth of other things.

Surgery for this day is over for Jannetta, and he now moves, if it is possible, even more briskly. He tears off his paper gown on his way down the hall to the surgeon's lounge, where he pours a cup of coffee, tilting the urn toward him to get the last remnants, dashes into the locker room, dons his white coat, comes back, looks critically at the wall clock, pauses, seems to collate for a moment, and ducks into one of the dictating booths in the lounge.

The booths, which resemble the booths for cutting one's own records that were popular in the late 1950s, have a low stool, a low counter, and a telephone. Presby has recently installed a sophisticated new dictating system, "so sophisticated," Jannetta says, "that half of us still can't get the damn thing to work right." The old system was a glorified phone answering machine into which the surgeons dictated their operative notes. This new system requires the surgeons to call the Transcription Department and then, via the touch-tone phone, enter their ID number, the patient's ID number, and a code for the type of information about to be dictated. Other codes allow them to back up and start over, to listen to what they have dictated, to dictate notes on another patient without starting all over.

From the pocket of his scrub suit, Jannetta takes a bit of note paper on which he has written the ID numbers of the three patients he has operated on and, after a few false starts, gets connected. The first dictation is for Janice Slater: "Title of operation, right retromastoid craniectomy, microvascular decompression of auditory nerve. The surgeon is Peter J. Jannetta, the assistant is Dr. Mark Dias. The anesthesia is general. Preoperative diagnosis was disabling positional vertigo, right-sided; postoperative diagnosis, same.

"Operative findings: The eighth nerve was compressed severely at the brain stem by the lateral branch of the anterior inferior cerebellar artery, which was adjacent to the nerve rostrally, grooving the nerve.

"Procedure: The patient was anesthetized, intubated, placed in the left lateral decubitus position in the usual way using the three-point head holder. The back of the head was shaved, prepped and draped in the usual fashion. A two-by-two-and-a-half-centimeter-in-diameter retromastoid craniectomy was performed through a five-and-a-half-centimeter incision in the usual way. The bone was waxed. Hemostasis was secured in the soft tissues with the bipolar. The dura was opened obliquely, sewn back out of the way and the microscope was brought into play. We came easily to the brain stem on the rostral side of the nerve after an initial attempt caudally. A direct electrode was placed on Eight on the rostral side, and opening the arachnoid, we saw the pathology as noted above. The branch of the artery was mobilized and held away with shredded Teflon felt, which appeared to give satisfactory decompression and, indeed, when the arterial branch was first mobilized, the BSERs and direct auditory potentials improved. There was no bleeding on repeated Valsalva maneuvers. Indeed, we had not taken any vessels. Retractor, rubber dam, and cottonoid were removed. The dura was closed in watertight fashion with Neurolon. Bony chips were replaced and the wound closed in the usual fashion. A dry dressing was applied. The patient tolerated the procedure well and left the OR in satisfactory condition. Estimated blood loss was less than one hundred milliliters, replaced, none.

"A videotape and some thirty-five–millimeter color slides were taken of the procedure. Dr. Aage Møller monitored BSERs, and direct auditory compound actual potentials."

And that was that. The operative report will be transcribed, added to the patient's records, and eventually find its way to the Medical Records Department, where it will sit in a manila folder in a stack awaiting Jannetta's signature. By then, Janice Slater will have long been back home.

Jannetta dictates the other two cases, Xavier Williams's taking a bit longer as Jannetta describes the scarring that made the operation so difficult. No mention is made of Xavier Williams moving during the surgery—no harm, no foul is the general attitude. Ellen Goldberg's takes the least time of all. Jannetta is watching the clock creep toward 1:30, which is when Clinical Neuroscience Conference begins. He remembers to mention that the videotape was running for only part of the exploration and notes that Ellen Goldberg tolerated the procedure "extremely" well. Other than changes in the specific findings, the operative notes are couched in almost identical language—"the usual fashion," "the microscope was brought into play," and so on. These are songs Jannetta has sung many times before.

Dictation done, Jannetta now heads for the Postanesthesia Recovery Room, or the "PAR." Xavier Williams and Ellen Goldberg are still there, but Janice Slater has already been moved up to NCCU, or the Neurosurgery Continuous Care Unit, on the eighth floor of the hospital. The PAR is brightly lit and bustling, and Jannetta stops at the desk and asks for his patients. A scrub-suited nurse leads him to Xavier Williams and Ellen Goldberg, lying next to each other on gurneys and covered with identical white cotton blankets. Williams is sleeping—snoring, in fact—but Goldberg is half-awake. Jannetta squeezes her hand and, bending to her ear, asks her how she is doing. Her eyes flutter. "You're going to be just fine," he tells her, and, with one last squeeze, he heads upstairs to NCCU.

On the eighth floor, he moves down a hall to Unit 83— Eighth Floor, 3 Wing—and into the visitors' lounge. There are fifteen or so people in there, most of them sitting, a few staring out the window. And when he comes in, everyone looks up expectantly. More than many surgeons, Jannetta is recognized and recognizable. Often he can return the favor, but not always. Dr. Goldberg, Ellen's husband, spots Jannetta and moves over to talk to him, as does Herbert Slater, Janice's husband; Xavier Williams's wife has never met Jannetta, so she looks up with the rest of the people in the room but doesn't rise.

Dr. Goldberg gets there first and shakes Jannetta's hand. Jannetta recognizes him and says, "Everything's fine, just fine. We found an artery just where we should have, and we took care of it. Her troubles should be over."

Goldberg asks where his wife is, and Jannetta replies that she's still downstairs. Goldberg thanks Jannetta profusely, asks a question or two about the operation—professional curiosity—shakes his hand again, and moves to the pay telephone on the wall of the lounge to call their children.

Herbert Slater moves up next, and just as Jannetta calls out "Slater?" Herbert reaches out to shake Jannetta's hand, too. "Oh, right here in front of me," says Jannetta, but Slater waves the apology away. "Everything's fine," Jannetta says, "just fine. We found an artery just where we should have, and we took care of it. Her troubles should be over."

Slater wants to know if they had the correct side after all—those conflicting test reports have been weighing on him and his wife for several days. They would hate, he says, to go through it all again. "No, no, we got the right side," says Jannetta. "We definitely found trouble on the right side, and we fixed it. I think she's going to be just fine. She's already up, by the way. Talk to one of the girls at the desk about getting in to see her."

Again, the profuse thanks, and Slater leaves the lounge. Jannetta looks around expectantly. No one moves. "Ummm, let's see," he says. "Campbell—no, Williams? Mrs. Williams?"

Xavier Williams's wife rises and crosses the lounge, and Jannetta moves to meet her. "I'm Pete Jannetta," he says, and he takes her hand in both of his. "He's doing just fine, just fine. We had a little trouble with all the scarring from the first operation, but we found the trouble, and we fixed it. He

153

should be just fine. You can check with the girls at the desk, and see when he's coming up."

It is said that the most grateful patients are the mothers of newborn babies. If this is so, they must be overwhelming to outthank the spouses and children of neurosurgery patients. Jannetta's patients are in a minority, because he does what he calls "happy surgery"—he makes people better. Most neurosurgery patients at big urban medical centers are not having "happy surgery"—they are having tumors removed or aneurysms clipped or emphatically unhappy results of trauma repaired. But Jannetta's patients, if things go well, are happy patients, and this makes their family and friends happy, too. Elva Williams, who is about five feet two inches tall, impulsively rises onto her toes to give Peter Jannetta a kiss on his cheek. He smiles, he laughs, he thanks her, and then, as quickly as he can, he extricates himself and backs out of the lounge.

As he turns the corner, he almost runs into Sharon Sell, Head Nurse for Unit 83 and NCCU. She has her chart with her, having been alerted that Jannetta was on the floor. "Oh," she says, "hello."

Jannetta squeezes her arms. "Hello, Ms. Sell," emphasizing the "z" sound in "Ms." and smiling.

"Are you doing rounds?" she asks.

"No, no, no. I've got conference. I'll be back up this afternoon," he says. "We'll do 'em all at once." He says this over his shoulder. It is exactly 1:30, and he needs to stop in the office to check with Patty and get a cup of coffee before he settles into the afternoon conferences.

Scaife Hall, which houses most of the offices, classrooms, lecture halls, and laboratories of the University of Pittsburgh School of Medicine, is connected with Presby by a tunnel, a cafeteria, and half a dozen floors of a building, called the A-Stem, cunningly inserted between them. As is apparently required in hospital architecture, the numbered floors in one building do not match with the numbered floors in the next. Jannetta zips down two flights of stairs, cuts through the A-Stem, and emerges in Scaife Hall, where he rides an escalator down to the fourth floor, to the offices of the Department of Neurological Surgery. Since the first two conferences are in a lecture hall almost opposite the offices, he is not delayed much by ducking into his office for messages and coffee.

Patty Caldwell is on the phone when he comes in, as are Judy Campbell and Gail Schwartzmiller, two other department secretaries who share the outer office with Patty. The phones in the office start ringing at about 8:00 A.M. and quit, after a fashion, when they are switched to the answering service around 5:00 each day. In between, there are calls from prospective patients, from current patients, from former patients; from residents, from colleagues, from laboratory staff; from business-office people, from medical-records people, from the medical-school administration; from referring physicians, from former colleagues, from physicians wanting a little more information; from Radiology, from Central Imaging (which does the CT scans), from NMR; from Pathology, Rehabilitation Medicine, Orthopedic Surgery; from medical-equipment salesmen, from computer salesmen, from office-supply salesmen; from Patient Accounting, from Patient Billing, from Patient Records; from financial planners, from accountants, from life-insurance salesmen; from medical-conference organizers, from travel agents, from medical journals; from old friends, from brief acquaintances, from total strangers; from reporters, from lawyers, from risk managers; from family, from Jannetta's squash partner, from his tailor, from an auto-rental agency. Patty does a triage of sorts with phone calls, listening intently for a few moments before deciding if (a) she can handle it without writing it down, (b) she can handle it, but needs to write it down, (c) someone else can handle it, which means it needs to be written down, (d) Jan-netta alone has to handle it, which means that not only does it need to be written down, but it needs to be handed to him with an explanation, or (e) not only does Jannetta have to handle it, but he needs to handle it expeditiously, which means it needs to be taped to his office door. Patty Caldwell spends as much time on the phone as Ellen Goldberg is plan-ning to when she gets home from the hospital.

Because she spends so much time on the phone doesn't mean that Patty doesn't get to do anything else. In fact, she is usually doing at least two things, sometimes three, or else she would disappear completely beneath the stack of correspon-dence, patient records, medical journals, journal articles, memos, videotapes, color slides, and phone messages that cover her desk and counter. Over time, the piles change in character but not in size. This afternoon, she looks up as Jan-netta comes in and starts reading the half-dozen pink mes-sages taped to his door. Patty hangs up the phone and briefs him on what they mean as he leafs through them gingerly. "The rental-car man will be here between three-thirty and four, you've got a squash court at five-thirty, and two of those"—she points at a separate group of messages taped to the door—"are about patients for clinic tomorrow, and the other three are calling about referrals."

Jannetta continues to leaf. "Who's Thomas Adams, M.D.?"

Patty thinks. "He is . . . let me see it."

Jannetta peels it off the stack and hands it to her.

"Oh, he's got a patient with torticollis and wants you to see her. But he needs to talk to you today, because he's going out of town for a week," she says, after deciphering her handwrit-ing. "Do you want him now?"

"I've got to go over," Jannetta says. "I'll come back before two-thirty and take him and the other three. Is there coffee?"

There is coffee, and, plastic-foam cup filled, Jannetta

crosses the fourth-floor hall and enters Lecture Room 1. He is seven minutes late, which means that he is arriving after about half—but, he likes to think, before about half, too—of the surgeons, neurologists, pathologists, residents, medical students, and nursing students who meet every Wednesday for Clinical Neuroscience, colloquially referred to as "brain cutting," for reasons that will soon become apparent.

7

The Brain Trust

The weekly calendar for the medical school runs to two pages of single-spaced entries, ranging in a given semester from something like Otolaryngology Tumor Review at 7:30 A.M. on Monday to Surgical Grand Rounds at 10 A.M. on Saturday. In between, specialists, subspecialists, generalists and their medical students, interns, and residents meet in a staggering array of configurations. There are lectures, conferences, clubs, rounds, and boards in pediatric ear, nose, and throat, the anatomy of rheumatology, mycology, emergency medicine, pediatrics, general medicine, neuropathology, biochemistry, renal electrolytes, endocrinology, radiology, ophthalmic pathology, ophthalmology, immunology, cardiology, neurobiology, anesthesia, patient management, gastrointestinal disorders, urological surgery, and critical-care medicine, to mention the events of one day, and, of course, every possible permutation of the neurosciences: the basic science of neurology, pediatric neurology, neuropathology (microscopic), neuropathology (gross), clinical case conferences, interdisciplinary conferences, multidisciplinary conferences. The centerpieces for the neurosurgeons, however, are the Wednesday conferences and the Saturday-morning complications conference. Around these the neurosurgeons try to work.

Observers of the neurosciences are quick to generalize on the differences—psychological, physical, and metaphysical—between neurologists and neurosurgeons. At many medical schools, psychiatry, with its own conferences, students, specialists, and residents, is also blended into the stew. At Pitt, primarily because of the existence of the huge Western Psychiatric Institute and Clinic, the psychiatrists tend not to cross DeSoto Street to mingle at Wednesday conferences. But neurology and neurosurgery provide enough distinctions to make such observations, while not completely accurate by any means, interesting enough. Neurology is like the science of the consulting detective; neurologists spring at clues like a bevy of Sherlock Holmes, contemplating for their Watsons the vagaries of the nervous system. By comparison, neurosurgery is pragmatic, down-to-earth, physical. It is a rivalry that varies in intensity from place to place—indeed, from country to country. In England, the neurologist tends to hold sway, and the neurosurgeons are the workmen; a charming analogy is the neurologist as a sculptor like Henry Moore and the neurosurgeons like the welders and foundry workers who execute the grand designs. In many medical centers in the United States, the roles are reversed, and the neurosurgeon is king. Pitt boasts the closest thing there can be to a truce, partly because of the personalities involved, partly because the sheer size of the institution means enough good work for everyone, partly because Peter Jannetta and his counterpart in neurology have worked to establish a truce. Neurologists have their jokes about neurosurgeons ("Neurosurgeons know nothing but will try anything"), neurosurgeons have their jokes about neurologists ("Neurology is what you do while you wait for the CT scans"), but collegiality generally rules the day, quiet snorts notwithstanding. (The quiet snort is an art in itself, practiced by residents in both neurology and neurosurgery. Since the neurologists all sit on the right side of LR 1 and the neurosurgeons all sit on the left side, quiet snorting involves equal parts of skill and the physics of sound. Ideally, only the resident on the other side of the room who has said something that one thinks is particularly wrongheaded hears the snort, but it is all right if, say, all of the residents on the other side of the room hear it, too. Points are lost if the chief or any of the attending physicians on the other side of the room hear the snort and look askance at *your* chief or attendings. Attendings, rather than snorting, practice the subtle smirk, seen only by the people on one's own side of the room. Perhaps once a week, the subtle smirk is accompanied by the rolling of the eyes heavenward. But an attending would rather die than be seen as criticizing someone on the other side of the room. Attendings are as comitous as members of the U.S. Senate, right down to referring to their "esteemed colleagues.")

The master of ceremonies at brain cutting and the conference that follows it is John Moossy, M.D., Chief of the Division of Neuro and Ophthalmic Pathology, who conducts the meetings with northern efficiency and southern charm. Generally, by 1:45, the group is assembled: half a dozen attendings from neurosurgery, a dozen from neurology, most of the residents from both programs, a row of medical students, another row of nursing students, a few pathology residents. Moossy gets things started by turning things over to the pathology resident who will present the case. At a table in the front of the room, there is a cardboard screen shielding a lidded glass jar containing a clear solution of Formalin (which years ago replaced the iconic formaldehyde) and, resting gently on the bottom, the brain of the patient whose illness and death form the center of the day's conference. On a tripod next to the table, a video camera is aimed at the brain, and it broadcasts a picture to two television monitors that hang from the ceiling of LR 1. As the resident begins to read his presentation, Dr. Julio Martinez, one of the attending neuropathologists at Presby, puts on surgical gloves and carefully lifts the brain out of the jar and places it on a slab. Then, with a large knife, he methodically begins to make gross serial sections of the brain—slices about half an inch thick, from the anterior aspect of the brain toward the posterior. Each section is placed in the order in which it was cut on a flat aluminum tray. The image of the sections is picked up by the camera and appears on the monitors.

Jannetta slouches in one of the theater-style seats of the lecture hall amid the other attendings; the residents sit in a similar group about five rows back. As the pathology resident reads, haltingly, from the case report he has prepared, most of the people in the room scan photocopies of the case report that were passed out at the beginning of the conference. It is part of the ritual of hospital conferences that the report be read aloud in all of its medicolingual opacity, including a history of the patient's ailments, results of the physical exam, results of lab tests, and the hospital course. Unlike the conference that follows this, the results of the hospital course are always made obvious by the presence of the patient's brain in a jar on the front table. The cases are selected because they represent interesting clinical phenomena, unusual pathology, classic clinical problems, or good opportunities to second-guess in a professional setting. This case has elements of at least three of the four—only the pathology is evident from both the report and from the flickering video images of the serial sections, which show a large damaged area within the right frontal lobe of the cerebrum.

The case is only of passing interest to Jannetta, and, in fact, to most of the neurosurgeons, because it is a pediatric case, because neurosurgery offers nothing for the kind of damage represented, and, perhaps more philosophically, because the patient is dead. They are there because their residents are there (the residents rotate through Children's Hospital during their seven years at Pitt), because the pediatric neurosurgeons are there, because the neurologists and John Moossy are there (neurosurgeons hate being chided for having anything less than a fervent interest in the kinds of neurological phenomena that passionately interest the branches of the science of the brain), and, finally, because Jannetta believes it is important for the neurosurgeons to be there. These reasons do not, however, prevent some of the neurosurgeons and their residents from writing notes about their own patients, reading reports, or glancing at the clock. One attending is methodically opening, glancing at, and sorting a large stack of mail.

"The patient was a two-and-a-half-year-old white girl admitted with increasing cyanosis and decreasing exercise tolerance due to a complex cyanotic congenital heart disease," the resident is reading.

The child had a very short and very hard life. At age three months, she had had open-heart surgery to partially repair a very damaged and deformed heart, and two years later, during a diagnostic procedure—cardiac catheterization, in which a thin tube (the catheter) is fed into one of the large veins in the leg, through the abdominal aorta and into the heart; once in place, dye is injected through the catheter and a variety of X rays are taken of the heart as it pumps the blood and the opaque dye—she had a cerebrovascular "accident," or stroke, which weakened her left side and affected her speech. A CT scan at the time showed old neurological damage in the left hemisphere of her brain but nothing new on the right side (the right side of the brain controls the left side of the body and vice versa). She was admitted to Children's for another open-heart procedure two weeks after the cerebrovascular accident, and a new CT scan showed a new area of damage in the right frontal lobe.

The open-heart surgery went well, but following the operation, the child began to deteriorate: the heart simply wasn't functioning. Two days after the surgery, the ventilator that was helping her breathe was disconnected, and she died—eighteen days after the cerebrovascular accident during the cardiac catheterization.

When the resident has finished his report, Dr. Martinez takes the aluminum tray and hands it to a neurology resident who is sitting in the first row. He looks at it briefly, then passes it on to the person behind him. In this manner, the tray slowly makes its way around the room as Dr. Moossy asks his customary leading questions. There is discussion of the old damage in the left hemisphere, which, on closer examination, is substantial. The damaged areas are called "infarcts" (from the Latin *infarcire*, "to stuff," as in "clog" or "obstruct"). Something blocked the blood vessel that brought blood and oxygen to that part of the brain and thus stifled that part of the brain. "How old is old?" Moossy asks, and the physicians in the room offer possibilities: at or shortly after birth; at or shortly after the first heart operation; at the time of the first cardiac catheterization, when the girl was three months old. Then Moossy asks, "How new is new?" and they contemplate the fresher infarcts on the right side of the brain. The neurologist who consulted on the patient when she was first admitted comments on the results of the neurological exam he conducted. He is quizzed on just how bad off the child seemed to be.

When the tray reaches Jannetta, he perks up and examines the sections with interest. The newer infarct on the right side is modest compared to the deep and profound damage on the left. "This was not a good kid to begin with," he murmurs, and he promptly raises his hand—like a child in school.

Moossy calls on him immediately, interrupting a resident by saying, "I think Peter is going to resolve all of this for us."

"I'm not presuming to resolve anything," Jannetta says with a smile. "But I wonder, I want to ask someone who saw this kid, did she seem to be okay? Was she mostly all there?"

Moossy modifies this before the neurologist has a chance to answer. "What Peter is getting at is the size of the old infarcts, I think," he says. "Are you wondering if she was out of it to begin with? How can we tell if the damage was, say, *in utero,* as opposed to at, say, age three months?"

The discussion then moves off into the realm of neuropathology, with several of the pathology residents trying to talk at once. When the discussion comes back to the neurology side of the room, someone notes that the child wasn't "extraordinarily" alert, but only "somewhat" alert.

Jannetta says, "I ask, because I don't think this was a good kid to begin with. I'm wondering what the cardio people were thinking they were doing, and I'm wondering what the parents were thinking they were doing. What about the parents? Were they with it? Or the other kids in the family—are they all good kids? Are they okay?"

There is a good-natured chuckle in the room every time Jannetta uses the phrase, "good kid." They know what he means: "neurologically intact," but also "well developed, neurologically," a good candidate for a series of cardiac operations.

A neurologist answers. "The other children are normal— this child has an identical twin, you know, and the parents report no problems with her. The parents themselves," he pauses, "no, I wouldn't say they're particularly on the ball. They're from . . . ," and he names a nearby state, "and I don't get the impression that the pre- or postnatal care was thorough. Not necessarily contributory, but the history is very sketchy and contradictory in places."

The tray has made its way to the neurology side of the room, and there are questions about the old infarcts again. Even with highly sophisticated tools like CT scans, it is still immensely valuable to see closely and clearly neurologic phenomena.

An older neurologist sitting back near the residents speaks for the first time, and his voice is the voice of authority. "I think you've got two issues here: you've got a relatively mild event that happened recently, and you've got an old, massive infarct whose effects would have eventually overshadowed the effects of the second infarct. I agree with Peter that the cardio people should have thought this through a bit differently, because the ball is really in their court."

"Is there anyone here from cardio?" someone asks.

Dr. Moossy answers. "We tried to get someone here, but he couldn't make it. What we were told was that they really didn't consider the neurological implications beyond the initial consult. They asked if they could do the surgery and didn't take it beyond that. Are you asking if they *should* have done the surgery?"

Several physicians start speaking at once, and Jannetta raises his hand again, and, again, Moossy calls on him almost immediately. "I wonder if this is a case that just sort of got rolling and kept rolling—if they lost sight of the big picture and treated the problem and not the patient?"

This is one of Jannetta's recurring themes, because what the physicians in the room are finally talking about is what medicine has become. Some would say they are talking in a roundabout way about social engineering or euthanasia or playing God, and to some degree they may be. But they are also specifically talking about a little girl with profound heart problems and a chancy neurological state being operated on with only the profound heart problems in the forefront of the medical strategy. Medical progress has, in essence, created the problem of medical progress. Physicians regularly save smaller and smaller infants and older and older adults and patients of all ages with more and more difficult problems because they have learned how to do it. The kinds of cases that come up more often in discussions among medical professionals are cases that a decade ago—or a year ago—wouldn't have come up, because there wasn't anything that anyone could do. Physicians in the neurosciences are particularly sensitive to these issues, because medical progress constantly reminds everyone that there is biological life and something that one might call "neurological" life. Is it good medicine or good ethics to "save" someone for a minimally neurological life? Or is it bad medicine not to "save" everyone that one can?

Jannetta raises the question gently. Most of the attendings have made their peace with questions like this, based on long and difficult experience; the residents, though—the residents are often asking each question for the first time. Medical specialties, particularly surgical specialties, are seductive: "I can do that" is what the residents are teaching themselves through their training to say. Cases such as this little girl's subtly raise the question: "Should I do that?"

Dr. Mark Dias asks a question. "What should be the components of a neurological consult? Is it just an answer to a question, or, in a case like this, is there more to it?"

One of the neurosurgeons murmurs, "Watch out, buddy." Dr. Dias is one of the most refreshing of the residents, because he is absolutely straightforward: most know him well enough to realize that he is not trying to tweak the neurologists, but really wants to know what they think. One of the neurology residents answers immediately.

"I think we're all aware of what you're talking about. But

you can't take over a patient. A consult is a consult, not an invitation to take charge." This could be a gentle jibe at neurosurgeons, who have the reputation for doing just what the resident has said one really shouldn't do. "You can't take away the patient."

The older neurologist in the back speaks again. "You can counsel. And I think in this case, in retrospect, we might have probed a bit more deeply, raised these questions then rather than now, because I think if we don't, you have other physicians going ahead and thinking that because we said it was all right, it was really all right."

The discussion is winding down, partly because of the philosophical tack that it has. Residents by and large want their philosophy in very small doses. Sensing that the end is near, Jannetta rises and slips out a side door and heads for his office. He has made it to conference, has raised a couple of issues, and now he is getting out with a precious fifteen minutes. If nothing has developed in the last forty-five minutes, he might not only get his phone calls made, he might be able to bring his records for the day's operations up to date as well.

As he enters the offices, Patty Caldwell, phone to her ear, raises a finger and points at him. Obediently, he stops where he is and waits until she puts the caller on hold. When she does, he asks, "Is that one of the five?"

"Well, there aren't five anymore—there are seven. But this is someone else." She glances down at her message pad. "Dr. Olson from Cleveland."

"Do we know him?"

"He says he met you at AANS last year, and you invited him to come sometime." AANS is the American Association of Neurological Surgeons, whose annual convention is one of the big events for the profession.

Jannetta is moving again toward his office, saying as he passes her, "Okay, give 'im to me. Is there any coffee?"

The inner office of the Chairman of the Department of Neurological Surgery is, as offices tend to be, reflective in many ways of the person who inhabits it, given the constraints of space and architecture. Some physicians make do for their entire careers using institutional metal furniture and fluorescent lighting, which is what universities tend to issue to everyone they possibly can. Other physicians will make an office into what could only be called an inner sanctum, replete with Oriental rugs, indirect lighting, and, in at least two cases at Pitt, mock fireplaces. The office of Dr. L. Dade Lunsford, a neurosurgeon at Pitt, resembles nothing so much as an English manor-house library, with leather-topped, Chippendale-style furniture and brass hunting lamps. All neurosurgeons' offices have couches, even Howard Yonas's, whose office looks bright and Spartan with the exception of the couch.

Jannetta is sitting on his own couch, an overstuffed brown affair, and he has his feet up on a contemporary glass-and-steel coffee table as he holds his phone and waits for Patty to transfer Dr. Olson's call. The couch is in the sitting-area part of the office, faced by contemporary armchairs; the office part of the office has a huge desk surrounded by floor-to-ceiling shelf and cabinet combinations in the same walnut veneer as the desk. On the shelves are hundreds of neurology, neurosurgery, neuroanatomy, and neuropathology books along with physician directories from professional associations, various *Who's Who*s, a small collection of antique medical books, rows and rows of videotapes and metal boxes of slides, a skull in a wooden box, plastic models of the brain, the ear, the eye, and the brain stem, knickknacks and gewgaws of the type that neurosurgical societies bestow upon their guests, a small stereo system. One whole wall is given over to videotape viewing equipment, and under one set of cabinets is Jannetta's banjo in a case. His desk is as deeply heaped as Patty's. The decor might be called "Institutional Contemporary." The furniture is well designed and tasteful, but the large gray sheetmetal cabinet, the acoustical-tile ceiling, and the gurgling radiator, in addition to the ton of paper, will keep it out of magazines. The walls are covered with old engravings of the brain at autopsy, certificates from medical schools and medical societies from Chile to Sweden to Japan, photos of Jannetta's house in New Hampshire, and a small water color of a jazz pianist.

When the call is connected, Jannetta doesn't repose, but rather picks up his record cards for the day's patients and begins filling them in as he talks to Olson from Cleveland. "Yes, yes, anytime," he says. "That would be just fine. Just give Patty a call when you're ready. Nice talking to you. Thanks for calling," and he breaks the connection with his finger, then dials Patty, even though she is only about three feet away. This is their system. If he gets up and opens the door, someone else might want something. "He's going to call you to come by in January. Set him up for any Tuesday or Wednesday when I'm operating."

Visitors come regularly. Neurosurgeons read Jannetta's papers in the journals, hear him, his colleagues, or his former residents at conferences, and take him up on the invitation to see him work. Visitors affiliated with other medical schools generally arrange to give a lecture or a clinic while they visit, and thus are advertised as "visiting professors." In return, Jannetta makes a dozen or so like appearances each year, with preference given to programs where he has friends or acquaintances, places he's never been and would like to be, and places he would just plain like to be: he has just returned from Colorado and is planning on trips to Italy, San Francisco, Long Beach, and Hot Springs, Virginia. Both of these activities—visiting and being visited—are integral parts of the "business" of microvascular decompression, that business being to see that the technique is presented correctly and well, to make sure that surgeons learn exactly what is involved in the procedure so that they may make an informed decision on trying it themselves or referring, and, finally, to try and continue to raise the consciousness of those in the profession whose consciousness is capable of being raised. This is part of a larger strategy on Jannetta's part that some might call "boring from within." One tack to take, when you've got what you think is a good idea, is to drop it in the lap of the profession: report your work, and let the profession take it from there. For reasons discussed earlier, this did not and, in retrospect, could not, work for microvascular decompression: the institutional inertia is very difficult to overcome. The other tack, whereby you get as many people as you can to do what you're doing and report their results, builds another kind of inertia, one where the procedure will ultimately be confirmed—or discounted—on the basis of widely reported results. This is the reason why Jannetta has as many people as are interested come to Presby and why he takes his show on the road.

While Patty is trying to reach one of the other physicians who wants to talk to Jannetta, he fills out his orange record cards and his record book. The orange cards are started for every patient he operates on and have spaces to confirm the receipt of medical records, the clinic visit, the operation, the operative findings, the date of dictation of operative notes, the date of dictation of a follow-up letter to the referring physician, the immediate postoperative results of the operation, the date of discharge, and the date of the follow-up clinic visit. The orange cards are filed by Patty and provide quick reference to the broad questions related to a particular patient.

Jannetta's record book, on the other hand, is a more personal affair. It is a spiral-bound message notebook, the type with carbonless copy paper, so that a copy of whatever one is writing is automatically made. Patty uses one of these notebooks when she takes messages that require Jannetta's attention: she gives him one copy, and keeps the other herself. Jannetta uses the notebooks to record the findings and results, via drawings, of every cranial operation he does. He writes the date and the patient's name at the top, and then draws what he saw at operation, noting what was where and what was causing the trouble. To the inexperienced observer, he draws a series of sticks or tubes lying across one another and labels one, say, "V," if it is the fifth, or trigeminal, nerve, and another, "AICA," if it was a branch of the anterior inferior cerebellar artery that was compressing the nerve. What Dale Carnegie's mnemonic devices did for connecting faces and names, Jannetta's drawings do for connecting neuroanatomy with patients: a glance at one of his drawings is all that is necessary to remember the particulars of the operation, the patient's history, and the patient's progress. Likewise, Jannetta can watch the videotape of an operation and remember the patient, the pathology, the procedure, and the result. He knows his patients from the inside out.

He does the three drawings in quick succession, one for each of the day's patients. And as he picks up the microphone of the dictating machine, the telephone buzzes—Patty has one of the physicians on the line. "Give 'im to me," he says to her, setting down the microphone. "Hello, Doctor . . ."

If contemporary American medicine has a vital organ—a heart or a liver—or a central nervous system, it is not its richly sophisticated medical schools with their honored faculty, nor its operating rooms bristling with technology. Or, if it is, it is so only incidentally. The crucial link that makes much of medicine happen is tied up in the concept of "referral." In olden days—say, before World War II—consulting physicians and specialists were secondary to the primary physicians that provided the bulk of medical care. Part of this was due to the fact that the body of knowledge held by the medical community was comparatively small, and part was due to the fact that the scope of treatments for any given ailment was correspondingly small. Someone with, for example, kidney failure could most often be followed by his regular doctor, because there wasn't a great deal that anyone else could do for the patient anyway. The exceptions to this tended to be the surgical specialties. The stereotypical G.P., or general practitioner, could remove an appendix or a cyst, for example, but a patient that needed a kidney removed was generally better off with someone that removed kidneys regularly. Other exceptions were those specialists who focused on chronic or systemic conditions, or the body's systems prone to complicated diagnosis—as in neurology.

As the amount that doctors knew *in toto* about medicine increased, so did the level of specialization. This was complemented by a rise in the number of possible treatments for any given condition. Increased knowledge led to increased specialization, which, in turn, led to a further increase in knowledge, and so on. Today, medicine is a highly specialized field, with whole communities of physicians devoted to the major organs (cardiology, nephrology, hepatology, gastroenterology), to specialized patient populations (neonatology, obstetrics and gynecology, pediatrics, sports medicine, geriatrics), to the blood, to the skeletal system, to cancer, to joint diseases, to the eye, the ear, the reproductive system; to surgeries in most of these fields (vascular surgery, cardiothoracic surgery, oncological surgery, orthopedic surgery, reconstructive surgery); to the study of the basis for whole galaxies of disease (bacteriology, virology, contagious diseases). Within each "major" specialty, it is not unusual for there to be several subspecialties as well. In neurosurgery, for example, pediatric neurosurgery is a well-defined subspecialty—Peter Jannetta would no more operate on an infant than he would operate on himself; and, likewise, the pediatric neurosurgeons don't get involved, except academically, in adult cases. Further, within the department at Pitt, there are informal subspecialties such as vascular neurosurgery, trauma, spinal surgery, tumor surgery, peripheral nerve surgery. In some cases—the last, for instance—subspecialties in one discipline overlap with another: the surgeon at Pitt who is most experienced with limb reattachment, for example, is a plastic and reconstructive surgeon who specializes in hand surgery. The day may soon come when the standard joke about medical specialization ("Oh, this is your *right* hand—I'm a *left-*hand specialist") is not really a joke at all.

The net result of all this compartmentalization is a sophisticated (some would say "Byzantine" or "bizarre") dependence on one physician sending a patient he or she cannot treat to another physician who can. The system can be considered sophisticated, because most people, no matter how unusual or esoteric their illness, end up fairly quickly being treated by a physician who is experienced in providing such care, the major exceptions being in cases where the symptoms of one illness are mistaken for the symptoms of another. This is why many of Jannetta's patients with trigeminal neuralgia start out by being sent to dentists, and why many of his patients with hemifacial spasm or disabling vertigo start out by being sent to psychiatrists—illness A is seen as being illness B.

The referral network is also complicated by the usual difficulties that arise when there are people involved, especially when those people are physicians. Physicians, like anyone else, think better or worse of other physicians on individual bases and, like anyone else, are sometimes guilty of stereotyping, possessiveness, turf-guarding, and succumbing to the effects of the ego. This is to be expected. Most physicians are justifiably sure of their diagnostic and therapeutic skills (who would want a physician who was not?) and may be forgiven for wanting evidence of another physician's skills before sending him or her a patient. If all things were equal, even these issues would not make referrals terribly complicated.

Imagine, for a moment, a medium-sized town with three doctors. The first is certified in "family practice," the newest board-certified medical specialty and one dedicated to addressing the developing shortage of general physicians. The second is a board-certified general surgeon. The third is a board-certified cardiologist, or specialist in the medical treatment of heart problems. If the family practitioner sees a patient with heart disease, he may treat the patient himself or, more likely, may refer the patient to the cardiologist, who is a specialist in heart disease. If the cardiologist sees a patient that needs her gall bladder removed and he likes or respects the general surgeon, he would likely refer the patient to the surgeon. If he didn't like or respect the local surgeon, he would refer the patient to a surgeon somewhere else. If all three of these physicians get along, they can provide the vast majority of the medical treatment needed by the town residents and have a relatively simple set of referral patterns. Each is, in essence, helping the other two out when he sees a patient that could be better treated by one of his colleagues, and he is helping himself out as well by letting his colleagues know that he knows when to refer. Further, town residents who have illnesses beyond the scope of the three local physicians—say, someone who needs a hip replacement—are likely to be referred to an orthopedic surgeon liked or respected by the referring physician, and another referral pattern is established. An orthopedic surgeon who sets up shop in this town will have to win the respect of the physicians already there as well as the respect of physicians in neighboring towns without an orthopedic surgeon, if she wants their referrals. In towns where there are already orthopedic surgeons (or cardiologists or general surgeons), physicians are in competition for patients. And this can make referrals complicated. Give all the orthopedic surgeons in the area identical skills, bedside manner, success rates for hip replacement, and the other physicians suddenly must make choices between two or three orthopedic surgeons. How they do it and how the orthopedic surgeons encourage or teach or suggest that they do it makes all the difference in the world in the referral patterns. Let one orthopedic surgeon be the son or daughter of a beloved and honored G.P. in the town and the others will have a hard time competing. The only thing more complicated than referral patterns are perhaps the patterns of how people choose their physicians in the first place, but being the offspring of a respected physician is well up on the list.

Small towns and even, to a large degree, small cities, however, sort these things out in time. A new physician in town has to establish himself, but if there is enough of a need for another physician, he can generally make good. The town's physicians treat the majority of the problems they see and refer the rest somewhere else, which establishes yet another referral pattern—say, of patients who need open-heart surgery from this town to the cardiothoracic surgeon who has won the hearts or minds of the local physicians. Again, he may treat the vast majority of the cases referred to him by the town physicians, sending on to a physician that he respects the cases he doesn't feel he can responsibly treat. The referral lines at this point are long but not impossible to trace: family practitioner to cardiologist to cardiac surgeon A to cardiac surgeon B. In most parts of the United States, though, the odds are very heavy that surgeon B practices in a large urban area where there are not two or five cardiac surgeons, but two hundred. How did surgeon A pick surgeon B? Answer that, and you could become a referral-pattern consultant.

Jannetta's position is analogous to that of cardiac surgeon B—with some differences: he has the advantage of being considered the major progenitor of the treatment he provides; the procedures he does are still considered so highly specialized that most neurosurgeons who have not made a practice of microvascular decompression are not inclined to begin on a whim; he practices at a high-profile, well-respected institution; he practices within a specialty that, although highly competitive, still generates a large part of its own referrals—that is, neurosurgeon to neurosurgeon. Because of these differences, he has no shortage of patients. Indeed, he has perhaps six hundred in the pipeline, either waiting to come to clinic, to come for testing, or to come for operation. But here his situation is similar to surgeon B, because in the situation above, surgeon B got the referral. Jannetta likes to operate, likes to help patients, likes to be busy, and likes getting the referrals. In spite of that, he does his best to become the victim of his own success, by training residents, fellows, and visiting surgeons, by helping residents and fellows become established at good medical centers, by spreading himself around. When Jannetta performed the first microvascular-decompression operation, the patient had a choice of one physician: Jannetta. Now, there are perhaps one hundred around the world who are qualified to perform the procedure, several of whom trained at Presby, many of whom came to Presby as visitors, most of whom have spent some time with Jannetta, and, gradually, some who have trained with people who have trained with Jannetta. His work is already making the generational leap.

But given the still somewhat controversial nature of microvascular decompression in general and the highly controversial nature of it in the specific (for example, in the case of its use to treat people with uncontrollable high blood pressure), Jannetta needs referring physicians. He needs to let them know what they feel they need to know in order to make the referral, needs to let them know that they're making the right decision, needs to let them know the results. A referral from a former resident or colleague is, if not expected, at least not surprising; a referral from a total stranger is an opportunity to establish a pattern. Hospitals, because they need patients to survive, often make sophisticated and colorful charts showing where their patients come from; areas of high referral are generally areas where their physicians have made a special effort to develop and maintain good relationships with the native physicians. Jannetta tries to do this all the time, and the other neurosurgeons in the department do so as well. The result is that well over 40 percent of the department's patients are from outside the ten counties of western Pennsylvania, a figure they constantly strive to improve upon, because of the wide range of active and sophisticated neurosurgical practices in Pittsburgh (the chiefs of at least two of Presby's competitors are former members of the staff and still teach at the medical school on a "clinical," or part-time, basis) and in the East. For patients with sophisticated neurosurgical needs, Johns Hopkins in Baltimore, Harvard in Boston, Mount Sinai in New York, and Georgetown in Washington, D.C., may as well all be in the same city. No one with a big tumor or trigeminal neuralgia is going to quibble about an extra two hundred miles.

So Jannetta talks with referring physicians as much as he is able, no matter how pressed he is. It's the Jannetta way of doing things, the way to keep the program moving, the way to keep the program and its physicians from seeming inaccessible. In combination with the numerous journal articles he publishes and the papers he presents at conferences, Jannetta manages to generate a large proportion of his work himself. He likes to operate.

The physician on the phone is a double bonus of sorts—he is both a stranger and a neurologist. He has already decided, primarily after consulting with a neurosurgeon at his own institution who knows Jannetta, to send on the patient, a woman with vertigo. The phone call is to find out how things are going lately, how soon Jannetta might see her, and how soon she might have the operation—her daughter is to be married in eight weeks' time. Jannetta's part of the conversation is mostly a series of "Yes, sir," and "I understand, Doctor"; at least two parts of his personality are evident as he patiently listens to the physician while fidgeting with the dictation machine and glancing at his watch: he wants the patient; he wants, in theory, to talk with the physician; but, in practice, he wants it all to be over with so that he can do something else. He winds up by telling the physician to make the arrangements with Patty. He puts the call on hold, dials Patty, tells her to take care of him, and in the minute or so he knows he has gained by leaving her to handle the details, he dictates a letter.

"This is to . . ." He glances at the orange card on his lap and reads off the referring physician's name. "Dear Doctor: Janice Slater was admitted to Presbyterian-University Hospital yesterday, and today I performed a right retromastoid craniectomy and microvascular decompression of the eighth nerve for her disabling positional vertigo. A small artery was compressing the nerve, and we were able to mobilize it away and keep it away with shredded Teflon felt. The procedure went very well, and Mrs. Slater is doing very nicely. I hope this procedure will help her, and I will keep you informed as to her progress. Paragraph. Thank you again for sending this nice lady to me. Best personal regards, etcetera, etcetera, and a copy to the guy in her hometown.

"Next is Williams. This is to . . ." Again, he reads the name off the card. "Dear George: Xavier Williams was admitted yesterday evening to Presbyterian-University Hospital, and this morning I performed a right retromastoid craniectomy and microvascular decompression for his recurrence of hemifacial spasm. The operation seemed to go very well, although we did run into a bit of scarring from his previous surgery. We found an artery on the seventh nerve that seemed to be causing the problem, and we were able to mobilize it and hold it away with shredded Teflon felt. As I say, the procedure appeared to go well, and Mr. Williams is doing nicely now. I hope this takes care of his problem, and I will of course keep you informed as to his progress. Paragraph. Thank you for sending this nice gentleman to me. Best personal regards, etcetera etcetera.

"Next is . . ." and the phone buzzes. He answers, and Patty tells him the next doctor's name. "Okay, give 'im to me," he says. He breaks the connection; the phone rings. "Hello, Doctor . . ."

This is a neurosurgeon in Iowa who has seen a patient with spasmodic torticollis, a condition characterized by involuntary movements of the neck muscles; when the muscles contract, it is as though the sufferer is trying to look over his shoulder. It is relatively rare, and Jannetta is interested in seeing more patients and operating on them, relieving pressure on the accessory nerve, which runs through the top of the spine. This fits in well with Jannetta's larger theory about microvascular compression, but he needs patients, needs to operate, to see. Thus far, the results have been slightly better than 50–50.

Jannetta quickly runs through the history of the treatment for torticollis thus far as well as the early results. "We've got about fifty percent who are perfect, twenty-five percent who are improved, and twenty-five percent whom we didn't help," he is saying. "No. No mortality, no morbidity at all with these. With the cranial-nerve cases, we've had mortality way below one percent, but we're in a different ballpark here." He nods, he agrees, he smiles as he talks. "I can see him anytime, anytime at all," Jannetta says. "Let me give you back to Patty, and she can make all the arrangements. Thank you, thank you very much, sir." He puts the call on hold, he buzzes Patty, he tells her to take care of the neurosurgeon, and he hangs up the phone. Neuroscience Conference began five minutes ago, and he moves out through the outer office, pausing only to refill his cup with coffee.

Neuroscience Conference differs from the Clinical Conference in several ways. Rather than focusing on the specific case of a patient beyond the art and science of medicine, it serves as a sort of update on state-of-the-art treatment or state-of-the-art perplexing problems, depending on who is presenting that day. The neurologists tend to present "open" cases—that is, cases of patients currently being treated by the neurology service that have the attendings hamstrung; neurosurgeons tend to use a current or recent case that came to surgery as a point of departure for talking about diagnosis and management. Again, the dichotomy between neurology and neurosurgery is apparent. Neurologists expect to see plenty of cases where no one knows what is wrong, but neurosurgeons expect to see cases where the problem is obvious and the points of discussion are arrayed around two central questions: Can one operate safely? What's the best operation to perform?

Today is a neurosurgeon's day. Dr. Dachling Pang, a pediatric neurosurgeon at Children's Hospital, is at the podium waiting for the Audiovisual Department technician to begin showing Dr. Pang's slides. There is, as there *always* is, some sort of difficulty with the slides or the slide projector (AV blames the difficulties on physicians using cut-rate production houses to develop and mount their slides, something that neurosurgeons scoff at), and several of the residents, including Dr. Mark Dias, are helping to sort the problem out. One cannot but note that two neurology residents stand near the projector, arms folded, and offer diagnoses, and that two neurosurgery residents have elbowed the AV tech out of the way and are grappling with the projector and the slide tray. They are a paradigm of the professions.

The difficulty is resolved, the lights dim, and Dr. Pang turns expectantly toward the screen. Dr. Pang is fortyish and smiling. He is one of the most popular of the attendings with the residents for several reasons, one being his ability to take a joke. Evidence of this quality flashes on the screen, because the first slide is not of an unusual spinal-cord deformity, as Pang is already talking about, but of a surprise birthday party thrown for him the previous week by the residents, with the gift, now shown in living color, a scantily-clad belly dancer with her arms around the neck of a very surprised Dachling Pang, whose glasses have been knocked askew by her embrace. Dr. Dias's voice booms, "Next slide," and the image is replaced by one of the belly dancer giving Pang a very sloppy kiss on the cheek. The room is awash with laughter, in part at the slides, in part at a very startled Pang, who is trying to retain some sense of decorum. The third slide shows Pang staring at the belly dancer as she dances in front of him. And the final slide is a shot of Dr. Pang's birthday cake, a gift from the residents, with a caricature of Pang in yellow icing, complete with glasses and cowlick. The laughter gradually subsides until Pang says, "I forgot what I was going to talk about," at which the residents start laughing again.

When things settle down, Pang begins again with the correct slides, starting with a short history of the particular deformity, an outline of previous methods of surgical treatment, and then a dozen slides of an actual surgical case. The audience in the room ebbs and flows as residents and attendings come in and leave, answer pages, confer with each other, doze. One of the attendings once noted the three stages of conference lectures: "The lights go down, the slides come on, and the residents go to sleep," which, while often accurate, tends to give a slightly misdirected view of medical education because of the way that the residency system operates. Residency is an accretive process, not a holistic one. In neurosurgery, the residents first learn to do simple things—taking a history, giving a physical exam, opening and closing—and then more complex things. As this progresses, the theory they get in bits and pieces is augmented by actually working on the cases. No one learns pediatric spinal surgery from watching a slide presentation, just as no one learns diagnostic skills in surgery. So the conferences differ from real practice by virtue of the fact that they are not real, and this takes off a bit of the edge in any clinical presentation. The resident who scrubbed on the case being presented by Dr. Pang already knows much of what Pang is saying, and the residents who didn't scrub on the case know that when they do, they will actually learn the nuances as one cannot by watching slides of someone else work. Pang's case today is of value diagnostically, which is something the neurosurgery residents rarely get except vicariously since most patients come to the neurosurgery service with diagnosis in hand. The residents will learn the surgery when they get to do a case. In cases such as this, the residents in fact suffer from an embarrassment of riches. The odds are very good that in their seven years at Pitt they will see at least one—but more likely several—of everything; the department is busy and well regarded, and this bodes well for the residents. The department as a whole—not just Presby, but the VA, Montefiore Hospital, and Children's—sees more than four thousand inpatients and five thousand outpatients each year, and performs, in aggregate, well over two thousand surgical procedures. This is one of the reasons that Pitt is such an attractive program to would-be neurosurgeons and why they are good: success breeds success.

When Dr. Pang finishes, the attendings all approach the podium, some to ask questions, others, like Jannetta, to say

"Nice case" and "Thank you." Jannetta is particularly thankful because Pang has ended early, and Jannetta heads back across the hall to finish correspondence and phone calls.

Settled on his couch, he picks up the dictation microphone and his orange cards, and begins exactly where he left off. "This is Goldberg," he says, "and send a copy to Ron"—Apfelbaum, then at Montefiore Medical Center, New York—"and what's-his-name at Mount Sinai. And to her husband. Dear Doctor: Ellen Goldberg was admitted to Presbyterian-University Hospital yesterday, and today I performed . . ." As he says the last "etcetera," his phone buzzes; Patty has another physician on the phone. "Give 'im to me," he says. "Hello, Doctor . . ."

Consult, transfer caller to Patty, take the next one. Consult, transfer caller to Patty, take the next one. In fifteen minutes, Jannetta has talked to six more doctors and has lined up four more referrals for clinic and surgery as well as two more that are possibles—one wants to talk to his own chief of neurology again and the other wants to talk to Aage Møller. Finished, Jannetta picks up the orange cards and dictates his own informal operative notes. As he does each dictation, he draws a little circle next to the numbers "1" and "2" on his memo-pad drawings. When the letters have been typed, he will fill in the little circle next to the number "1" with an "x"; likewise, when his own notes have been transcribed, he will do the same for number "2." Thus, by looking at his drawings as well as his own notes on the case, he can tell if letters to referring physicians have been dictated and transcribed. As he does this, he hums.

The only thing left to do for his surgery patients is rounds on the eighth floor, but that will have to wait until after the Residents' Conference, which is convening across the hall in a small classroom. When Jannetta enters, most of the attendings and residents are already present, and Dr. Dias is passing out stapled packets of text to accompany his presentation and his slides. Residents' Conference is primarily for residents to present what in other disciplines might be called "research papers." The residents prepare a certain number of presentations each year and use them as dry runs for the time when they will be presenting papers at hospital, regional, and national conferences. It is also a way of addressing the scattershot aspects of their medical education in that they are required to research the history of treatment as exhaustively as is possible and reach some conclusion about recommended therapy for some illness. The subtitle of Residents' Conference might be "Everything You Always Wanted to Know about. . . ." Some of the residents refer to it as "Show and Tell."

8

Show and Tell

It is enlightening to see how thoroughly the present-
ers prepare their talks for Residents' Conference. They are on
stage in front of their mentors and their peers, a different
audience than the more anonymous atmosphere of the joint
conferences and at which residents rarely have the privilege of
presenting, and thus they prepare accordingly. For forty-five
minutes or so—a long, long time in the chaotic and distrac-
tion-filled days of academic surgeons—the resident has the
floor.

Dr. Dias begins briskly. He is talking about vein of Galen
aneurysms, and, after the usual momentary difficulty with the
slide projector, a slide appears that says "VEIN OF GALEN
ANEURYSMS," because a slide presentation isn't a slide presentation unless there is at least one slide that tells you exactly
what the presenter has just said. It is as though presentations
were designed for the hearing-impaired.

After a brief discussion of the history of the name, which,
like many names in medicine is a misnomer—actually, a vein
of Galen aneurysm would be called an "arteriovenous malformation of the vein of Galen"—Dr. Dias plunges into the anat-

omy of what he is calling the "VGA," pronounced "vee-gee-ay." His talk moves effortlessly (later, he admits that he has rehearsed it several times), and his slides, culled from illustrations in half a dozen anatomy texts, are crystal-clear and pertinent. The discussion is so precise and objective that it only slowly becomes apparent how troublesome and frustrating treatment of a patient with a VGA can be; and as this becomes clear, a great deal about the practice of neurosurgery becomes clearer as well.

There is, finally, no analogy for neurosurgery—there is nothing in medicine that can compare to it, even though there are many operations that can be just as long and just as fundamentally dangerous to the patient. Those who undergo, say, a liver transplant, endure a long and complicated preoperative period, a dramatic operation in which one of their most vital organs is removed and replaced with an organ from a stranger, and a lifetime of convelescence, where even if the new liver functions properly, there are regular follow-up visits, daily medications, strictures on both physiological and psychological behavior—a transplanted liver can, after all, begin to fail at any time.

But surgery on and within the brain is different, because it is the brain that reminds us that the body is finally a repository, a moving container, for the brain. There is a rudimentary artificial heart, the equivalent of an artificial kidney, work in progress on an artificial pancreas, but no conception possible for anything like an artificial brain.

Some would say that the medical specialties of neurology and psychiatry are better suited for contemplation of what it means to talk about the brain, or that social specialties such as philosophy are where one seeks to understand the relationship among the brain (the physical structure), the mind (an abstract concept), and the being (the organism, the container for the brain and the mind). But it is interesting to contemplate the brain as those practitioners who alone touch it, manipulate it, and try to understand it on a physical basis contemplate what "brain" means.

The vein of Galen is named for Claudius Galen, a Greek, who was physician to the Roman emperor Marcus Aurelius. His extensive writing about anatomy and medicine was always linked to one overriding concept: "Nature does nothing in vain." He sought, as many of the ancient and medieval physicians did, to portray the function of certain structures or organs in terms of a grand schematic: every anatomical structure, every physiological process, had a particular purpose. He was a proponent of the "humors" theory—that blood, phlegm, black bile, and yellow bile must be in perfect balance for the body to be healthy.

Although he did not "discover" the vein of Galen—Galen himself never dissected a human cadaver—it is fitting that such a structure, one of the most deeply hidden and buried of any in the anatomy, be named for a theoretician.

The vein of Galen lies within the center of the brain, the cornerstone of the deep veins that drain blood from the interior of the brain and interior structures such as the thalamus: It is the junction of two sets of paired veins, the internal cerebral veins and the basal veins. Although it is only about three-quarters of an inch long in an adult, the vein of Galen is a vital passageway for blood returning from the brain to the heart.

An arteriovenous malformation is a defect of the circulatory system whereby an artery and a vein—the former carrying oxygenated blood to the body, and the latter returning "used" blood to the heart—that are in close proximity to each other are fused, rather than separate. Vein of Galen aneurysms are thought to form around the fourth week of life, when the embryonic circulatory system is beginning to develop and differentiate. Because these rudimentary vessels are only one layer of cells thick, there is the potential for an artery and a vein to develop with common, rather than separate, walls, and oxygen-rich blood never reaches its destination but, rather, is drained off by the venous system. When this happens, one has an arteriovenous malformation. When the vein of Galen is one of the vessels, not only do you have a vein of Galen aneurysm, but you have a newborn or very young child with a serious circulatory defect in the most inaccessible part of the brain, a defect that causes a wide range of dangerous and difficult-to-treat problems.

In a newborn, a vein of Galen aneurysm is almost always suggested by a very overworked heart. At birth, the output of the heart increases dramatically, and the normal newborn heart is working at almost maximum capacity. The added strain of increased blood volume, pressure in the venous system, and the consequent increase in blood pressure within the lungs caused by a vein of Galen aneurysm means that the heart has to work even harder, even though the heart itself is getting less blood than it should because of the decrease in arterial vascular pressure. (The arterial system is essentially a closed system under pressure, and a vein of Galen aneurysm lowers this pressure.) In newborns and very small children, it is also instructive to remember that everything is much smaller than in an an adolescent or an adult: the total volume of blood is smaller, the blood vessels themselves are smaller, the heart is smaller, and any anatomical defect is magnified in terms of its effects.

When a vein of Galen aneurysm is diagnosed, then, it is usually diagnosed in a small child having heart problems. The aneurysm itself is dangerous because of the effect it is having on the heart, and thus any attempt at therapy must be at the cause.

But the vein of Galen is so deep. The neurosurgeon is not asked to contemplate the brain or the mind or the being; he is asked to open the skull and retract—move away—the right occipital lobe of the brain, move deeper within the brain to almost the very center, where he will find a vascular confusion: arteries and veins in a tangle. In this tangle, he must then try and tie off the branches of the arteries that are feeding the vein of Galen aneurysm; he is to turn the aneurysm itself, so as to reach vessels on the underside and tie them off, too. The arteries are tied off so that the blood flowing through them does not enter the vein of Galen. Thus, if all of them can be reached and blocked, only venous blood flows through the vein of Galen, as Nature intended and as Galen himself ("Nature does nothing in vain") would understand as necessary for a balance in the bodily humors.

Or, if surgery is deemed too risky, the surgeon might try to block off the feeders through "embolization," a process in which a tiny balloon is fed, under radiographic guidance, through the arterial system into each of the arterial feeders and then inflated, blocking off blood flow. Or, if not a balloon, an acrylic glue. Or, if not glue, a bit of wire called a "Gianturco coil" that winds up tightly when released, blocking the blood vessel. Or a combination of surgery and embolization, where the surgeon exposes the aneurysm and then tried to block off the arteries with bits of glue or wire or tiny balloons. Neurosurgeons have tried all of these things, in all combinations; some surgeons have even meticulously sealed off all of the arteries feeding the vein of Galen, and then snipped out the whole mess. Neurosurgeons, the neurologists scoff, will try anything. They have tried lowering the patient's blood pressure, the patient's body temperature, and they have had cardiac surgeons temporarily stop the patient's heart, all to try and give the neurosurgeon a chance to do his work.

If the problems caused by the vein of Galen aneurysm are relatively mild, one can wait for the surgery; four year olds do relatively much better, have a comparatively much better chance of surviving than do children younger than four years, who, in turn, have a better chance than infants, who may have a slightly better chance than newborns.

All of this is preparation for understanding what Dias is talking about to a room full of neurosurgeons and neurosurgical residents. What he is talking about when he is talking about surgery in newborns with vein of Galen aneurysms is a mortality rate that "approaches," in medical parlance, *100 percent*. What he is talking about, and what his colleagues are hearing about, nodding at, and making notes about on his meticulously prepared outline, is very complex surgery in which the overwhelming odds are that the patient will die. Dias cites series of patients operated on by other neurosurgeons, such as a series from Canada in which 45 newborns with vein of Galen aneurysms were seen, 39 were too sick to operate on, and 35 of them died. Three of the 4 survivors were neurologically impaired. Of the 6 who went to operation, 4 died, and 2 survived with neurological impairments. Some of the techniques he describes have mortality rates of exactly 100 percent. The most encouraging series, a group of infants with only mild heart problems, had a mortality rate of about 40 percent.

And, on top of this, Dias mentions one other series of patients, 7 infants who died of vein of Galen aneurysms. At autopsy, only 1 of the 7 had a normal brain apart from the aneurysm in the first place. The rest had neurological damage that antedated birth by at least several weeks. Dias ends on what would be, to a group of any other than neurosurgeons, a discouraging note. "In neonates, at least," he says, "it seems that severe neurological damage has already occurred, and that surgical intervention after birth, no matter how well intentioned, may in fact be futile."

When he finishes, there is no awkward silence, no shuffling of feet, no one apparently uncomfortable at the prospects of 100 percent mortality, of newborns whose brains are severely damaged before surgical intervention, of infants with what may be insoluble problems. There is none of this. Instead, there are questions about the possibilities for *in utero* diagnosis or the latest innovations in embolization. "The Gianturco coils seem like an excellent idea," says one of the residents, "What problems have they had with those?"

Dachling Pang answers. "The big problem has to do with the frailty of the arteries," he says. "I've talked to people who've tried this—this is unpublished data—where they've blown out the walls of the blood vessels completely. The vessel just explodes."

"Well, that's data for you," says Jannetta, and they all laugh.

An attending asks about waiting to do the surgery. "That's finally what everyone thinks is the best thing to do," says Dr. Dias, "and in any given case, that's probably what I'd recommend. The problem is that no one's been able to do this, though. They all die."

"What that means is that you're basically an optimist," says Jannetta, "which is why you're a neurosurgeon. If your brother had a kid in this situation, what would your treatment be?"

Dias answers promptly. "At this point, I'd say, 'Wait until the child is two years of age.' "

"Even though no one has done that?"

"Yep."

This is taken as fact. Jannetta rises and moves to the front of the room. "That was an excellent rundown," he says. "Any other questions? Okay, thank you, Doctor. All right. Go to work, and have a ball." And the conference is dismissed.

Such a discussion is, in a way, disorienting when viewed from the outside, unless you realize that what makes it so is that the underlying questions are, for neurosurgeons, different than those of anyone else. It is startling, but neurosurgeons *are* different from everyone else. They are different from neurologists and psychiatrists and philosophers, because at some point along the way of becoming a neurosurgeon their contemplations of the brain become rooted in the physical structure. This is not to say that neurosurgeons are not aware of the function of the brain, of the existence of the mind, but rather almost as if they have come to understand that the physical structure of the brain is primary—that the mind exists because of a properly functioning brain. A newborn child has a problem, and the child's physician suspects there is something wrong within the skull; tests are ordered and performed; the tests show a vein of Galen aneurysm; a vein of Galen aneurysm is a defect in the physical structure; the neurosurgeon seeks to correct the defect. That it happens to be an almost insurmountably difficult defect to repair only makes it a more difficult and challenging repair to attempt, and without the attempt, the defect will certainly remain. Neurosurgeons do not throw up their hands at the failures, the losses, of others. The neurosurgeons listening to Dr. Dias's report on vein of Galen aneurysms did not close the book on surgery or embolization or a combination of the two; they wondered how it could be done differently or better. Jannetta's offhand comment to Dr. Pang on the disasterous attempts at using Gianturco coils—"Well, that's data for you"—is in fact an aphorism for neurosurgery, because to the surgeons in the room it *is* data.

Some neurosurgeon—perhaps even in the near future—will figure out some method for treating vein of Galen aneurysms: a variation, a new technique, an improvement over previous attempts. That neurosurgeon will do so, because, finally, neurosurgeons don't say "no."

At another Residents' Conference on another day, Dr. Rosa Pinkus, the department's ethicist, reported on controversies surrounding the so-called "Baby Doe Rules," which tried to require that life-sustaining treatment be provided to severely handicapped newborns and infants regardless of how hopeless the prognosis. She says later that she was trying to get a sense of where the residents stand on the relationship between autonomy and paternalism on the part of the physician, truth-telling and lying, privacy and confidentiality. What she got were statements like "At the bedside, you're not worrying about whether something is right or ethical, but what you can get away with medico-legally" and "The fact that we even have to discuss these things reflects our collective fear of being prosecuted for something" and "There's really no need for ethics—these aren't ethical issues; they're *medical* issues" and "Ethicists simply change their rules depending on the situation; the question is never whether or not to withhold treatment, but simply who decides."

It was a tough audience but one that she was used to, given that the residents are already, at least psychologically, neurosurgeons. They *know* what they think, know what are to them the pressing questions facing them as physicians, and few of those questions have to do with ethics. Even the attendings are resistant to discussing such questions. Jannetta's sole contributions to the ethics discussion were, first, the comment "It's important to understand these processes, so that if you're criticized at some point, you have something in your armamentarium" and, in closing, "It's very important to keep up in this area." The final sense of Residents' Conference is that the neurosurgeons are not talking about the mind or the spirit; they're talking about the *brain*. This is to them a big difference. All else is confusing the issue.

As the Residents' Conference breaks up, the residents crowd around Dr. Rob Parrish, the chief resident, getting and trading their assignments. Two attendings—Jannetta and Sekhar—have clinic the next day, at which time they see patients in for office visits, and two others—Yonas and Nelson—are operating. Assignments are made on the basis of seniority: the longer one's tenure as a resident, the more choices and the more say one has in terms of assignment. At one end of the spectrum, the newest residents will take histories and give physical exams to newly admitted patients; at the other end is Dr. Parrish himself, who will do one particularly interesting vascular case with Dr. Yonas in the morning and then see patients in Jannetta's clinic.

Jannetta himself has little to do with any of this; it is a job delegated to the chief resident, and, thus, it occupies none of his attention. If the schedule is screwed up, he doesn't even have to tell Parrish about it, because Parrish, being a good chief resident, will, of course, know about it (Parrish's instructions when he became chief resident basically consisted of his being told to take care of things).

Jannetta leaves the conference room and heads back through the labyrinth of the A-Stem toward the hospital in order to make rounds. Along the way, he muses about Dr. Dias's presentation. "Those are tough, tough cases," he says, referring to vein of Galen aneurysms. "It's a tough place to work, especially on a sick kid. That's why so many of them don't come to surgery. It takes a super surgeon to pull that off. But," he says as he enters an elevator, "someone will figure something out." There is no doubt he means that that someone will be a neurosurgeon.

Unit 83 is bustling. It is change of shift for the nursing staff, and the nursing station—an island in the hall—is full of nurses, nurse's aides, unit clerks, a smattering of social workers, pharmacy aides, nurse practitioners. Dr. Eric Altschuler has beaten Jannetta to the floor and sits on a stool, writing notes into a patient chart.

Jannetta says to one of the nurses, "I want to go around real quick," and the nurse promptly summons Sharon Sell, who emerges from her office carrying her clipboard. Jannetta will see, as he does every day, all of his patients, starting with those on the regular unit before stopping in at the other end of the hall at the Neurosurgical Continuous Care Unit. When she can, Sell accompanies Jannetta as a sort of Minister of Protocol: she gives him at the door of each patient's room the patient's name, current condition, and date of discharge.

Patients, even the sickest ones, are delighted to see Peter Jannetta. His manner with them is part natural warmth and concern, and part a conscious effort to be nice. For all the progressiveness of the medical world, he still believes emphatically in the quaint notion of bedside manner. He smiles, he holds hands, he looks his patients straight in the eye, he tells them that he cares. If you listen to the hallway wisdom of the hospital, you are given to understand that the women on whom he has operated are particularly susceptible to Jannetta's charms. Dr. Steven Haines, a neurosurgeon who is now at the University of Minnesota, did his residency at Pitt and, like most residents, was skeptical of the concept of microvascular decompression. Unlike most residents, though, he wrote a song about Jannetta, trigeminal neuralgia, and a prototypical patient, "Mrs. Snodgrass." (In the song, Dr. Lunsford is L. Dade Lunsford, M.D., then chief resident and now head of Pitt's program in stereotactic neurosurgery.)

I've got pain in my fingers, I've got pain down in my toes,
I've got lancinating pain in the right side of my nose.
And the Tegretol's not working and my Ripple's wearing off,
So please tell me, Dr. P.J., what you are thinking of.

Don't worry, Mrs. Snodgrass, everything will be all right;
We will do a little test or two that will keep you up all night.
And then early in the morning, this will be our strategem:
We'll cut a little hole in your head, and tickle your brainstem.

Oh, don't go, Dr. P.J., there's much more I've got to tell;
You're the thirty-second doctor that's tried to make me well.
This pain is unpredictable, it moves from left to right,
It's burning in the morning, and prick-ally at night.

Don't worry, Mrs. Snodgrass, every patient here is cured,
Even if there is a year or two of pain that they endure.
Now this is Dr. Lunsford, he'll explain the rest to you,
And I really must be going, for I take my nap at two.

God Bless You, Dr P.J., all my pain has gone away,
I only have it now and then, when I have something to say.
That's the secret, Mrs. Snodgrass, if you want to live pain-free,
You must never say another word about your pain to me.

When Jannetta heard Haines sing his song, he laughed and laughed. The song is close (the nap, the rap that the patients don't tell him about any postoperative pain because they don't want to hurt his feelings), but not too close for comfort. Copies of copies of copies of the tape of Haines playing his folk guitar and singing the song surface regularly throughout the department, usually during the department Christmas party. All of the administrative staff know the words by heart.

"Guilty as charged" is what Jannetta says when he's asked about his patients liking him. "What's wrong with liking your doctor?"

Everyone on Unit 83 this afternoon likes the doctor just fine. Tomorrow is discharge day for two patients on whom he operated the previous Tuesday, and five from the previous Wednesday. Jannetta charges down the hall, Sell at his elbow until she stops, and he stops, too, and backs up. She consults her chart, tells him the name of the patient, to which Jannetta says, "Oh, yeah, okay," and he enters the room, smiling. The patient is famous in medical and social circles. He is the president of a large charity organization for a common progressive disease; he is a regular on the New York party circuit. Last Tuesday, Jannetta had removed a "middling large" acoustic neuroma, a benign tumor that arises within the auditory canal from the auditory nerve, and tomorrow, the man is going home. He is thrilled to see Jannetta, calls him *paisan* (both patient and surgeon are of Italian heritage), invites Jannetta to come to New York anytime to go to the best damn restaurants in the city ("And you know what New Yorkers say," the man says, " 'in the city' really means in the whole damn world!"). Jannetta probes at the incision, which is just behind the patient's right ear. "Any pain? Any soreness?" he asks. There is none. "Well, you're out of here tomorrow," Jannetta says. "I'll see you in about four weeks. Call Patty to set it all up. Good luck to you—I think you're a winner."

"Well, I think you're a winner, too!" says the patient, laughing. They shake hands again, and Jannetta is gone.

"Next," he says to Sharon, who has been waiting patiently in the hall.

"Next is thirty-two, Bed one, Mrs. Cavanaugh. You did her eighth nerve on Wednesday," she says.

"How is she?"

"She's doing pretty well—some dizziness when she walks around. She doesn't get up as often as she should."

They reach the room, and Jannetta enters, smiling his smile. "Well, well, well," he says, sitting next to Mrs. Cavanaugh on the edge of her bed and taking her hand in his.

"Oh, good after*noon*, Doctor!" she says, smiling brightly. She is fifty-two years old, diminuitive. She suffered from progressively worsening vertigo for almost five years before coming to Pittsburgh from Chicago for surgery.

"How are they treating you?" he asks, getting up and turning her head slightly to press on her incision.

"Just fine. Everyone is so kind!"

"Well, what I want you to do is get around a little more,"

says Jannetta. "Get one of these wonderful people to take you on a stroll or two this evening, work out the kinks. You're going home tomorrow? Well, you need to get out of bed."

"Of course," says Mrs. Cavanaugh. "Certainly."

"And we'll see you in a few weeks. Call the office and set up the appointment," he says, taking her hands in his. "Have you been having any dizziness?"

"Just once or twice. Nothing, nothing like before—I can't tell you the difference!" She smiles again brightly.

"Well, good luck to you. Take a walk this afternoon; get someone to go with you."

"Thank you, Doctor," she says, reluctantly releasing his hand.

In the hall, Sharon says as they walk, "She's been a bit of a complainer."

"Ahh," says Jannetta, "she's fine." He doesn't see Sharon roll her eyes. Since hardly anyone ever complains about anything to Jannetta, he can hardly be contradicted. But patients, being patients, sometimes—and sometimes often—do complain. And when they do complain, they complain to Sharon or the Unit 83 nurses, who then witness what they sometimes refer to as "the Transformation," in which a patient who has been an absolute pill dissolves into milk and honey the moment Jannetta crosses the threshold. Some of the nurses wish, tongue in cheek, that he would spend all of his time on the unit so that "the Transformation" would hold for the entire period of hospitalization.

"Next," says Jannetta.

"Twenty-six, Bed one. This is Mr. Bowles, another Eight. He's fine. You did the left side three years ago. His wife's here."

Mr. Bowles is healthy and vigorous-looking, belying what can only be termed his unusual luck: he is one of Jannetta's patients who has had truly bilateral disabling vertigo. Jannetta did an operation on the left auditory nerve three years previously and, last week, did the right side. Mr. Bowles is ready and raring to go, claiming that he's sure he's good for another fifty years. Jannetta chats for a moment but generally reserves his send-off of "You're a winner" until the follow-up clinic visit for cranial-nerve-compression patients. He wants to make sure things take.

Next is the other acoustic neuroma from Tuesday, a young woman from the Pittsburgh suburbs. Because acoustic tumors arise within the posterior fossa, Jannetta removes a fair number of them, sometimes because some friend of a friend asks him to, but most of the time because yet another innovation that Jannetta has made in posterior-fossa surgery is a method for removing large acoustic tumors without the loss of facial function that commonly accompanies such surgery and word of his success has gotten around. By monitoring the function of the facial nerve in much the same way they do for neurovascular-compression cases, Jannetta and Aage Møller can quite often get all of the tumor but leave the facial nerve function.

And so go rounds. Into the room, smile, chat, take a peek at the incision, pleasantly reinforce any instructions from the nursing staff, a smile, a handshake, a reminder of the clinic visit, and then on to the next room. Described schematically, one might suspect that the patients don't see much of their surgeon, but "much" is relative. Not all surgeons see their patients every day, because many surgeons rely on the resident handling the patient's care, who does see the patient every day. Some patients *never* see their surgeon after the initial office visit, which is something that Jannetta feels is wrong. "What's the first thing that family members ask when they come to visit someone in the hospital?" Jannetta asks as he walks up the hall toward NCCU. "They ask, 'Did you see the doctor today?' Some doctors get tremendously busy and forget that while this is all just routine to them, for the patients this is probably the biggest moment in their lives. They're in a strange place, surrounded by strangers, being poked and prodded by strangers, and they have to believe that some other stranger is going to make them well. They ought to at least get to see the guy. Sure, it's five minutes a day, but it's a *big* five minutes to someone who's just had his head opened up. Some doctors are too busy to remember that these are people. That's why doctors make such terrible patients—they're used to knowing exactly what's going on, and they can get pretty annoyed if they don't. I put 'em in the hospital, and I make sure they don't think I've forgotten about 'em. It's part of the business."

NCCU is brightly lit and busy; all but one space is taken. All patients who have had surgery within the skull routinely spend a night or two in the Continuous Care Unit, where they are watched closely—checked every fifteen minutes immediately after coming up from the Postanesthesia Recovery Room and then less frequently, but still much more often than a patient on Unit 83. Mostly, the nursing staff watches for a hint that something within the skull is awry—bleeding, for example. Because the skull is a physically limited space, bleeding from, say, a nicked blood vessel builds up pressure within the skull, and that pressure can be exerted on the brain or the brain stem. Cut a fingertip with a razor blade, and blood flows freely; a similar cut within the cranium means the start of life-threatening trouble as the blood presses on neural tissue. NCCU also allows for more focused care as patients recover from anesthesia. Some people get very sick from inhalation anesthetics—nausea, dizziness, headaches—and there is also the pain from the incision to contend with.

Jannetta's three morning patients are in NCCU. Janice Slater is awake and resting comfortably, her eyes closed. She half-opens them when Jannetta touches her hand. "How are you?" she asks, and he laughs.

"I'm fine," he says. "How are you doing?"

"I feel terrible." If only Sharon Sell were present to hear a patient tell Jannetta this. But she isn't—he can find his own way around NCCU.

"That's normal," he tells her. "That's from the anesthesia. Are you dizzy?"

"I don't know."

"Well, I think things went pretty well. I think you'll start to feel better pretty soon."

He squeezes her hand and takes his leave.

Xavier Williams and Ellen Goldberg are both sleeping. Williams has been awakened several times by the nurses, not to be contrary, but to make sure that he's sleeping because he's sleepy, not because of pressure from a bleeding blood vessel. Jannetta doesn't awaken him, but instead just asks one of the nurses if he's been okay. He has.

Ellen Goldberg awakens when he comes to the side of the bed, and she lifts her hand. "Hiya, Doc," she says weakly. "I'm sick as a dog."

"That's from the anesthesia," he says. "I think you're going to be fine." As he says this, her eyes close.

"Are they all okay?" he asks a nurse at the NCCU desk. And she tells him that they are. "Has the resident been around?" he asks, hand on the doorknob.

"Dr. Altschuler is on the floor," she tells him.

"Okay, thank you," he says, and rounds are done.

He hums as he winds his way back toward Scaife Hall. It is 4:00 P.M., so he will be able to have his nap after all.

In the office, a young man wearing the uniform of a rental car company is sitting in a chair, holding a clipboard. Patty says to Jannetta as he comes in, "This is the man from the rental car company," and Jannetta turns and smiles at him.

"Hi. I'm Pete Jannetta. How are you today?" he says, and he sticks his hand out. "C'mon in and let's get this squared away," and he waits until the rental car man enters the inner office door first. "Do you want some coffee?"

Two days before, Jannetta's car was stolen from in front of his house in the Squirrel Hill section of Pittsburgh—a minor annoyance. More annoying was the concomitant loss of two cases of Italian wine in the trunk. Most annoying was the loss of his squash gear, including a treasured pair of metal-framed eyeguards. Patty Caldwell had spent the previous day calling sporting-goods stores, trying to locate another pair, but the best she could come up with were eyeguards with plastic frames. Car theft he can understand, but his *eyeguards*. Salt will be rubbed in the wound a month later when the car is found, stripped and abandoned. The eyeguards, bent and crushed beyond use, will be lying on the floor of the trunk. By then, Jannetta will have a sporty new Nissan, with antitheft door locks and an alarm system, but he will be playing squash for the duration, it appears, wearing plastic eyeguards. Later, he gets a pair with prescription lenses, and his game, already very good, improves.

The rental car will relieve Jannetta in the interim of borrowing and riding in his daughter Carol's car, which he has done since the theft. While the rental agent fills out his forms, Jannetta engages him in small talk—where the young man is from, how he likes his work. When the agent is done and gives Jannetta the keys, Jannetta gives them to Patty and asks her to move it, because he is going to take his nap.

As the mothers of children know, taking a nap doesn't always mean sleeping. For Jannetta, it means twenty minutes or half an hour stretched out on the office couch, doors closed, shades pulled, lights dimmed. Sometimes he reads the newspaper, sometimes he stares at the ceiling. Once in a while, the soft strumming of a banjo can be heard in the outer office, which can be startling to visitors who have been told that the chief is busy and cannot be disturbed. But who are they to question? Have they performed any surgery today? Some physicians collect stamps, others have aquaria and exotic fish. Paul Nelson runs his five or ten miles each day, and Howard Yonas has his Porsche. Peter J. Jannetta, previously of Philadelphia, Los Angeles, and New Orleans, has his banjo. Some evenings, a ragtag group of amateur musicians assemble on the stage of a bar called Mad Anthony's Bierstube. No one would know that they are physicians one and all, perhaps least of all Jannetta, who introduces himself as "Pete—I work at Pitt." Indeed, he does, which is why no one begrudges him his nap.

When he emerges from the inner office, it is almost five o'clock. Sitting in the same chair that had been occupied by the rental car man—the only chair, in fact, in which a visitor to the outer office can sit—is a medical student, a friend of Jannetta's daughter Carol, who is midway through medical school at Pitt herself (her older sister Joanne is a surgical resident at Pitt, after having followed her father to medical school at Penn); he is holding a squash racquet. Jannetta tends to like rather than dislike medical students and friends of his daughters', and he particularly likes medical students who play a good game of squash. Jannetta gathers his gear, including the annoying plastic-framed eyeguards, and the men head out to the rental car and depart for the Pittsburgh Golf Club, where Jannetta has a court reserved for five-thirty. Patty Caldwell is the only person left in the outer office, and, as Jannetta makes his exit, she calls out, "By the way, Secretary's Day is ——"

He interrupts her. "I know, I know. Take care of everybody but yourself." He laughs. "Take care of it, and we'll go out and have a terrific lunch. Okay?"

Patty laughs, too, and then calls "Good night" as Jannetta

moves out into the hall. The office is quiet for the first time since early morning—until a phone rings. She stares at the blinking light on the phone console for a moment and then answers. "Good afternoon, Neurosurgery. . . . No, he just went out the door."

9

Clinic

The newly renovated quarters on the third floor of the University of Pittsburgh's Falk Clinic, where the neurosurgeons see their patients, are quite different from the old quarters, which were in Falk's basement. The old quarters, reached by a creaky and impressively slow elevator, are dark and cramped, especially in the waiting areas. The neurosurgeons have one side of the basement, the transplant surgeons the other, and on Thursday mornings, when Jannetta sees his patients, the transplantation team sees liver patients—many, many liver patients. Since Jannetta sees quite a few patients himself and since neurosurgeons and transplant surgeons both see quite a few patients from out of town, the waiting areas in the old quarters sometimes look, as one of Jannetta's patients put it, "like Ellis Island."

The examining rooms, however, are completely anonymous and interchangeable—the decor could be called "contemporary interchangeable." The walls are painted in institutional lemon, institutional beige, institutional orange; the small desks in each are white Formica; the examining tables are topped by identical bronze-colored vinyl cushions. In each room is a low, wheeled stool and two fiberglass chairs. The framed prints on the walls are variously Holly Hobby, covered bridges, still lifes of a vase of flowers, or forests primeval. The neurosurgeons who see patients at Falk Clinic take turns using the entire wing of six examining rooms, and Rose Carter, the secretary in charge of the logistics, sees to it that there is a patient in each room at all times. The first six patients are scheduled for 8:00 A.M. and the last six for 11:15. At 7:45, the patients, most accompanied by a spouse or a child or a sibling, have already begun to gather in the waiting room and leaf through relatively current but extraordinarily worn magazines.

Roughly half of the clinic patients this morning are here for postoperative visits, which were scheduled when they were discharged after surgery. The rest are new patients, preparing to see Peter Jannetta for the first time. All but three of the new patients are straightforward—for Jannetta anyway—referrals for well-described problems: disabling positional vertigo (four patients), trigeminal neuralgia (three patients), hemifacial spasm (three patients). They will each in turn be examined, quizzed, prodded and probed a bit, and, generally, scheduled for a series of preoperative tests. Then, depending on their availability, Jannetta's availability, OR availability, and the severity of the problem, they will "go into the pipeline"—the fast track to surgery. Some patients will come to operation within a week of the clinic visit, while others may wait much longer. Some choose to get it all done right away, and some choose to return home and ruminate. Some are as busy in their own professional lives as Jannetta is in his, and must schedule the surgery and the consequent recuperative period around stockholder meetings, important court cases, or their own busy medical and surgical schedules. One patient postponed his surgery because his corporation became the object of a hostile takeover, while others schedule the trip to Pittsburgh around previously announced "vacations" because of the difficulty in explaining to friends and associates why they need brain surgery when they look perfectly healthy. Some must fit clinic visit, testing, and surgery all into one visit, which Jannetta does his best to accommodate. But he is only one surgeon. And while on his aggressive and chipper days he might feel as though he could operate on all of them at once, his schedule and the hospital's don't always mesh.

This Thursday is not a particularly chipper day. Jannetta comes into the small conference room a little after eight o'-clock carrying a cup of coffee. He has been bothered in recent months by a sore hip, and he has been to see an orthopedic surgeon who took X rays, which Jannetta wants to see but hasn't yet. Already in the conference room are Rose Carter, who has the appointment sheet and a stack of charts in front of her; David Bissonette, the department's Physician's Assist-ant, who spends most of his time in neurosurgeons' clinics seeing patients and doing the initial work-ups; and Ann Monroe, a Falk Clinic RN who works not only neurosurgery clinics, but other specialties as well. There is no resident yet. Dr. Rob Parrish, the Chief Resident, is supposed to be helping out this morning, but he has called from the Emergency Room and said he would be late. The first six patients are already in the examining rooms, and Bissonette, after ex-changing pleasantries for a moment with Jannetta, leaves the conference room to see the first patient of the day. During the course of clinic, his path and Jannetta's will cross many times. In theory, he or the resident will see every patient before Jannetta does to do an initial exam and gather a brief history. Until Parrish arrives, however, Jannetta will see some of the patients without the benefit of anyone else ahead of him. This makes a difference because Jannetta sees every patient, and if no one paves the way, the visits take a bit longer and the schedule suffers. Reality prevails in this way far more often than theory does, and the net result is that nine-o'clock appointments are seen at, say, nine-thirty, and ten-fifteen appointments are seen around eleven. Jannetta's day is already looking as if it will be an hour longer, and it has barely begun.

And, at this moment, a further complication in the schedule rolls down the examining-room hall in a wheelchair in the person of a young woman from Argentina, her head still swathed in postoperative bandages and her eyes bright as she speaks excitedly with the three people accompanying her. Her name is Maria, and she and her parents are returning to Argentina today, ten days after Jannetta had removed "a monster pair of bilateral acoustic tumors—real biggies." Maria is the daughter of a friend of a friend of a professional acquaintance of Jannetta's who referred her to one of the more successful surgeons who isn't intimidated by large acoustic tumors—that is, to Jannetta himself. Jannetta goes into the hall, shakes hands all around, probes the bandages on Maria's head as everyone smiles and laughs and chats through the hospital escort/interpreter. Jannetta receives a kiss from Maria's mother, another hearty two-handed handshake from her father, edges them back up the hallway where he wishes them a bon voyage, and then returns to the conference room. He sips his coffee, puts on his half glasses, glances at the appointment sheet, and says to no one in particular, "Well, let's get this show on the road," and moves down the hall to Examining Room 1.

At the door, he pulls a manila folder out of a clip on the door and shuffles through it for a moment before knocking twice and entering the room. Inside is a couple in their mid-fifties, she seated on the edge of the examining table, he in a fiberglass chair. Both rise expectantly when Jannetta comes in. "Hi," Jannetta says. "I'm Dr. Jannetta, and you're . . . ?" Introductions all around, handshakes all around. (On his days spent in clinic, Jannetta shakes more hands than two average politicians—his handshake is his calling card.)

The woman suffers from hemifacial spasm and wears the secret badge of hemifacial-spasm sufferers: large stylish sunglasses with lightly tinted lenses. When she takes them off, the right side of her face draws slowly up into a squint and then relaxes. She looks sheepish at this impromptu sample of the symptoms.

Jannetta stands in front of her and holds her head in his hands, one hand on each side of her neck. "Close your eyes. Open your eyes wide. Blink. Open. Close. Bat your eyelashes. Close tight: squeeze like you've got soap in 'em. Harder. Harder. Okay, relax."

He steps back a step. "How long have you had this?" he asks.

She glances at her husband. He says "three years" at the same moment she says "almost four years."

They both smile, and the woman explains. "The first time was almost exactly four years ago—four years ago next month. Then it went away, and came back about ten months later."

"How many times a day do you get it?" asks Jannetta.

Again the glance at her husband, who smiles but doesn't answer this time. "Oh, on bad days twenty-five, on good days maybe fifteen."

"Does it bother you? Does it ruin your life?" he asks.

"Yes," she replies promptly. "I can't read; I can't sew; I can't write a letter to the children."

"How many do you have?" asks Jannetta, as he scribbles a sentence into the manila folder.

"Five."

"Hey, I've got six," he replies. He steps up to her again and places his hands again on each side of her neck. "Look left. Look right. Look up. Look down." Again, and only for a moment, the spasm draws the right side of the woman's face up, and then relaxes. Again, she blushes.

Next, Jannetta takes a cotton-tipped swab on a wooden stem from a jar on the examining room's counter. He breaks it in half so that one end of the stem is pointed and sharp. Then he tugs a bit of cotton on the tipped end until it stands up, one thread in diameter. Both of these movements are so practiced as to seem unconscious. "Close your eyes, please," he says. And when the woman has done so, he raises the cotton-thread end toward the side of her face. "Tell me when you can feel this tickle," he says.

He touches her with the wisp of cotton in an irregular pattern along the side of her face, beginning up near her eyebrow. For most of the touches, she says a soft "yes."

"This will feel sharp," says Jannetta, and he reverses the swab and touches her very lightly in the same irregular pattern, and again she says "yes" to most of the touches.

A person with all cranial nerves functioning properly (what physicians describe as "neurally intact") might normally have no reason to know that different nerve endings respond to different stimuli—sharp points, like the broken swab; dull stimulus, such as the intact swab end; light touch, such as the wisp of cotton or the wisp of a spider web as it brushes across the face. But to neurosurgeons and neurologists, this is significant information, because it is a way of finding out how well the patient's cranial nerves are functioning. Anesthesia, or lack of sensation in certain areas of the face, might mean a tumor rather than hemifacial spasm or, in a patient with a clouded medical history, a more comprehensive nerve dysfunction. A weakness in the facial muscles on the afflicted side of a hemifacial-spasm sufferer's face is fairly common and grows more common with time, and weak facial muscles have different responses to stimuli than strong ones do.

Because of this, one of the components of the physical examination that neurologists and neurosurgeons perform on virtually every patient they see is this sort of sensationally opposite cotton and point test. Many physicians carry a pin of some sort in the lapels of their lab coats, ranging from an ordinary safety or straight pin, common among residents and harried house staff, to ornate and bejeweled pins given as tokens of esteem or appreciation to senior attending physicians. Predictably, since physicians scrutinize everything they or their colleagues do with the avidity of philatelists, the practice of using the same pin on multiple patients has come in for its share of attention. A letter to the editors of the *New England Journal of Medicine* recently suggested that these pins could conceivably carry and spread contagious diseases such as hepatitis. Counteropinions followed, but no consensus has yet been reached. Jannetta carries no pin not out of fastidiousness, but simply because it would be one more thing for him (or, more likely, Patty Caldwell) to keep track of, and life is full enough as it is. Every examining room in Falk Clinic has a jar of cotton swabs, so Jannetta travels this much lighter.

Jannetta steps back. "Well, I think we can help you."

The woman opens her eyes and smiles. "How wonderful," she says. "What do you do?"

Jannetta draws over the small stool with a foot and sits down directly in front of the woman. "Sit down, and I'll explain it to you," he says.

Jannetta draws in his breath and begins. "We've done several hundred of these already," he says, slipping into the "these" and "it" method of talking about disease, a form of distancing prominent among surgeons, because disease, after all, is a foreign object, an enemy, a thing that inhabits nice ladies and young girls from Argentina. He says, when he thinks it is so, "I think we can help *you*," but what he is helping you overcome is an "it."

" . . . and we think that it's caused by a blood vessel pressing against the facial nerve, a way back on the underside of the brain. When we operate, we go in right behind your ear"— and he turns his head and places his index finger exactly two centimeters distal to the mastoid process—"move back that part of the brain, and look around with the microscope. What we generally find is a tiny blood vessel pressing on the nerve there, and we move it away and put a little pad in there to keep it away, and that usually takes care of it.

"Risks?" he asks himself and then answers. "Basically, the biggest risk is hearing loss on that side in about one or one and a half percent of the cases. We've done a great many of these kinds of operations, and we're very, very good at it." He smiles.

"Oh," says the woman, "we know you're good. Dr. Baumgartner said you were the best." The couple has traveled from their retirement home in South Carolina on the advice of Dr. Baumgartner.

Jannetta smiles again. "We do our best. Now, if you want to go ahead, we'll get a whole series of tests—the usuals, like X rays and CT scans, and then some tests of nerve function on that side. We would want to do all of that before you came into the hospital. Questions?" There are none. "If you decide to go ahead, call the office and schedule the tests, and we'll fix you up." Jannetta stands up, shakes hands all around, and, humming, leaves the examining room.

Into the conference room, where he picks up a dictation recorder from a stack on the table. He speaks into it, recording the date, the patient's name, the diagnosis, and a summary of his consultation. "And send a copy to Dr. Baumgartner." He clicks off the recorder, picks up his coffee cup, and says to Rose Carter, "Next?"

David Bissonette comes in, shaking his head. "You'll want to see these two," he says, gesturing toward the examining room next to the conference room and handing Jannetta a very thick sheaf of medical records, bound with a very thick rubber band.

"Two?" Jannetta asks.

Bissonette just shakes his head again. "It's the woman you talked to on the phone yesterday. Her son is with her."

Jannetta still doesn't make the connection—he probably talked to eighty people on the phone yesterday. "The one with the tumor?"

"No, no. The one with scleroderma."

"Oh, oh, Okay. Where is she?" Jannetta takes the rubber band off the chart, reads the top sheet as he walks to the door, and taps twice before going in.

Handshakes, introductions, smiles—or, rather, one smile, Jannetta's—and he plops himself down on the wheeled stool. "How are we doing today?"

This is the last thing Jannetta says for the next three minutes, as the woman, fidgety, fiftyish, and her son, fidgety and thirtyish, both begin talking, rapidly, at once. Jannetta nods, trying to sort out the voices at the same time as he leafs through the chart, flipping the pages as though it were a none-too-interesting magazine.

The "chart" takes its name from what were once literally "charts," which were, and are, graphic representations of the fluctuation of some variable such as pulse or body temperature. It lives on in this form in medical cartoons, where it hangs at the foot of the patient's bed, and its peaks and valleys are either in the punch line or present simply for verisimilitude. When the chart and its impedimenta became too bulky to hang at the foot of a bed without tipping it—or perhaps when physicians began relying on a telephone call to a nurse to check on patients' progress rather than the room visit—the chart migrated up hospital corridors to nursing stations, where it took up residence in, first, the "chart rack," which hung on a wall, and, more recently, in "chart wheels," which are lazy-Susan devices that allow nurses, residents, and unit clerks to look for a particular chart by spinning the wheel. When a patient is in a hospital bed, the "chart," which has long been a synecdoche for test results, nursing notes, progress notes, operative notes, postoperative notes, discharge notes, and medication notes, is kept in a snap-backed binder that fits, in typical hospitalizations, smartly in the chart wheel. When the patient—and, hence, the chart—leave the patient unit, the patient leaves the building and the chart stays in the hospital.

Charts of office visits never get the snap-backed binder, and they never repose in hospital medical-record departments. Instead, they line the walls, halls, offices, and conference rooms of physicians' offices. Every patient who visits a neurosurgeon who practices in the University Neurosurgical Associates has a chart on the ninth floor of Presby. When a UNA physician refers a patient to another physician, the chart travels to the new physician; when, as is much more common, a physician refers a patient to UNA, a chart ends up in the color-coded, overstuffed bookcase of a filing system on the ninth floor. Whatever physician ends up with a patient ends up with the chart, too.

It is a relatively recent phenomenon that patient charts became the repository for so much information. In the lobby of Presby, inside a glass case commemorating the hospital's history, is a large ledger book from the turn of the century. Patients' names run down the left hand side of the ledger, each name followed by a diagnosis, the name of the physician, the date of treatment, and the result, usually "Cured," "Improved," or "Died."

The chart Jannetta holds has been swollen by technology (for example, the results of an electromyographic scan and their interpretation), fiscal prudence (to prevent the unnecessary repetition of tests and consultations), and medico-legal concerns. (Doctors chart virtually everything that they do so that later they can demonstrate that they did it. More and more often, critics of contemporary medicine say that this motive directly conflicts with fiscal prudence, as physicians "protect themselves" by ordering a panoply of tests and consultations. *Dorland's Illustrated Medical Dictionary* lists thirty-seven pages of tests in small, double-columned type, and new tests are being invented almost daily.) Such a panoply confronts Jannetta—the woman sitting in front of him on the examining table has been to see enough physicians to staff a moderately large medical center, and each has added his batch of tests to the stew. The woman is here to see Jannetta on the advice of a neurologist who has confirmed that the woman has scleroderma and that she suffers from episodic pain and numbness in the left side of her face. Scleroderma is a chronic hardening and shrinking of the connective tissues of the body. Since nerves travel through connective tissue such as skin, neural difficulties are not unheard of. They are also devilish to isolate and almost impossible to treat conservatively.

The woman's son is reaching the peroration of his own diagnosis, having managed in the first minute to talk over her loud enough so that she has given up trying to get a word in. She waits patiently as her son delivers what can only be called a speech, one liberally salted with references to medical literature. He has made a second career out of understanding his mother's illness and talking about it with doctors. Some patients and some patients' relatives would rather vanish through a hole in the floor than ask a question of a physician. Others ask questions every step of the way. A few cross the line between questioning and lecturing, and as the son takes one last glance at his note cards, he finishes, saying, "So what I think we're looking at here is not trigeminal *neuralgia*, which as you know can sometimes be addressed through microvascular decompression, but rather trigeminal *neuropathy* with pain, which is a different animal entirely." He sits.

Jannetta snaps the rubber band back around the chart and smiles at the woman. "Tell me where it hurts."

The son's diagnosis turns out to be accurate, as far as Jannetta can tell, but Jannetta is not a rheumatologist, which is what he thinks the woman should see. "I'd like you to see someone here from Rheumatology," he says, standing up. "Surgically, there's not much we can do. If the pain is really bad, if it's really ruining your life, we can cut the nerve, but I think you ought to explore some other options first. Have you seen anyone here from Rheumatology?" he asks.

The son says no.

"Well, that's your best bet, I think. The girls upstairs can help you set up an appointment." He shakes hands and takes his leave.

He and Bissonette enter the conference room at the same moment. Bissonette grins as Jannetta dictates a terse note, stopping the recorder to say to Bissonette that he thinks "they're basically fishing around. No one seems really involved in the care, so they're out shopping for doctors." The recorder goes back on, and he recommends the rheumatology consult. "Next?"

Next is Anna, a woman Jannetta first treated for atypical facial pain nearly eight years ago and who is a regular patient at clinic. Her medical history is emphatically atypical as well for a neurosurgery consult, but Jannetta has continued to see her because most other physicians won't: she is on welfare in a neighboring state known for particularly anemic reimbursements through Medicaid; she is a former heroin addict being maintained on methadone; she has recently had tuberculosis and has lost forty pounds. She also lost a nearly full prescription bottle of Tegretol, and no local physician would prescribe it for her, so she has come back to Pittsburgh on the bus to get a refill. She gets the smile and the handshake and an unreimbursable chat, during which Jannetta counsels her to look after herself and not to be a stranger. He leaves the examining room and tells Bissonette to give her a double refill this time around and to send the consultation notes to the physician who oversees the methadone program. "Tell him it's a pain in the ass to ride around on the bus to get a prescription filled," he adds as he heads out of the conference room. "Where am I next?"

Next is a woman from a coal town in central Pennsylvania. She was operated on for hemifacial spasm four years ago, during the period when Jannetta was using a bits of muscle tissue to slip between blood vessel and nerve. Unfortunately, the muscle is gradually reabsorbed, and the patients he operated on during that period gradually reappear for reoperations. This woman knows the ropes and is, in fact, looking forward to the surgery. "I'm afraid to drive to the Foodland," she tells him. No handshakes here. The woman gives her surgeon a kiss on the cheek, demonstrating for posterity that the Jannetta Effect is never reabsorbed and, in fact, may even be more long-lived than the Teflon he uses in surgery now. In his dictation, he mentions that she is "a nice lady."

Jannetta's face and posture change slightly, depending on whether he is in an examining room or the conference room. In the conference room, he sits to dictate his notes, even if they only take twenty seconds; he sips his coffee, looks at the ceiling, and hums. The change occurs during the ritual tap-tap-tap on the examining-room door: he takes a breath, squares his shoulders, and marches in, smiling. When he leaves an examining room, the smile is replaced immediately by a more thoughtful look, which is replaced by a more distant look that carries him into the conference room and his chair. Occasionally, a patient might peer into the conference room on the way to an examining room and not even see Jannetta, even though he is sitting right there. He looks like a different person in the tiny interstices when he is off-duty and humming.

He is humming "The Yellow Rose of Texas" as he knocks on the door of Room 5 to see a patient he has been waiting for for several weeks, a young man from Louisville referred to Jannetta by the Veterans Administration. The man is thirty-one years old and looks, Jannetta tells him, "terribly healthy." The young man is, in fact, terribly healthy, but for one terribly nagging problem: following the removal of an abscessed tooth and, later, "a partial V_2 neurectomy," or excision of part of the nerve branch that served the now-absent tooth, he has had excruciating jaw and mouth pain, so excruciating that he was mustered out of the army with a 30-percent disability. He has seen and been seen by most of the specialists within the VA system, and the system has now sent him outside the VA to Peter Jannetta. The man's chart is easily double the size of the woman with trigeminal neuropathy.

Jannetta is fully engaged by this patient's problem. Jannetta stands in front of him for a full thirty seconds, just looking at the man's jaw, as though he can see through skin. He strokes his own jaw thoughtfully and hums a Gershwin tune.

"Tell me where it hurts."

In addition to telling, the man shows him, running a finger along his jaw line but not touching. It hurts him, he says, even to shave.

"Open up," says Jannetta, and the man opens his mouth wide so that Jannetta can peer in. "Does your tongue hurt?"

The man shakes his head.

"Do your gums hurt?"

The man nods.

"Does it hurt when you're not doing anything, when you're just sitting around?"

Vigorous nods.

Jannetta turns to the counter and finds one of the trusty

cotton swabs, but instead of breaking it, he uses it as a soft-tipped probe. "Open up," he says, and the young man opens his mouth again, having closed it when Jannetta turned to get the swab. He also seems to know exactly what Jannetta is going to do with it, because he closes his eyes and braces himself on the examining table. Under his polo shirt, his shoulder muscles tense.

He is exactly right. Jannetta ever so gently probes the socket where the tooth was removed, just the barest touch, and still the man winces. Jannetta touches the gum line, and the man winces again. Jannetta removes the probe and tosses it into the wastebasket. "Okay," he says.

The man looks at Jannetta expectantly, and Jannetta looks back at him. "I need to think about this for a few minutes," Jannetta says. "I want to sit down and look over your history and think this through. Do you have any questions?"

The man answers promptly. "Yeah. Can you do anything about this pain?"

"That," says Jannetta, "is what I want to think about. Have you seen Dr. Patterson?"

"Who's he?"

"He's an oral surgeon here, a big guy."

The man shrugs.

"I'm going to find Dr. Patterson and talk about this. Make yourself comfortable for a few minutes," Jannetta says. "I'll be back in a little while." He hoists the chart and leaves the room.

Jannetta sticks his head into the conference room and tells Rose Carter, "Page Gary Patterson for me. I want to see him, if he's around. I'm going to hide in the coffee room and read this guy's chart."

The coffee room is behind an unmarked door halfway down the hall toward the suite where the transplant surgeons are seeing patients. The overflow from the waiting room reaches almost to the coffee-room door. Patients on both sides of the hall look hopefully at Jannetta as he comes toward them—is he the doctor they've been waiting to see? But their hopes are dashed as Jannetta ducks into the coffee room and shuts the door behind him.

The room is the size of a large broom closet. A table surrounded by five chairs fills the room in such a way that if five people managed to squeeze inside, no more than three of them could sit at any one time, even if they used laps. On a small counter next to a small sink sits an institution-sized Braun coffee maker gurgling out a fresh pot of coffee. Jannetta selects a foam cup from a stack on the counter and fills it to the brim before sitting down at the table and beginning to read the young man's medical history.

To the typical person suddenly struck with a neurological disorder that requires consultation with a neurosurgeon, the disorder itself, the tests required to diagnose it, and the recommended treatment may all seem astonishingly mysterious. The language used to describe the ailment and the treatment is often opaque, even—or especially—when "translated" into layman's terms. Some physicians take translation to the extreme, referring to a tumor as "a bad thing that doesn't belong there," to bleeding blood vessels as "leaky pipes," to occluded blood vessels as "clogged pipes," to aneurysms as "weak pipes." Such attempts at synonymy are often less than helpful even to weekend plumbers. Despite well-intentioned efforts at making the strange seem familiar, there is an abiding mystery attached to problems of the nervous system, and busy physicians do not often enough take the time to explain what a problem is and what a certain course of treatment means. An apocryphal story told by (and about) neurosurgical residents has to do with a patient who is diagnosed as having an operable tumor and who is admitted to the hospital to have the tumor removed. The patient undergoes the operation, recovers, and is discharged. When he returns to the surgeon for a follow-up visit several weeks later, he is surprised when the nurse asks him how he is doing after surgery. "I didn't have *surgery,*" he is supposed to have said. "All I had was a craniectomy."

Nevertheless, a surprising fact about neurosurgery is that in the vast majority of patients, the surgeons know exactly or almost exactly what is wrong. They may not know how to fix it, but anomalies of diagnosis are relatively rare, thanks in part to sophisticated diagnostic tools such as CT scanners and magnetic resonance imagers, both of which provide the diagnostician with unprecedentedly detailed "pictures" of what patients look like deep within their skulls. Further, the most common neurological disorders have been so comprehensively described and chronicled that the diagnosis is most often made by a second- or third-year resident. Unusual cases, even at a major medical center, are so relatively unusual that they are the cause for interested observation and consultation.

Unfortunately for the young man waiting in the examining room, no one has been able to decide exactly what is wrong. Jannetta knows that *something* is wrong ("Pain: Nature's way of telling you that something is wrong" reads a small poster attached to the coffee-room bulletin board), but he isn't sure what. The V_2 neurectomy was performed in an effort to alleviate the pain that persisted after the removal of the abscessed tooth. But now it seems to Jannetta, as well as to one of the VA physicians whose notes are included in the chart Jannetta is reading, that the man has two sources of pain: the original pain and pain from the neurectomy. Because of Jannetta's success at treating certain chronic pain conditions, he has acquired a modest reputation in the peripherally-related field of "pain management," a specialty that has evolved around the need to treat symptoms when the cause is untreatable, unresponsive, or unknown.

At this moment, Gary Patterson comes in. When Jannetta

referred to him as "a big guy," he might have been referring either to his institutional stature, because Patterson has a reputation as a careful and talented oral and maxillofacial surgeon, or his physical stature, which approaches that of a tight end.

"What are you doing in here?" Patterson asks, gesturing.

"Hiding out," answers Jannetta. And then, ever the host, he says, "Have some coffee."

Patterson pours coffee and sits down next to Jannetta. "What've you got here?"

"This is a guy who had an abscessed tooth and then a neurectomy for persistent pain," Jannetta begins.

"Oh, I saw this guy already. I saw this guy yesterday," says Patterson, beginning to leaf through a stack of pages from the chart.

"I don't think he should have had the nerve cut. I think he should have had the nerve explored," says Jannetta, meaning that the neurectomy might have been a bit precipitate: the surgeon might rather have surgically examined the course of the nerve, looking for the cause of the pain, such as a dental neuroma, rather than just treating the symptoms.

"I was surprised," said Patterson, "that he hurts so much." Jannetta nods vigorously. "Oh, let me tell you, that socket is exquisitely sensitive. I gave it just a touch, and I thought he'd go through the roof."

"Maybe he still ought to have the nerve explored," says Patterson.

"That's what I've been thinking. Get Shake"—Laligam Sekhar, another neurosurgeon in the department—"to explore the nerve, because this guy has two problems now: he's got pain, and he's got new pain," says Jannetta. "You know what else? I would love to see the numbers on long-term relief from dental neurectomies. I don't think they'd be that hot."

"I don't think there *are* many numbers on that," says Patterson.

When physicians talk of "numbers," they are not simply talking about number of patients treated or operations performed. Instead, they refer to the results of certain operations, expressed when the number of cases is relatively small through a sort of round-number proportion ("Two of the five are perfect, two are good, and one was a washout," a surgeon might say). Larger numbers of cases are cited as percentages of successful results, generally for a specific time period following surgery. Physicians who acquire series of patients publish their results in medical journals so that other physicians can use the information to judge the efficacy of certain procedures. What Jannetta wonders is how successful the results are from operations performed to cut the dental branches of nerves for relief of pain. His suspicion is that the numbers would not be that good. Patterson wonders if anyone has even done a long-term study of results.

Jannetta pours more coffee. "I wonder if it's time that we had a regional conference on dental neurectomies," he says, "just get everybody together in a big room and try and see how we're doing. I think we're overdue for something like that."

Patterson does, too, although both of them know that such a conference might be ticklish to arrange. Because Patterson works regularly and closely with the neurosurgeons (Jannetta tends to introduce him as an "enlightened" maxillofacial surgeon), he more often than not can see the need for such pooling of efforts and information. Some oral surgeons—and, for that matter, some neurosurgeons—tend to be a bit more . . . parochial. Sometimes they get together, and sometimes they don't. One of Jannetta's more triumphant bridge-building efforts was an appearance, in 1980, at the Annual Meeting of the American Institute of Oral Biology, where he presented a paper on atypical trigeminal neuralgia. Such crossovers, while not actually rare, are still to some degree unusual.

"I don't think there's anything I can do at this point," Patterson is saying. "If Shake wants to explore the nerve, I'd like to be there. But I think he should be the one to have a look."

Jannetta agrees and then looks at his watch. "Do you want to see this guy again?" he asks.

"No," says Patterson. "I'll see him when he sees Shake."

They rise and leave the coffee room, Jannetta a bit regretfully. He has had fifteen minutes of peace and quiet.

When Jannetta returns to the conference room, David Bissonette is dictating notes on a patient, and Dr. Robert Parrish, the chief resident, is standing at the viewing box, gazing intently at a CT scan. "Reinforcements!" Jannetta greets him. "Busy morning?"

Parrish shakes his head. He has been most of the wee hours of the morning in the Emergency Room. First, there was a victim of an auto accident who needed a neurological evaluation, and then a stroke victim who apparently had a second, more severe stroke in the ambulance ride from the community hospital, where he had first been taken, to Presby. The double duty of being both chief resident and on-call resident has resulted in Parrish's meticulously planned schedule for the day being disrupted. He had hoped to work on a case with Howard Yonas, but decides that he has to stay and help Jannetta, which means a reshuffling of the other residents' schedules as well. If clinic goes smoothly, he might catch the last hour or so of the operation; if not, it won't be the first time.

Jannetta goes back to Exam Room 5, where the man with the pain is waiting. Quickly, Jannetta tells the man that there's something wrong, that the most likely thing to have done is another operation to explore the course of the nerve that seems to be causing the problem, and that the best person to do that is Dr. Sekhar, who has clinic on the following day.

"Tell them to set you up with an appointment for tomorrow morning and to make sure that Dr. Patterson is called when you go in." He helps the man on with his jacket and walks with him a short distance. "You take care of yourself," Jannetta says in parting, then stands in the hall until the young man goes through the swinging doors at the end. One of the prices of Jannetta's excellent success rate is that it is easy to forget that there are lots of people that one cannot help, and sometimes he seems to take it personally. "What are ya gonna do?" he asks rhetorically as he goes into the conference room and picks up a tape recorder.

As he sits down to dictate, Parrish comes in. "I did two postops real quick," he says. "They're both fine." He picks up a tape recorder, too. But he doesn't sit down, because, while there are four chairs in the room, one of them is broken, its metal legs bent at a curious angle, and the other three chairs are all occupied. At the exact moment he finishes his dictation, speaking in an undertone like a golf announcer, Bissonette and Jannetta finish, too, and the three of them leave the room simultaneously. It is 9:45, and clinic is finally in full swing.

Exam Room 3: a stately woman in her sixties, here for a three-month postoperative visit following surgery for hemifacial spasm. "Look up," Jannetta says. "Raise your eyebrows. Squint hard—squeeze your eyes shut like you've got soap in 'em. Tighter, tighter, c'mon. Okay, whistle."

The woman opens her eyes and whistles the first seven bars of "Yankee Doodle Dandy." If anything is going to trigger an episode of hemifacial spasm, it is usually whistling.

"You look terrific," Jannetta says. "How do you feel?"

She feels terrific. Handshakes, smiles, a little help with the coat, another handshake. "Send me a card," Jannetta says. "Send me a card at Christmas or on your birthday, and let me know how you're doing."

"*My* birthday?" the woman asks, smiling.

"You never forget your own birthday, do you?" he says and laughs. "Keep in touch."

It is not because he likes to get mail that Jannetta asks to be sent Christmas cards: He believes in aggressive follow-up—in some ways has staked his reputation on keeping in touch with as many of his patients as he can. Upstairs, in one of the department offices, records on past patients are continually updated; questionnaires go out regularly to try and ascertain longer- and longer-term results. Inevitably, a few patients are lost forever to follow-up—they move without notifying Jannetta. The ones who send a card every year can be reached, when necessary, to see how they are doing, and it is a very efficient way of keeping addresses current. Some physicians have specially printed forms that they give to patients to be sent in case of a change of address. But a form lost is a form lost to follow-up, while Christmas, although but once, does come every year.

Exam Room 2: an attractive woman in her mid-thirties from West Palm Beach with trigeminal neuralgia. "Tell me where it hurts," Jannetta says. "How often? For how long? What brings it on? Does anything make it stop? For how long? Close your eyes." Cotton wisp. "Does it bother you? Does it ruin your life? Well, I think we can help you."

"What do you do?"

"Sit down, and I'll run through it for you."

He describes the operation. He describes the results. The tests. The hospitalization. The risks. "We're very good at this; we're very careful. We feel we know what we're doing."

The woman sits silent for a moment. "You'll want to think it over," Jannetta says.

But the woman says no. "The sooner the better. Can you do it tomorrow?"

Jannetta laughs. "We're not that good. Talk to the girls upstairs, and tell 'em you want to go as soon as you can. I'll be away the last week of the month, but anytime after that should be good. You can try for the tests tomorrow though. Questions?"

There are none. Handshake, then Jannetta helps the woman on with her coat, hands her her purse, opens the door for her.

"Thank you," she says.

And Jannetta replies, "Thank *you.*"

Exam Room 1: another woman from Florida, mid-fifties, lightly tinted designer sunglasses, which means, in Jannetta's clinic, probable hemifacial spasm. Her husband stands when Jannetta comes in. Introductions. Handshakes.

"How long have you had it? How often? Anything start it? Anything stop it? For how long? Look up. Raise your eyebrows. Look left. Look right. Squint hard. Squeeze your eyes shut like you've got soap in 'em. Harder. Okay." Cotton wisp. Broken swab handle. "Tell me when you feel this. Now? Now? Now? Okay. I think we can help you."

"I knew you could. I knew it the moment I talked to Marilyn." Marilyn is her next-door neighbor, whose aunt Jannetta operated on for hemifacial spasm the previous year.

Most of the patients that Jannetta sees have been diagnosed long before he sees them. All of them have tried more conservative treatments, such as medication, before making their way to Pittsburgh. Estimates vary widely as to how many people have symptoms of cranial nerve dysfunction that are treatable with medication, but most agree that it is the majority. Thus, the patients Jannetta sees are generally already somewhat psychologically prepared for the possibility of surgery before they ever see him, because the spectrum of choices always includes the status quo. One may leave Jannetta's clinic and return to Florida, or Iowa, or New Kensington, Pennsylvania, and pretend the visit never occurred. This makes his clinic patients subtly different, in most cases, from those of neurosurgeons like Laligam Sekhar, who spends most of his time diagnosing and removing very tricky and very dangerous tumors, or the clinics of the pediatric neurosurgeons, like Leland Albright, where anxious parents learn that sometimes the worst is far worse than they had tried not to imagine. In cases where, say, a patient is diagnosed with a malignant brain tumor, that patient is asked to assimilate a real and dramatic threat to his or her own mortality, to participate in a life-and-death decision. Some patients diagnosed with tumors faint when told of the diagnosis; others dispute, some argue, almost all ask, "Are you sure?" The tension can be debilitating.

By contrast, Jannetta's prospective patients—at least those who might benefit from microvascular decompression—have generally exhausted all other possibilities and thus come *looking* for surgery. Sometimes the symptoms are physically and psychologically debilitating; other times, they are only annoying or distracting. But the symptoms are always a presence, a new fact of life that must be either tolerated or confronted. And neurosurgeons like Jannetta are the embodiment of the confrontation.

A few clinic patients do go home and forget about undergoing surgery; some go home and try to, and come back in a month or a year. Many say, "The sooner the better."

This woman and her husband listen patiently while Jannetta explains the operation, the risks, the hoped-for results. Then, they don't even confer but, rather, just exchange a glance and a smile, and the woman says, "Will you do the surgery?"

"Sure," says Jannetta. "Tell the girls to get you set up for the tests, and we'll go from there."

"Thank you, Doctor."

"Thank *you*."

Exam Room 6: a woman from Long Island with hemifacial

spasm. "Look up. Look down. Raise your eyebrows . . . "

Respite. Into the conference room for coffee and a cigarette and a doughnut from an orange-and-white box on the table. Dr. Parrish sits down, too, and he and Jannetta chat about the stroke case in the Emergency Room.

"What did you have?" asks Jannetta.

Parrish looks at the ceiling. "He was out of it before he got here," he says. "His family took him to the local ER at two, and by the time they decided to transfer him, I expect he was either going or gone. They said he was alert when he left, but he sure wasn't when he arrived."

The patient is now in the NCCU, deeply comatose; one of the attendings is probably talking with the family right now. The stroke or strokes, Parrish suspects, were for all practical purposes fatal; the man is respirator-dependent and completely unresponsive. Jannetta and Parrish speculate idly and a bit darkly about suspicious transfers of patients that are more and more often flowing uphill from smaller community hospitals to the major medical centers. The city of Pittsburgh has been insulated, by and large, from the phenomenon of "dumping," primarily because there is no municipal hospital into which patients are readily dumped. But the large city medical centers seem to be seeing more and more transfers that might be more questionable medically than they are fiscally—that is, patients very ill or moribund with little or no health insurance. Macroscopically, it is all in a night's work. But microscopically, no resident likes to admit some other hospital's dead or dying patient. In a case like this, there were no clear ethical breeches—patients sometimes do suffer a series of strokes, and there is no reason why such strokes cannot occur in an ambulance. But it is still hard to deal with, because there was nothing to be done.

"By the way," Jannetta says, "I got a call from you know who yesterday."

Parrish indeed does know who. "I know, I know. I'll get over there . . . tonight or tomorrow."

At the hospital previous to Presby in his rotation, Dr. Parrish left some unfinished business in the form of a stack of unsigned charts. When Jannetta's charts pile up, he might get a courteous note or phone call reminding him gently of his duties; when a resident leaves a stack of unsigned charts, his chief gets a phone call telling him to keep his people in line.

"I have absolutely nothing I can say to these people," Jannetta says. "If you don't keep on top of this, they're going to be unpleasant about it. It's part of the business, and they know it, and I know it, and you know it. So take care of it." There is the slightest edge to his voice.

"I'll take care of it."

"Good," says Jannetta. Case closed, he is back to his normal self. "Who's next?"

Next is a woman from Tennessee, here for a three-month follow-up after surgery for hemifacial spasm. "You look terrific," Jannetta tells her. "How do you feel?"

Look up. Look down. Squint. Harder. Harder. Okay, now, whistle.

The woman purses her lips and tries, then tries again. Jannetta laughs. "You never learned to whistle, did you?"

She says no.

Jannetta looks as though he has half a mind to teach her, but not on a day when the clinic is full. "You know what?" he asks, "I think you're a winner."

This is the professional opinion Jannetta's patients dearly hope to hear.

Handshakes. "Send me a card once a year at Christmas, and let me know how you're doing," he says, holding the door open for her.

"Thank you *so much*, Dr. Jannetta. You know, I'm a different person, now."

"You're the same person you were, only happier," he says.

"Thank you, again."

"Thank *you.*"

Into the conference room, where Rose Carter says, "Ooh. Patty has a call for you." She points at the phone.

Jannetta says, "Who?"

"A doctor from Boston."

"Where?" Meaning "Where's the call?" not "Where's Boston?"

On the table are two phones. One is the sort of phone seen frequently in businesses: beige, traditionally shaped, with a row of buttons across the front that light up when it rings. Next to it is a device that has the distinction of having earned the enmity of almost the entire huge, heterogeneous population of the University Health Center hospitals. The device has one tiny red light blinking furiously. The device is the dreaded New Phone.

Hospitals, it seems, get new phones nowadays about as frequently as they get new patients. The phones are designed, physicians are told, to make their lives easier. Physicians may be forgiven for being suspicious of this claim when they see that New Phones come with thick instruction books full of diagrams and hypothetical situations that use capital letters at the beginning of words to provide needed emphasis ("Imagine you are in the middle of an Overseas Conference Call, and a call that you have previously Programmed the Receiver to Pass Through does not Pass Through. . . . "). Suspicions are sharpened when physicians are told that their office staff must attend a half-day seminar in order to learn how to use the phone. The suspicions are realized when physicians are themselves asked to come to a half-day seminar in order to learn how to use the phone. One half-day seminar for physicians at Presby had exactly one physician, and he left during the break. At any given moment, somewhat less than half of the phone users throughout the University Health Center are absolutely confident that they can use the New Phones as they can the Old Phones. The New Phones, however, do have a distinction in that they have added a new phrase to telephone etiquette. Imagine you are a powerful and influential physician at a Major Medical Center. You call a colleague at another Major Medical Center, perhaps to discuss the Future of American Medicine or maybe a Large Grant. The physician you are calling is not at the number you have called, and the offer is made to transfer the call. You are told, "I'll try to transfer you. But we have these new phones, so I'll give you the number . . . " You, of course, understand completely, because your institution has just gotten New Phones, too.

Jannetta looks at the New Phone as though it is a puzzling neurological disorder. "What," he asks, "do I do?"

"Just pick it up," says Rose, and Jannetta does so, saying, "Hello?"

No one answers. Out of habit or neurosurgical nature, Jannetta presses a button. Nothing. He presses another button. "Hello?"

He turns to Rose. "Nothing."

"Try the button that's blinking."

He does so. "Hello?"

He turns back to Rose. "Nope, it's gone. It's going da dah da dah da dah da dah." He shrugs and hangs up. "How do I call Patty?"

Rather than explain, Rose calls Patty on the Old Phone and hands it to Jannetta. "Hi. Who was it? Uh-huh. Uh-huh. Call him back and tell him I'll call him back. Uh-huh. Okay." The wonder of technology.

Exam Room 2. Bissonette is just emerging as Jannetta arrives. The patient is thirty-two, newly married, newly moved to the Detroit area, newly diagnosed with disabling positional vertigo. Her new husband stands next to her holding her hand as Jannetta comes in. Introductions. Handshakes. The woman has been to clinic a few weeks earlier, when Jannetta was out of town, and has been through a series of tests of her auditory nerves. Jannetta skims the report from Margareta Møller as he asks the woman questions. "When did it start? . . . How often do you get it? . . . What brings it on? . . . What stops it?"

The woman answers promptly and precisely. The vertigo was coincident with her marriage, almost sixteen months earlier. "We thought at first it might be some sort of allergy," her husband says, "and then we thought it might have something to do with . . . you know, getting married and moving and everything."

He looks sheepish. How many spouses have said in pique, "You're driving me out of my mind!"? The psychiatrist was anything but encouraging, recommending weekly sessions and suggesting it might have something to do with the early death of the woman's father. A neurologist disagreed and prescribed medication that alleviated the symptoms by making the woman so sleepy she would doze off during meals. The husband hunted around a university's medical library, where his unfamiliarity with a computerized searching system for medical literature turned up, by accident, a reference to Jannetta cross-listed under something like "Vertigo, Other Cases." Referral patterns for disabling positional vertigo are still tenuous.

"Dr. Møller thinks we may have something," Jannetta is saying as he pulls up the wheeled stool and sits in front of the woman. "The results aren't conclusive, so we ought to run through some tests again. But there's a chance we can help you. I think you ought to try a different medication, though, in the interim. Does this bother you? Does it ruin your life?"

"You have no idea," the woman replies.

"Okay, what we'll do is run some eighth-nerve tests again,

233

and I want you to try this other medicine. And if you don't shape up, come back and we'll see what we can do."

"I want the operation," the woman says, quietly but emphatically.

Jannetta smiles. "Let's cover the bases first. You may feel terrific tomorrow." He writes out a prescription. "Have them set you up for the tests, and let me know how you're doing." He stands and shakes hands all around before leaving the room.

In his dictation, he says, "The symptoms are compatible, but ——" he switches the recorder off for a moment to think. Recorder on. "The symptoms are compatible with an eighth-nerve problem, but the first set of tests were inconclusive——" Recorder off. Recorder on. "I expect that a second series may indicate a problem but recommend that we wait a bit and try to make sure. Dr. Margereta Møller should see this woman again, and her neurologist should follow her on the medication for four weeks." Recorder off. "So much for my knife-happy reputation."

Exam Room 1. "Hiya, Doc! What's the good word?" The patient is a young woman, appearing at clinic for her three-month follow-up following surgery for trigeminal neuralgia. She is effusive, she is effervescent, she is on top of the world. "I told ya, Doc, I'm a mill hunkie. I can get through anything. So, am I all fixed?"

She does indeed appear to be all fixed. All through Jannetta's exam (Look up. Look down. Close your eyes . . .), she chats on. She tells mill-hunkie jokes. She tells what she calls "dago" jokes. She tells Jannetta that her sister is getting married in three weeks, and Jannetta must—*absolutely gotta*—come to the wedding, when Jannetta admits he has never been to a hunkie wedding. "We eat, we drink, we dance, we swing from chandeliers. Doc, you gotta see my dress." She describes her maid-of-honor dress. "Hey, my sister is outside waiting for me. Do you wanna meet my sister?"

Jannetta, of course, does wanna meet her sister and accompanies his patient to the waiting room. "Hey, Amy! Come and meet Dr. Jannetta!"

Amy shakes Jannetta's hand. "Hey, when are you gonna do a brain transplant on her?" She invites Jannetta to the wedding.

Exam Room 6. A woman who can only be described as from the aristocracy, in manner ("How do you do, Peter?"), in dress (a page from Lord & Taylor), in accent (Back Bay Boston). She is at clinic for a follow-up after surgery for hemifacial spasm. Although she doesn't put it quite that way, she, too, is all fixed. Cranial-nerve disorders are emphatically democratic. She allows Jannetta to help her with her coat. Jannetta says, "I think you're a winner."

And she replies, "Why thank you, Peter!" She is off for Australia.

Parrish has not been idle during Jannetta's spin through the social spectrum. He and Bissonette have teamed up to see an entire time slot's worth of patients, bringing them up almost to on time. To celebrate, the three crowd into the conference room and reach for the doughnuts. Rosa Pinkus comes in, carrying her own cup of coffee. She tries to spend at least some time in the clinics, observing, occasionally offering suggestions and advice. Her role in the department is sort of as a Minister without Portfolio; she is invited to be as involved in the workings of the neurosurgical world as she wishes to be, and for her, that includes watching the surgeons interact with their patients. Parrish and Jannetta, who happen to have the two available chairs when she comes in, both rise and offer her a place to sit. Jannetta offers her a doughnut.

The remaining patients to see are, if possible, even a slightly more mixed bag than has come through the clinic already. They include a follow-up visit by a patient who had an acoustic tumor removed (Parrish will see him); a woman who is almost a year postop for a successful operation for vertigo and who shows up every three months for a clinic visit, nominally to make sure that everything is all right but, Jannetta suspects, because she has a void in her life now that the dizziness has gone—nothing has replaced it and she is unable to move on (Jannetta will see her); a woman who has had surgery, also for vertigo, but without good result (Bissonette and then Jannetta); a woman with possible spasmodic torticollis, referred to Jannetta by an old friend in the Midwest (Parrish and then Jannetta); and, finally, a prospective patient whose reputation has preceded her by several weeks: she has an acoustic tumor and has managed to miss connections at two previous clinics, first because Jannetta was out of town and she refused to be seen by Sekhar, second because she got tired of waiting one morning when things were more behind schedule than usual and she left rather than pay for another hour of parking. She is accompanied by her daughter, who has already berated Rose Carter for the high cost of parking in Pittsburgh. ("Why can't the doctor come to the house, like they used to? It's the same goddamned thing back home.") They live in a middling large town about an hour from Pittsburgh, from whence they—the records forwarded from the local physician refer to the woman and her daughter as a "they," which is an ominous sign—were referred. Parrish will see the patient first, and he begins hanging CT scans, X rays, and angiograms on the viewing box. "Don't lose any of those," says Rose, smiling. She has also gotten an earful from the patient's daughter about how some goddamned doctor lost one of the envelopes containing CT scans and they had had to pay for another set. Parrish gives Carter a withering look, terminated by a rueful smile.

Jannetta starts with the persistent vertigo patient, preferring that, at the moment, to the patient with the persistent vertigo. "How are you today?" he asks as he comes in. The woman is fine. She feels fine, she looks fine, she is absolutely pleased with everything. She is here, however, just to make sure.

Jannetta does a cursory examination of the incision site. It is completely invisible. This woman is—well—fine.

The woman talks, with some bitterness, about what she went through to find help: the doctors, the hospitals, the "run-around." She has taken to doing volunteer work at her local hospital and gives the impression that she is doing a bit of diagnostic work as well. She has visited as many of her local neurologists and neurosurgeons as would see her, offering her help and letting them know that Jannetta is helping people like her.

As she talks, Jannetta nods and says, "Uh-huh," every minute or so, occasionally interjecting a "That's good." He stops short of accepting her offer to come once in a while and visit with his patients, suggesting instead that her work might be more valuable in her own area, which is, after all, four states away. As soon as he is courteously able, he takes his leave. She shakes his hand for a long time.

In the conference room, he tells Rose Carter, "I don't want to see her anymore," meaning not that she is banished, but that if she insists on future visits, she is to see someone else. He was the epitome of politeness with the former patient; he is slightly curt now in recompense. "She's gotta put this behind her, and I can't help her do that," he says, picking up a tape recorder. The note takes ten seconds to dictate: "Patient appears to be completely recovered from operation and has no complaints of symptoms. No clinic visits are indicated at this time, but patient should receive usual follow-up question-naires."

Exam Room 3. Possible spasmodic torticollis. A few months after seeing this patient, Jannetta will score a modest medical coup when he operates not only on a patient referred to him for torticollis, but also on the referring neurosurgeon, who has torticollis himself. Both will have good results, and Jannetta, in addition to some ink in the Pittsburgh and Iowa newspapers, will establish a referral pattern to end all referral patterns. Getting a good result in an operation on another neurosurgeon is an excellent way of establishing one's bona fides.

This woman, though, and another dozen torticollis patients must come first. Thus far, he has only done a small number of these cases, and the follow-up is so relatively short that nothing conclusive can be drawn. But the operation *feels* like the right thing to do, fits well within the conceptual framework of microvascular decompression, seems to make sense. Jannetta is positively charming as he examines the woman and makes small talk with her husband.

Torticollis, more familiarly known as "wryneck," is a name formed from the Latin words *tortus,* or "twisted," and *collum,* or "neck." It is not in and of itself an unusual condition, because it can be caused by any number of things. Congenital torticollis, for example, is caused by an injury to one of the neck muscles during birth; dermatogenic torticollis is caused by the contraction of the skin of the neck; rheumatoid torticollis by rheumatism; ocular torticollis by, interestingly, severe astigmatism or, sometimes, ocular muscle palsy.

But, as is the case with so many cranial nerve dysfunctions, there are also cases of torticollis characterized as "neurogenic," as "habit," as "mental," as "intermittent." Occasionally, exhaustive diagnostic work may lead the physician to an identifiable cause. Almost as often, one finds no identifiable cause, and patients are variously medicated with muscle relaxants, sent to psychiatrists, treated with hypnosis, with acupuncture, with cold baths and hot towels, with exercise, with bed rest. Since 1981, when a neurosurgeon in West Germany thought to extend Jannetta's theory of microvascular compression to the eleventh, or spinal accessory, nerve, several surgeons, including Jannetta, have been trying and refining the procedure. This is exactly what Jannetta wants to do now, and he is telling her so. "I would like you to think about the possibility of surgery," he says. "I'd like you to talk it over with your physician, but I think we can help you."

The woman asks several questions about the operation, and Jannetta pulls up his stool to answer them. He is candid, saying that the results are mixed. "About fifty percent are perfect, about twenty-five percent are improved, and about twenty-five percent aren't successful at all. We've done about two thousand procedures for other conditions—for people with facial pain, with facial twitches, for dizziness, and the results have been very good for those. But we haven't done enough of these to really have a good picture."

The woman is polite and hopeful; she has had torticollis for nearly five years.

Her husband seems hopeful, too. "We've heard marvelous things about you, Doctor," he says.

"Don't believe everything you hear," says Jannetta, and they all laugh. He takes his leave, and he hums on his way back to the conference room, mulling over the possibilities.

Next is the woman whose vertigo was not helped by the operation, and Jannetta can add little to what Parrish has already told her. "Do you feel any better at all?" Jannetta asks. The woman estimates that the episodes have decreased by perhaps 10 percent, which is not encouraging. Jannetta says he'll review the operation and that he'd like to see her again in a few months, but that some cases don't turn out for the best.

"Can you operate again?" the woman asks.

"We can," Jannetta says. "We'd have to feel like we had some reason to, have a pretty good sense that there was something we could do. Before we do that, we should sit down and consider cutting the nerve. But let's wait a bit to talk about that."

Into the conference room for one more cup of coffee and another look at the CT scans and other radiography of the woman with the tumor. Parrish is looking at them again, too, having just come out of the examining room. He looks annoyed.

"How is she?" Jannetta asks.

Parrish exhales loudly. "Well, she's nuts."

"Bad?"

"Ridiculous. We spend ten minutes talking about parking and then ten minutes talking about how it's her goddamned *doctor's* fault that she has the tumor, which she doesn't believe that she has anyway."

Jannetta points with his pen to one of the CT scans. Computed tomography has changed medicine in much the way that X rays did—in some ways more profoundly, because CT allows physicians to, for all practical purposes, "see" inside a patient, one level at a time. The principle is remarkably similar to the principles by which X rays work: different structures, different tissues, different spaces within the body are penetrated to different degrees by a beam of radiation and thus, in the case of X rays, affect a piece of photographic film differently. Tomography used to be the moderately well-developed science of directing the radiation beam in such a way as to illuminate structures in a certain plane only and obscuring structures in different planes, thereby increasing the detail of the radiographic image of the structure in question—for example, a tumor. When tomography was linked up with the computer, however, the entire universe of diagnostic radiology was changed in an instant, because CT uses computer software to recreate the radiographic image, rather than the comparatively poor resolution of photographic film. The computer "sees" subtle differences in the depth of penetration of the radiation beam and can be programmed to ignore completely any information that falls outside the requested spectrum.

Imagine, for example, a traditional skull X ray of a patient with a tumor, an X ray taken in profile. The physician may see the tumor right there in the center of the skull, but how does he know if it is, say, two centimeters from the right side of the patient's skull or two centimeters from the left side or exactly in the center?

He knows, because he immediately orders a CT scan of the patient, which generates images of the patient's skull and its contents in a series of "slices" taken in cross section. Radiologists explaining CT invariably use the analogy of the automatic bread-slicing machine in one's favorite bakery, the one with the row of vibrating blades one slice away from each other, which is why many physicians don't allow radiologists to explain CT to their patients. Instead, surgeons usually draw the little slices themselves on a sheet of paper, preferring not to cloud patients minds with images of bread slicers. The analogy, however, is a good one for those sufficiently distant from the specter of surgery.

CT scans have grown from being the diagnostically exotic to the pedestrianly commonplace—virtually all hospitals in the United States have at least one, and big medical centers have dozens. Further, the software developed to generate the images has become more and more sophisticated. Color CT, for example, is highly valuable for some applications; physicians who suspect aneurysms or arteriovenous malformations can inject radiopaque dye into blood vessels, so that the blood vessels and their defects show up stark white on a field of gray. Jannetta's colleague Howard Yonas, in conjunction with several of Pitt's radiologists, has patients inhale xenon while undergoing CT; the gas moves through the bloodstream and shows up within the brain's circulatory system wherever blood is, so that Yonas can tell if blood flow is high or low or absent. A sideline of xenon-enhanced CT is that it may prove to be the definitive test for "brain death": a physician who can demonstrate that there is no blood flow within the brain can demonstrate that a patient is dead, not deeply comatose. With CT, neurosurgeons can see with unprecedented clarity if a tumor is present, where it is, how big it is, and the extent to which it contains blood vessels—all crucial information before and during an operation. CT has had a long reign as one of the most important diagnostic tools available to surgeons, and only recently has its outright supremacy been challenged, most notably by magnetic resonance imaging, or MRI, which is not a radiographic device at all, but rather measures the response of the molecules of a person to a strong magnetic field. Parrish, who is staring at a CT scan just now, happens to have picked up a Ph.D. in MRI along the way to becoming a neurosurgeon, which is the newest wave in a field of new waves.

Jannetta taps his pen again. On three successive slices of the CT scan, a roughly round whitish spot can be seen within the cerebellopontine angle. It is the shape of a typical acoustic tumor; it is in exactly the right place for an acoustic tumor; the symptoms are right for an acoustic tumor; so the odds are very good that it is an acoustic tumor and that it wasn't put there by any doctor. In fact, the woman is lucky that it was caught relatively early. It seems to be about the size of a marble, and many acoustic tumors are much, much bigger before they are diagnosed.

Jannetta recites this, half to himself. "Well, let's see what the lady has to say," he says. "Anyone coming along?"

"How are you today?" Jannetta asks.

"Are you the doctor?" the woman's daughter asks.

"Yes," he says. "I'm Peter Jannetta."

"I'm doing just terrible, Doctor, just *terrible*," the woman sitting on the examining table begins. "The other doctor won't give it to me straight. I don't think he knows what he's doing. Do you think he knows what he's doing? I think he's full of crap, that's what I think. Sending me all the way up here. This is the third time we've been up here, you know, trying to see you——"

The daughter interrupts. "This place is a real zoo, do you know? We spend an hour in the car to see the doctor, and when we get here, you're not here. Do you think that's a good thing? Tell me, Doctor, do you think that's a good thing?"

Jannetta, through this, is smiling. If the room were silent (which it is not), you could hear him humming (which he is) "Begin the Beguine." He waits patiently for a lull in the tirade, but one does not occur.

"You know, I think that son of a bitch doesn't know what he's doing," the woman is saying. "I think you're all a bunch of dummies, that's what I think. A tumor. Do I look like I have a brain tumor? And the gobbledygook about the surgery. No one says, 'Oh, we'll take it out, and you'll be fine.' No. You say, 'We'll do the best we can.' What the *hell kind of thing is that to tell someone with a brain tumor?*"

"Did you lose the X rays, too?" the daughter asks.

"Probably," her mother answers. She turns to the daughter. "You know the only thing they care about is their goddamned money." She turns back to Jannetta. "Do you know how much it costs to park in the damned parking garage?"

There is a pause, a moment of silence when Jannetta thinks he might have a chance to gain control of the conversation. He is still smiling. He stops humming and begins talking in a very soft voice. "We took a good look at the films—at the X rays and other things—and we can see the tumor very clearly. It's a small tumor, as tumors go, but it's definitely there. And if you don't do anything about it, it's going to get bigger and bigger. We know that. You know that. You came here to see what we thought we could do, and I think we can operate—should operate—and get the tumor out. This is basically what you were told by the other doctor, and I agree with him. I know that it's very disturbing to have something like this, and I know that it's upsetting, but it is something you're going to have to deal with. I'd be happy to help you deal with it, but you're going to have to deal with it."

Both the women erupt simultaneously into very fast and very loud speech. Neurosurgeons learn to be meticulous sorters: Jannetta can sort out the subtle gray distinctions between scar tissue, nerve tissue, connective tissue, and tumor, but he cannot sort out what the woman and her daughter are saying to him, to each other, to themselves. A CT-scan is of little use in this consultation—he needs a parliamentarian.

" . . . other doctor said it might go away . . . "

" . . . had been here three weeks ago, this wouldn't be happening . . . "

" . . . don't like this hospital, because this hospital is . . . "

" . . . can't get a straight answer from anyone . . . "

" . . . never sure what is wrong . . . "

" . . . lost X rays . . . "

" . . . radiation . . . "

" . . . parking . . . "

" . . . neighborhood . . . "

" . . . think you're all so smart . . . "

Jannetta raises a hand, both hands, as though acknowledging applause, but to no avail. The woman with the tumor stands and starts putting on her coat. Jannetta steps forward to help her, but she brushes his hand away. He leaves the room. The woman and her daughter don't even notice that he is leaving.

In the conference room, he lights a cigarette and stares at the viewing box. Then he carefully pulls down the films, slides them into their respective envelopes, and places them neatly on the table. He sits. "I've been as nice to her as I can. I tried to be nice, and now I'm through being nice. Screw it." He turns to Rose Carter. "I can't do anything for her." He turns to Parrish, who is sitting at the conference table, says, "Take care of it," stubs his cigarette out, and says again, "Screw it."

The woman and her daughter move past the conference room, still talking loudly at each other.

"Nothing."

It is said so emphatically that there is little doubt that this is the last word. "You're an optimist, which is why you're a neurosurgeon," Jannetta once said to Dias at a Residents' Conference, which is true, but only half of a larger truth. The other half of that truth might be: "A neurosurgeon also knows when to quit." For every hour that Jannetta has spent in the operating room since coming to Pittsburgh, he has easily spent two or three hours doing the kind of work that builds and supports a neurosurgical service. One of his largest successes institutionally may be, in fact, the making of the department into a known—and a well-known—quantity. And one of the side effects of that is the development of not actively looking for trouble. With a word, the woman with the tumor could have had at her service all the resources of a highly regarded, highly skilled team within a highly regarded, highly skilled institution. Without that one word, though, the woman might as well not even exist. In this sense, Jannetta's comment to Rose Carter, "I can't do anything for her," takes on a resonance, an emphasis on the pronouns. Jannetta has determined that *he* cannot do anything for her, and, to a good neurosurgeon, that is that. Asked about the woman a few weeks later, Jannetta can only vaguely remember having seen her at all. "Her?" he says. "She went back where she came from and had the surgery there."

Rose Carter begins packing up the tape recorders. "Is there anyone else to see?" Jannetta asks. There is not. "In that case," he says, "who wants to go get a hot dog?"

Ritual and Dogma

Introspection as a personality trait is not highly conspicuous in the neurosurgical profession. Introspection requires an acknowledgment of the self, which in and of itself might seem common in a profession that owes much of its most dramatic progress to strong personalities, strong egos, almost toxic levels of self-confidence. Neurosurgeons as a group do tend toward self-confidence, self-control, self-assessment. But these traits are "now"-oriented: they are exhibited day to day only in present time. Introspection requires a sense of past, present, and future; it requires a level of abstract thought; it may occasionally result in self-criticism or self-reproach; and it always requires a pause to reflect. Ask around at large medical centers about the neurosurgeons, and people will tend to call them—off the record—"cowboys," "gunslingers," "knife-happy," "cut-happy," "scalpel-happy," "trigger-happy," and, perhaps in deference to the fact that the overwhelming majority of neurosurgeons are men, "peacocks" (at least one neurosurgery department at a dignified medical school is thus referred to as "NBC"). Academic medicine is such a protocol-steeped profession that it matters little if the neurosurgeons happen to be as good as everyone says they think they are. They give off the aura of shooting from the hip and thus live with the consequences, if they take the time to notice it. And, like Paladin, there is never a shortage of people waiting to shoot them down.

Watch, for example, a stream of residents entering the cavernous cafeteria that links Presby's main towers and Scaife Hall, where the school of medicine resides. At any given moment, it is virtually impossible to predict where one's peers may be—residents seldom try and arrange to meet at a specific time and place, because they have little control over time and place—but the cafeteria serves very well as a place where someone will likely be, if he or she doesn't have to be somewhere else.

Some residents come in alone, stand on line, gather a meal, and find a sunny or shady place to sit—alone. Others might come in in pairs, and it is certainly not unusual for a pair of residents to grow into a small group. Residents in medicine (as opposed to surgery) almost unfailingly perform introductions, engage in polite conversations, talk about diverse subjects. The time in the cafeteria is for them a sort of respite.

Now look for a table of residents where the majority are wearing surgical scrub suits and long, white lab coats. There may be several. Find the group that is engaged in the most heated discussion, the group that seems the most oblivious to casual passers-by, the group that isolates itself not through polite silence or talk of politics or sports or difficult physicians. Find a group where the center of the conversation is always the work that they have just completed or are about to begin, where one resident might be drawing furiously on the house stationery (paper napkins) and talking rapidly about the One Right Way to do something while the other residents are talking just as rapidly about several other One Right Ways. Presto! You have found the residents in neurosurgery.

Neurosurgeons work in what can be an extremely isolating profession; even at their most collaborative, they finally work alone. And because the stakes are so high, a neurosurgical resident is only as good as his last operation, and in a busy place like Pitt, his last operation was probably no more than twenty-four hours ago, and his next operation will probably be no more than twenty-four hours in the future. If a neurosurgeon in training screws up, there is very little time to brood; if he does a spectacularly good job, he has very little time to savor the success. Neurosurgeons are asked to prove themselves, to be king of the hill, top of the rock, the last man standing, the best gunslinger, every time they enter the OR. It is little wonder that the expressions associated with good work that gain currency among neurosurgery residents are terms not of endearment, but of conquests grisly and absolute, as if these people are an auxiliary of organized crime: when you do something very difficult very well, what you've done is "blow the attending away." You are, until your next operation, The Best.

Which is not a state of mind amenable to introspection.

Some neurosurgeons, however, learn a sense of history, and some good neurosurgeons learn a sense of having a place in history. And as they acquire that sense, they can grow introspective. Also, as they amass a lifetime of work, they can afford a bit of self-reproach, of self-examination. If the lifetime of work is very full, they may lose some of the tension associated with needing to prove that they are the best. The best neurosurgeons grow to be what might be called conservative; the best neurosurgeons learn to say no; the best neurosurgeons learn what they see as the limits of the profession and carve out a place within those limits to work. They have enough patients, they have enough surgery, they are busy enough that opportunities to prove themselves are frequent, and they needn't seek opportunities to do so. Paradoxically, this is a difficult thing to teach to the residents, however, because the way that you learn to be a good neurosurgeon is to be asked to prove yourself at every opportunity. So residents are given a mixed message. Residents who don't lunge at every challenge gain the reputation of being "lazy" or, worse, "overcautious." So they learn to lunge at challenges, even while their mentors are learning to be more conservative. And the same apparent contradiction exists in the profession as a whole: one of the noteworthy things about the "establishment" in neurosurgery is that there is an establishment at all. If neurosurgeons didn't grow at least a little introspective, there would be five thousand plus chiefs and very few Indians. Some think that this is already the situation that neurosurgery faces, while others chafe at the conservative—"hidebound" is the word most often used—majority. As if the young physicians learning their craft were not called upon to perform enough delicate balancing acts within the operating room, they are asked to develop a delicate balance emotionally and intellectually within their profession.

It is of some help to the residents at Pitt to have a chairman who is anything but hidebound and who has recruited a faculty given to independent thinking. Such a situation is not a prerequisite for a good residency program—some of the neurosurgery training programs in the United States that are generally categorized as the best also happen to have some of the most rigid hierarchies—but it does make for a certain kind of open communication when the attendings feel free to speak and, perhaps just as importantly, think freely and feel free to encourage the residents to do so as well. More interestingly, even the most conservative surgeons in the department tend to retain a very open-minded view of the profession: they are conservative in radical ways. Paul Nelson, for example, likes to consider himself one of the most conservative neurosurgeons in the business ("My idea of an ideal operation is one where the chance of a good result is ninety percent or greater," he said once). But he is also a neurosurgeon who took time to learn endocrinology and to develop a multidisciplinary treatment program for patients with pituitary tumors. In order to do so, he works very closely with the endocrinologists at Pitt, which once could be seen almost as heresy; since pituitary tumors are generally operable, many neurosurgeons operate instead of sending the patient to the endocrinologists. To *team up* with an endocrinologist once was, to the conventional wisdom, almost akin to teaming up with a phrenologist, but that is what Paul Nelson does, because he is made free to do so. Howard Yonas, who does most of the vascular surgery in the department—aneurysms and the like—regularly performs operations that can, unfortunately, only be described as "breathtaking." How can one describe an operation twenty hours in duration, in which the surgeon, in Yonas's words, is "absolutely on the edge of being out of control the entire time, where nothing you touch doesn't have the potential for catastrophe, where it's sweat and terror through the whole operation"? Because he is a neurosurgeon, he likes this: "It's all tough, but sometimes these cases are *tough* tough. You're going for the big win, the big score. There's no question it's a high when you do something very difficult very well, when you can send somebody home. It tests what you are. You're not judged by what you did five cases ago, but by the case that's in front of you."

And yet Yonas, who in terms of the stereotypes by which neurosurgeons are pigeonholed has more right to be a cowboy than anyone (until recently, when Pitt recruited a neurosurgeon to be a specialist in trauma, Yonas was the neurosurgeon responsible for patients coming in through the Emergency Room—"Oh, let me tell you, that's incredible duty; somebody comes in on a stretcher, minimal history, minimal information about onset of symptoms, and you've got about thirty-four seconds to decide what to do"), does not stalk the halls chafing for surgery. Instead, he is at work on developing cerebral-blood-flow studies using xenon, a procedure that may ultimately result in *eliminating* some of the surgery that he so dearly loves to do, the principle behind the xenon studies being that if blood flow to the vital parts of the brain is unaffected by, for example, clogged arteries, then surgery is perhaps not indicated. Yonas doesn't know at this point how valuable his cerebral-blood-flow studies will turn out to be (preliminary results are very good), but he does know that he was encouraged, both by Jannetta and by what Yonas calls the "milieu created by Jannetta," to be creative, to work with a team made up of physicists and mathematicians and radiologists, to be adventuresome. "I don't know if there are too many chiefs of neurosurgery who would allow someone to spend so much time and energy doing other things," says Yonas, "things that are not directly refundable, that soak up time and resources and people. I got involved in a unique collaborative effort through the blood-flow studies, and it has been as though because Peter has done *his* own creative thing, he has created an environment that says, 'You're going to be left alone to fly to your own level.' At most places, one wouldn't dare to deviate beyond what the chief says is necessary. But that's where progress is made—when you dare to deviate. What Peter does is get the right people together and let them bounce off each other."

Which is not to say that Pitt is the only place where neurosurgeons are testing the limits of the profession or exploring new frontiers. However, it is unusual to have such a wide range of activity going on in areas so far afield from the chief's own interests: Laligam Sekhar is developing a sort of microphone to detect aneurysms and intracranial hemorrhages; Dade Lunsford, in addition to developing and managing the stereotactic neurosurgical service, is overseeing a new radiation device for the treatment of tumors and arteriovenous malformations, and so on. The department, in addition to all of the surgery, is a full-scale R & D facility as well. Surgery, Howard Yonas said once, is the basis of any surgeon; surgery is the art and craft that the neurosurgeons practice and teach. But beyond that, the department thrives on a decidedly unusual group of novel thinkers whose leader expects them to develop those ideas, to push themselves, and, above all, to explore. "Around here," says Yonas, "you can't do *anything* just because granddad did it that way. That's the one thing that Peter doesn't allow."

Thus, the role models whom the residents have are immensely competent and highly skilled surgeons who range in surgical aggressiveness across the spectrum, like some sort of demographic sample, but who also tend to be introspective rather than not, because they are able to spend as much time as they can trying to make better mousetraps, confident that they've got the support of their chairman and, through him, the institution. If someone comes to Jannetta for "celebrity surgery"—someone who wants Jannetta to do an aneurysm or vascular surgery because he is the chief—he sends the patient to Howard. "Nope," Jannetta will say. "You don't want me to do that; you want Howard to do that." For back surgery, he sends them to Paul Nelson, malignancies to Bob Selker, cranial-based tumors to Laligam Sekhar. He won't even see a pediatric case unless the pediatric neurosurgeons ask him to.

It is 7:45 on a magnificent sunny Saturday morning, and the residents and attendings are starting to gather for what might be called Introspection Clinic, but which the university calls "Neurosurgery Morbidity and Mortality Conference." All teaching hospitals require some form of complications conference as a sort of exercise in quality control, a (it is hoped) nonjudgemental review of the difficulties physicians on a given service have encountered the previous week. The neurosurgeons and the residents gather in Presby's Dining Room II, which during the week serves as a "physicians only" hideout but which on Saturdays, like much of the rest of the hospital, is quiet and cozy.

The chairs are arranged in rows facing the front of the room, and in them the residents sit, several of them writing, incongrously, in those black-and-white–speckled "composition" books such as small children carry back and forth to school. In a cabinet in Jannetta's inner office are rows and rows of identical notebooks, filed by hospital—Presby, Children's, Montefiore, and the Veterans Administration—and year. Inside the notebooks are lists of every single surgical procedure performed by neurosurgeons in the department since Jannetta became chief in 1973, along with brief and emphatically unofficial descriptions of the operation, the outcome, and any complications. The residents are required to have the notebooks completely up-to-date by the beginning of Saturday Conference, which is why several residents are writing furiously as the attendings come in and pour their coffee. This day, two residents will write in what they think is a surreptitious fashion through the first hour and a half of conference, only to overhear Jannetta remind the chief resident during a break that the residents need to learn how to get their homework done on time. Both residents look as sheepish as if they had been caught passing notes.

The notebooks seem like an interesting anachronism at first, but they serve the residents, Jannetta, and the department well. In five minutes, if necessary, Jannetta can look up an operation performed five days, five weeks, or five years ago, see who did the surgery, who the attending was, who the patient was, what happened, and why. In addition to the practical uses, they also serve as a sort of informal history of the department, containing as they do the names and cases of residents long gone into the larger world. Roberto Heros, M.D., now at Harvard. Steven J. Haines, M.D., now at Minnesota. L. Dade Lunsford, M.D., once chief resident himself, now Director of the Specialized Neurosurgical Center at Presbyterian-University Hospital. Howard Yonas, M.D., once a Fellow in Neurosurgery at the University of Pittsburgh, now Associate Professor. Albert Camma, M.D., now in private practice in Ohio. Many residents find an excuse at least once to browse through the older notebooks, often thinking they are the only ones to have done so. The notebooks, breathtakingly low-tech, seem at once marvelously complex and startlingly primitive: complex, because they re-create in brief phrases and almost incomprehensible abbreviations the work of many thousands of hours; primitive, because the residents sit a few rooms away from Dr. Lunsford's new "toy"—the Stereotactic Radiosurgical Unit, or Gamma Knife, a $3-million example of the cutting edge of neurosurgery, a device that uses focused radiation to do what literal cutting edges—scalpels—once did. The covers of a few of the notebooks even have absent-minded doodles on them, as though their very appearance drew from within the residents the last vestiges of schoolboys inside a gray building on a bright and sunny day.

The residents are slightly subdued, compared to their heated discussions earlier this morning over coffee in the hospital cafeteria. The ones who had complications during the week know that those complications are about to be discussed; they will be discussed frankly and openly, without rancor, but they will be discussed all the same.

The attendings come into the room in twos and threes. A few carry, again just slightly incongruously, what appear to be baseball togs. Indeed, today is the annual department softball game—residents (and former residents) against attendings, with OR nurses and social workers filling out the rosters. This

Saturday is also the one day a month reserved for the Tri-State Conference: neurosurgeons from outside the academy come in for a presentation, usually by a visitor to the department. The private-practice surgeons will come at 10:30, but the visitor is already here, having already given one lecture yesterday afternoon.

Jannetta arrives, as does Dr. Sidney Wolfson, who is Chief of Neurosurgical Research at Montefiore Hospital, and Dr. Ricardo Segal, Chief at the VA. Jannetta gets coffee and a sweet roll from a tray, turns a chair from the front row around, sits facing the group, and convenes the meeting, mentioning first the visiting surgeon, who stands and smiles, and then the softball game. "All right," he says, consulting a slip of paper that lists the complications. "Is Mr. Mulcahy of interest?"

A resident rises to report. "This was an eighth-nerve case—patient presented with intractable dizziness. We did the operation and had no problems, found nice compression of the nerve and relieved it. But on postop exam, patient had no hearing at all on the affected side."

Aage Møller speaks. "We hadn't noted any difficulty during the operation. But afterward, we went back and reviewed the data, and found a place where a one-millisecond delay jumped up to a two-millisecond delay and went back down."

What apparently happened was that during the moving of a retractor, the nerve was stretched and thus damaged. After it was damaged, but without the surgeon knowing that any damage had occurred, the retractor was moved again, and the readings from the device monitoring nerve function returned to normal. However, the damage had already been done.

"Why didn't the tech catch it when it happened?" a surgeon asks.

Møller shrugs. "The readings improved again. It's not so

unusual to see a spike like that, but it is somewhat unusual to have it happen and not know it."

"Was the monitor unattended?" asks an attending. "I wonder if that's important in terms of the legal ramifications."

Møller answers promptly. "No, the technician was right there. It was just a case of not being aware of the significance at that moment. There is no black-and-white line that says, 'Oh, this is too high.' "

Sekhar nods vigorously. "There was just an article in *Neurosurgery*, where they had spikes up to two and a half milliseconds, with no problems. You can't always tell what's good and what's not."

An attending: "What can you do to avoid this?"

Jannetta: "It's gonna happen occasionally; it's pretty much a fact of life. I think we've had about three or four percent in the last hundred cases where there was a problem."

An attending: "What are you going to tell the patient?"

Jannetta: "Well, we've gotta tell him—no question. We had a problem."

An attending: "Tell the family first?"

Another attending: "Why?"

Jannetta: "I'm gonna tell him tomorrow, but I'm going to have the resident right there with me!" Everyone laughs. The next day, a resident is going to learn how to talk about mistakes.

Jannetta: "Okay, tell me about Mrs. Golden."

Sekhar: "This is a nursing error. She had a transient weakness in [cranial nerve] Nine and Ten, and her husband tried to feed her. No order was written, but the nurses on the floor all knew. She was given some food by her husband, and she coughed all over and aspirated. And now she's got a little pneumonia."

Patients with weak ninth and tenth nerves, the glossopharyngeal and the vagus, cannot control their swallowing. Normally, they stay off solid food until nerve function returns.

Jannetta, to the residents: "Let's write the orders." "Nursing error" may fit the letter of the law—the woman probably should not have received a meal tray—but not necessarily the spirit.

Jannetta: "Mrs. Caponik?"

Resident: "This is a sixty-three-year-old woman who presented with seizures and staring. She had a left medial sphenoid meningioma. During operation, we nicked the third nerve with the sucker, and now she has some third-nerve loss. In sweeping the tumor off the nerve, the nerve got nicked. She can open the eye, but that's about it."

The third nerve, the oculomotor, controls the movement of the eye.

Jannetta: "What's amazing about this woman is that she can still talk. This was an eleven-hour case, and they were really hauling back on the frontal lobe."

Sekhar: "In a case like this, the prognosis for the third nerve is really very good."

Jannetta: "We're optimists. Joyce Carter?"

Resident: "This was a large ruptured disk on a twenty-eight-year-old woman. We did the op through a three-centimeter incision, and it went really well. Discharged four days postop, and she came back two weeks later with an infection. We opened the wound and took out a lot of fluid, and she's progressing fine."

Jannetta: "What caused it?"

Resident: "It could have been anything," and several residents laugh, one saying *sotto voce*, "Brilliant diagnosis." But, in fact, the resident is right—it *could* have been anything: something at operation, something with a suture, something with a bandage, something after discharge.

Jannetta: "Anything else at Presby? Okay, Children's. Johnny Merryweather?"

A resident: "This is a twelve year old with intractable seizures who's in the epilepsy protocol. Did a procedure for deep electrode placement, and afterward the CT showed a small epidural hematoma. Neurologically, he's fine—no problems at all—and it's resolving."

Jannetta: "Dwight James?"

A resident rises and looks very sad: "This is a seven-month-old infant, young parents—very young, unmarried. Was initially placed in a foster home after birth; the mother got signed up for assistance and took the infant home. Next day, the father says he 'spanked' the infant for urinating on the couch, and the day after that, the mother brought him in with fixed bilateral pupils, moving randomly to deep pain; tiny fontanelle was tense. The next morning he was worse—virtually brain-dead—and a CT showed massive edema: the ventricles were just collapsed. Did have some interesting movements after brain death—motor movements like a frog, very eerie movements. He was pronounced on Thursday after the CT." The resident sits back down.

Jannetta: "Mechanism for suspected child abuse?"

The resident: "The normal procedure is to call Child and Family Services and get a restraining order, but the mother had already called the police; the father is in jail right now. Normal protocol is to alert Child and Family through the social worker."

Pang, one of the pediatric neurosurgeons, stands. "We had another one like this about nine months ago—turned into a homicide. The father admits to beating the child, has a trial, and gets three years in jail." It is clear from the way he says "three years" that he thinks the sentence was too lenient.

"If it's something 'minor' "—again his voice drips with sarcasm—"something like a fracture, it goes to the Juvenile Services people, which is worthless."

Sekhar: "The judges let them off all the time with probation. The judges are so lenient, and then the police get frustrated."

Jannetta: "If you suspect child abuse and report it, are you liable?"

Pang: "Well, you point your finger at them, you fill out the form, and it becomes part of the complaint. We had one, which was clear, clear abuse, and the child was taken from the parent, so the parent is suing the courts and me. The parent was found guilty of abuse but is still suing me." An undertone grows in the room, with talk of lawyers and lawsuits and judges, none of which are terribly popular with physicians in general and perhaps neurosurgeons in particular.

Jannetta: "Anything else at Children's? Okay. Lamont?"

("Lamont" is not a person, but a place: Montefiore Hospital.)

A resident begins speaking almost inaudibly, from near the back of the room. Jannetta interrupts him by saying, "Who's this? Mr. Wilson? Start over."

"This was a patient in for a laminectomy, and during closing, a needle was left in the fascia. The needle count was incorrect, so we looked at the wound but didn't see anything. So we sent him to Recovery. The error was no X ray in the OR. A postop film showed the needle near the midline of the incision, not anywhere near the canal. We told the patient about it, and he elected not to have it taken out."

While not dire, this is not the kind of complication that surgeons like to hear about. During a routine back operation, one of the needles being used to sew up the various layers of muscle and connective tissue (the "fascia") was inadvertently lost in the wound—a not very uncommon occurrence. What was uncommon, at least in hindsight, was that when the needle count came up short, the resident sent the patient to the Postanesthesia Recovery Room (PAR) before investigating more thoroughly. Needle counts come up short on occasion. Since needles come prethreaded with the sutures, they are disposable, and a needle can fall to the floor or be wrapped in a sponge. Normal procedure would have been to bring in a portable X ray unit and take a film of the wound to see if the missing needle had been stitched up inside. If it had, the resident could reopen the wound with the patient still under anesthesia, find the needle, and reclose.

Jannetta: "Can this cause any trouble?"

A resident: "It can, if it migrates." Foreign bodies inside the body are said to "migrate" when they move. It is conceivable that the needle could migrate toward the spinal cord and cause difficulties there, or toward the skin, where it might break through and allow a path for infection. If it stays where it is, it may never cause a problem.

An attending: "I gotta tell ya, I would have gone back and got it. It's going to migrate—it *will* migrate."

A resident: "There was a case just recently, in urology. They left a pad in, the patient got mono and sued—successfully."

The resident who lost the needle: "The patient is recovering nicely, feels fine, doesn't feel any danger."

A resident: "This guy may be fine until he starts chatting about it with his next-door neighbor, who turns out to be a lawyer."

Jannetta: "I take it you didn't know it was in the wound. Why didn't you know it was in the wound?"

Resident: "The error was not getting the film when the count came up short."

A resident: "Some people feel that it shouldn't be taken out."

An attending: "Was the postop film done in the PAR?"

Resident: "No."

Attending: "Why not get the film at least in the PAR? You got the film after the patient was on the floor?"

The resident says nothing. He knows that the speckled notebooks contain stories of other residents in other times who have misplaced a needle, but it is of small comfort right now to know that they were probably discussed in just this way in their time. Neurosurgeons are well known for good eyesight. Their hindsight, however, is perfect.

Jannetta: "You have got to learn to separate ritual from dogma. So many things that have been done in neurosurgery were done for the ritual; but you've got to remember what's ritual and what's dogma. This is a perfect example. You went for the ritual—the ritual of the needle count, the ritual of the X ray—but it was just that: ritualistic. There's no good reason to do things for the ritual. If you're not going to look for the needle, why do the count? If you're not in a position to do anything about it, why do the film?"

An attending: "Are we talking about a medical risk here or a legal risk?"

An attending: "The risk of putting him to sleep again is far greater than the risk from the needle."

Jannetta: "You're talking about a risk of infection at most."

The resident: "I would say that we didn't take it out for medical reasons."

Jannetta: "Anything else?" There is nothing. "Okay, Mrs. Heil?"

A resident: "This is a woman in her late sixties, with TIAs from a left carotid occlusion. There was lots of trauma at intubation for anesthesia, and postop she was hoarse. We told her it would resolve, and she went home and came back two weeks later still hoarse. ENT [i.e., ear, nose, throat] exam showed one vocal cord paralyzed. There's the question of whether it was trauma or nerve damage in surgery."

This woman suffered from transient ischemic attacks—transient interruptions in blood flow to the left side of her brain because her left carotid artery, which runs along the throat, was clogged with fat. The indicated operation is a carotid endarterectomy, in which the carotid artery is sliced open, cleaned out, and sewn back up. Among the many things that can make this operation tricky (such as jostling loose pieces of debris that then move up to the brain and cause more TIAs or a stroke) is the location of the recurrent pharyngeal nerves, which are very close to the carotid artery; the recurrent branch in part controls the vocal cords. The question here is whether the damage to the vocal cord on that side was caused by the neurosurgeon or by the anesthesiologist during intubation prior to surgery.

Jannetta: "How do you hit the recurrent nerve when you're doing a carotid artery?"

Half a dozen residents at once: "Retraction!" This is something they've been told about many many times.

An attending: "I don't think this is our fault. When we were dissecting the artery, we were not that deep—I don't think we were down by the nerve. This woman was intubated five times before they got it right."

A resident: "Were the five attempts documented on the anesthesia record?"

The attending: "Excellent question. I don't know."

Jannetta: "You can't be sure where the nerve is. There's a syndrome that race horses get that prevents a lot of horses from running. When they run, the aorta dilates so much that it presses on the nerve and the horses can't breathe. It's called 'the blows.' How do you prevent this?" meaning, of course, not the blows, but damaging the nerve.

Howard Yonas, turning to look at the residents: "Simple.

You don't cut anything if you don't know what it is, and you don't retract anything unless you're absolutely sure. You have got to have a constant awareness."

Jannetta: "Anything more at Montefiore? Okay. There's one more here from Presby. Is Carmen Paul of interest?"

It is a curious way of examining mistakes or errors of judgment or mishaps. Visitors might be surprised at what seems to be an almost casual attitude on the part of the attendings and the residents, a sort of blasé view. To make that assumption—that this is all very casual—is to misunderstand something fundamental about the way that neurosurgery is practiced, taught, learned, and, finally, perceived by its practitioners.

In terms of perception, it bears noting again what is for many something infuriating about neurosurgeons: their concreteness. They are challenged to have all of their faculties immediately present when those faculties are required, primarily during preoperative evaluation and surgery. The profession has evolved this way because it is during preop and surgery that the surgeon has the power to affect the patient's situation. Indeed, as diagnostic devices such as the CT scan and magnetic resonance imaging become more and more sophisticated, the surgeon has the opportunity to gain correspondingly more control over the obvious challenge to his talent that surgery presents. During surgery itself, good neurosurgeons are masters of their own ships, and they extend this control, with a fair amount of forethought and judgment, to their residents. Neurosurgeons relinquish their control with a great deal of circumspection, because whatever they give up at any given moment is gone forever: much of what the residents do or do not do when they are operating can be irrevocable. Some neurosurgeons hover, coach, instruct, curse, interrupt a lot more than others, but all neurosurgeons are conscious to some degree of their relationship to control.

But once control is gone, it is gone, and this is the essence of neurosurgical concreteness: neurosurgeons simply do not cry over spilt milk. A complication can be the result of a misjudgment, misinterpretation of data, misinformation, a physical anomaly, or Fate. Any of these can happen at any time. But once something goes wrong, it has gone wrong, and the surgeon is not faced at that moment with self-reproach, but with how to get out of the trouble he is in. When an operation ends, the surgeon's most direct involvement also ends; and short of taking a patient back into the operating room (which is sometimes necessary), much of his control is relinquished, and the case becomes—well—academic. It is no coincidence that most neurosurgical progress is documented in professional journals in the form of cases: case reports, retrospective series of cases, prospective series of cases, summaries of cases previously reported in the literature. The abstractions of the profession are consistently overshadowed by the concrete facts.

The method by which the practice of neurosurgery is taught and learned also has an effect on the way that its complications are discussed. A prospective resident has been through, by the time he shows up at a hospital on July 1 (the New Year's Day of resident years), a series of selection processes intended to preordain a certain level of success in his chosen field. He has been accepted into medical school, he is expecting shortly to graduate from that medical school, and he has selected several hospitals at which he will be interviewed. Hospitals, in turn, select candidates to interview based on their academic records and the recommendations of their medical-school professors. And while, in theory, a new medical-school graduate has not been trained in any specialty, the reality is that those who want certain specialties (neurosurgery among them) have already made that choice long before they begin visiting hospitals for interviews. The members of the specialty, in turn, already know what they are looking for: the students most likely to make the best neurosurgeons, transplant surgeons, anesthesiologists. Neurosurgeons look for—and most often find—students who are on fire to be neurosurgeons. One neurosurgical resident at Pitt, for example, answered the question "Why would you like to do your residency here?" by saying, "Because you guys are very, very good, and I intend to be very, very good." In, say, the field of insurance or advertising or accounting, such an answer might be seen as a transparent attempt at flattery; at Pitt, the answer was taken as being honest, because the resident was telling his interlocutor something that he knew to be true.

So when the resident shows up on the first of July, certain expectations are already established, and the resident's day-to-day goals are to fulfill those expectations. As with residents in all specialties, the neurosurgical resident is expected to learn a great deal, often under tremendous pressure, so he must learn to learn things under pressure. As a prospective neurosurgeon, he learns how to adapt, to survive. He learns the concept of control, and he learns what to do when control eludes him. He learns about misjudgment, misinterpretation of data, misinformation, physical anomaly, Fate. And he learns to see his world as a long and complex series of events, each of which he must keep ordered in his mind. A professional golfer can easily remember what clubs he used throughout any given tournament; a Formula One race-car driver can remember when and where he shifted throughout the course of any given race; a neurosurgeon, by his third year of residency, can easily recount in casual conversation all of the operations in which he has participated in any given time period: what he did, why he did it, what went well and what did not. The ranting and cursing of an attending at the stupidity of a resident rarely occurs when the resident does something wrong the first time; it invariably occurs when he does it the second; the third time a resident makes the same mistake raises a red flag to the attending, because if you're going to be very, very good, you can't keep making the same mistakes. At the same time, the residents are encouraged, as the attendings are, to "fly to their own level"—to begin to make their own decisions about what to do and how to do it. As they progress through their training, they make more and more decisions until they reach their chief-residency year, when they operate, for all practical purposes, as a sort of shadow attending physician. They do cases from start to finish. They have patients whom they admit, work up, operate on, follow, and discharge, because the chief-residency year is the big push to do the kinds of cases that neurosurgeons need to have done to have a good list of cases to present to the American Board of Neurological Surgery when applying for certification.

In between first year and chief residency, the residents acquire power ceded to them by their teachers and, thus, responsibility as well. Residents at Pitt, mostly because of Jannetta's unusual sense of democracy, tend to be far more autonomous than residents at more hierarchical institutions. They get to do cases that assistant professors fight over at other hospitals, while some residents produced by the most rigid institutions often find themselves, although meticulously trained, having to work an extra year or two to acquire the skills required by the ABNS.

None of this is easy to learn. Roberto Heros, the Harvard neurosurgeon who trained at Pitt, remembers one case in particular. "Early on at Pitt," he recalls, "I was very cocky, and I wanted to do an operation on a very difficult tumor—very deep. The patient was a young woman who had just had a baby, and I thought I could get the tumor. Peter said it couldn't be done, but I was young and I thought it could be. Peter said okay. The operation took all day and into the night. Peter checked in with me about nine or ten that night, when things were really getting difficult. About midnight, all hell broke loose—bleeding, swelling. I had to close without having the bleeding under control, and that meant that this woman was going to die. About two in the morning, I called Peter and told him what had happened, and he must have sensed how I felt, because about forty-five minutes later he showed up at the hospital. He said he couldn't sleep. We sat and drank coffee, and he told me about some of his difficult cases. He could sense the way I was feeling and he was worried about the patient, but he was also worried about me. That is not the kind of thing that you forget. There were lots of difficult cases I had early on, and what he would say is "Someone has got to do it: go do it." I think I would have never developed the expertise I have if he hadn't backed me up that way. He is better at that than anyone else I know."

What Heros felt that night is what neurosurgeons-in-training will inevitably feel at some point in their careers. Saturday Conference is intended not to ameliorate those feelings as much as it is to remind the surgeons what can go wrong and why. Too much self-reproach can be devastating to a surgeon, because it can make him tentative; but a surgeon without at least some private self-reproach is a surgeon who has lost feeling for what he is doing and why. The residents know this, too, and become expert at very private self-reproach. Saturday Conference intentionally takes their self-reproach and makes it public. It is of use, of course, for the other residents to learn of possible pitfalls, but is also of use for the residents to learn the part of neurosurgery that doesn't happen in the OR. If in the operating room they learn to be technicians, during Saturday Conference they learn to be physicians.

So Jannetta asks, "Is Carmen Paul of interest?" meaning "Is

there something in Carmen Paul's hospital course that good neurosurgeons should learn from?"

There is, or Jannetta wouldn't have asked. Carmen Paul is, or was, a woman in her fifties who presented at another hospital with subarachnoid hemorrhage from an aneurysm—that is, a weak spot in a blood vessel (the aneurysm) burst, and the blood vessel bled within the skull. Subarachnoid hemorrhage is dangerous—often deadly—because the blood, having no place to go within the confines of the skull, presses against the brain. In Paul's case, the pressure led to cardiac arrest, and she underwent two hours of resuscitation before she was revived. When she was stable enough to be moved, she was transferred to Presby and, after ten days, had recovered enough to undergo surgery to clip the aneurysm.

The resident: "The aneurysm was large and atherosclerotic, but it was clipped without incident, and she did real nice postop. She was in ICU for six days, was eating, no deficits at all. She was transferred to Unit Eighty-three, where she continued to do well. Then she became somewhat lethargic, and CT showed some swelling in the temporal lobe and the posterior fossa. She became comatose, pupils fixed and dilated, and ended up being intubated. Subsequent CT showed a large hemorrhage in the upper brain stem, and she's very close to being brain dead."

Jannetta: "Was it sudden or gradual?"

Resident: "I don't know. No notes in the chart that she was deteriorating."

A resident: "How many days postop? And how many days after the first incident?"

Resident: "Seven days postop and seventeen days after the hemorrhage."

Howard Yonas: "This is something you're going to see with patients who've been CPRed: two weeks out they seem to be doing fine, and then they go to hell and die. You see it a lot in burn units with patients who've been resuscitated like this. CPR is a very imperfect system—thumping on the chest. They're okay, and then they go."

Paul Nelson: "Did she have another aneurysm in the posterior fossa? This might be a PICA aneurysm."

Resident: "We didn't have a right-side angiogram. The pathology was all on the other side."

An angiogram, in which radiopaque dye is injected into the blood vessel, will show an aneurysm. Since the resident knew that the patient had an aneurysm on the left side because of the subarachnoid hemorrhage, he didn't get an angiogram on the right side.

An attending: "How can you establish the cause of the bleeding if you don't have the angiography?"

Jannetta: "This is a post you've got to get," meaning "postmortem"—an autopsy, which is generally the only way to get absolutely definitive information. Neurosurgeons like to see autopsies on inconclusively diagnostic cases so that they can find out what went wrong.

Resident: "All I can do is ask."

Jannetta: "You get your papers in order and sit down with the primary person."

There is some more talk about the missing angiogram. Attendings and residents speculate as to what it might or might not have shown.

Jannetta: "It's up to the surgeon to see that the angiography is complete and satisfactory. Okay. What do we have at the VA? Jho?"

Jho is Dr. Hae-Dong Jho, a former fellow, now a resident at the VA hospital. "No complications this week," he says, smiling.

Jannetta: "The only way there are no complications are if there's no surgery or you're a liar; which are you, Jho?" But he is smiling, too, and Jho laughs. "One of these days we'll have a magic Saturday with no complications at all. Okay, let's take a break and get set up for our guest."

Most of the physicians stand up and stretch. Coffee cups are refilled, and the medical student who is on the neurosurgery rotation wheels the slide projector over and begins setting it up. The neurosurgeons from other hospitals begin filing in at this time as well, and most of them immediately go over to be introduced to the visitor, who is from a distinguished medical center on the East Coast. Most of the "tri-state" neurosurgeons are dressed casually in sport shirts and pants that were called "chinos" when they themselves were residents. The once-a-month Tri-State Conference counts toward the one hundred hours per year of continuing education that licensed physicians are required to accumulate. The stereotypical medical conferences that are held in places like Vail and Venice, Paris and Puerto Rico, Brisbane and Brasilia have grown around the one-hundred-hour requirement: a physician who travels somewhere for a continuing-education class is permitted to deduct his or her expenses for the trip, and physicians might be forgiven for choosing to gather some of those credits in interesting places. But the bulk of the hours are accumulated in far less prosaic locations that are closer to home.

This morning, the topic of the talk is surgical removal of craniopharyngiomas—tumors that arise deep within the skull in an area referred to as Rathke's pouch, which is an anatomical dead end left over from the embryonic development of the mouth. At one end of Rathke's pouch, the pituitary gland arises during fetal development, and occasionally, at the other end, a craniopharyngioma can develop. The tumor is troublesome to treat because it is difficult to reach, because it often calcifies or contains calcium deposits, and because it is almost impossible—some neurosurgeons say that it *is* impossible—to remove completely, which means that at some point it will recur. Left untreated, it can grow to a point where it increases intracranial pressure. Therefore, removal—even partial removal—is indicated in patients with a healthy life expectancy.

The visitor's talk is very cavalier and dashing, full of jokes and asides. Of main interest in his presentation is a videotape of an operation and a series of slides, both of very high quality. The videotape opens with orchestral music and an aerial view of the visitor's medical center, and the slide presentation opens with approximately the same aerial photograph. When the slide projector jams, six residents approach it as though they were about to drop it out a window. Instead, they prod and poke. A new slide drops in, and several of the residents step back; but Jannetta, diagnosing from the front of the room, calls out, "It's going to jam again." It does. He is half out of his chair when the residents manage to get it going again. The visitor picks up exactly where he left off.

When he finishes, he gets a nice round of applause and a few perfunctory questions. His presentation, one of the residents says later, was perfectly adequate, accurate, and informative. The only problem with it is "around here, that's a pretty basic operation; there's not a whole lot going on that we don't do here. You seldom get a chance to think about the range of cases that you see here until you get someone in from outside. Nice resolution on the videotape, though."

The conference breaks up into twos and threes, and Jannetta stands and thanks everyone. "Now, don't forget we've got something else on the agenda this afternoon," he says, referring to the softball game. The residents certainly haven't forgotten. Last year, the attendings won 26–25, and the residents are out for revenge.

II

Banter

The end of Saturday Conference nominally marks
the end of a Peter Jannetta work week, and, as at the end of
any given week, Jannetta is tired. During the previous six
days, he has, among other things, done eleven operations,
seen a clinic full of patients, attended two long and very tense
administrative meetings (the medical school being in the process of a search for a new dean), and finished a paper for
presentation at a medical conference later in the month. He
has also played squash twice. As he stands at the trunk of his
car and pulls on sweatpants, he muses on yet another of the
duties of being a good chief that is never seen in a job description. "After the past three days, I don't want to be here. I want
to be alone. I don't need this kind of competition today; I have
enough things to be competitive about. I want to go home and
relax, but I'll never let them know that, because this is the
kind of thing that's important, so it's got to be treated as important." He pauses. "Sometimes I like to play squash alone,
because you need to be competitive to play squash and I can't
always be competitive." He pauses again. "On the other hand,

sometimes the best thing in the world is to go out and try and destroy someone in squash."

Not surprisingly, Jannetta felt much the same at last year's softball game—or at least before it. This feeling, according to Mark Dias, lasted about five minutes into the bottom of the first inning, when Jannetta led off with a single and took the extra base with a beautiful hook slide. His emphatic non-noncompetitiveness culminated seven innings later, when Jannetta was on second base with one out and the score tied. "There was a single hit up the middle," recalls Dias, "and PJ rounds third and heads for home, just *barreling* toward the plate. The catcher was a second-year resident. He gets the ball in time, he plants himself, and here comes PJ, right into him, up *over* the catcher's shoulder, up in the air, lands flat on his back on home plate with a resounding *thump*, gets up, dusts himself off, and says, 'I was safe!' What are you gonna say when the chief says he's safe?" This is also a perfect example of Jannetta doing his rendition of being noncompetitive. If his critics in the neurosurgical profession could watch him play softball, they would fold their tents and never say another word again, even if they had heard Jannetta acknowledge, laughingly, that the run didn't count after all.

The barren and windswept softball field up behind the VA hospital is chilly and bright this Saturday afternoon as a long straggling string of physicians, department personnel, and family members wander toward home plate. They could be any group of friends and acquaintances out to celebrate the spring but for small telling details like surgical scrub shirts that are doubling as softball jerseys, the array of beepers attached to the waistbands of sweatpants, and the way the residents squint in the sunlight as though released from some dark cell for the first time in too long. For a couple of the residents, this is in fact true. They have been inside the warrens and tunnels and emergency rooms of the Health Center for the past thirty-six hours, and now they slowly adjust to being out of doors by swinging their arms, jogging in place, tossing softballs.

The wives and children in attendance gather on one sideline and talk of—what else—neurosurgery. "He had three nights in a row again last week," says one, which identifies her as a resident's wife. She has a little girl with her, and, as a group of residents crosses the infield, the woman stoops down next to the little girl, points, and says, "See, Honey? That's Daddy!" at which all the wives laugh, some, however, a tiny bit ruefully.

The little girl's face lights up. She smiles. "Daddy!" she says to Rob Parrish, who scoops her up and holds her.

"You remember him, don't you?" her mother asks.

"Of course you do!" says Parrish, just as another resident shouts "Let's go!" and the residents take the field. Parrish sets his daughter down, grabs his glove, and trots out to his position. The little girl's smile vanishes, and she turns to her mother.

"See? He left again, didn't he?" Parrish's wife says, and they all laugh again, just as ruefully.

As the residents toss each other ground balls and pop flies, Jannetta stands a bit apart from the other attendings and runs through his assessment of the opposition. "He's a superstar," he says of a resident who has just booted a ground ball. "He's a real superstar," he says of another, who throws a ball fifteen feet over the first baseman's head, "He's gonna be a superstar. He's damn good, but damn lazy. He's gonna be a great one." He is not, of course, talking about their on-field talents, which run from rusty at games to plain terrible. He is talking of their talents inside someone's skull.

The first batter is Leland Albright, who is built less along the lines of a softball player and more along the lines of a marathon runner. He swings at the first pitch and misses, spinning all the way around in a circle. "One thing we have got to get are some more jocks in this profession," Jannetta says. "Hey, we've got a resident coming next year who was a starting defensive back and a quarterback in college—a real jock. Neurosurgery has a shortage of jocks. Orthopedics has all the jocks; ophthalmologists are worse than we are—all their kids have glasses. Way to go, Leland!" he shouts as Albright runs out a clean single into center field. He takes a major-league turn at first and trots back, clapping his hands and shouting, "Let's go!"

Howard Yonas pops out to shortstop. Laligam Sekhar, whose enthusiasm for everything, be it a cranial-based tumor or a first-inning rally, surprises everyone, including himself, by lining a smart drive to right field. He stands for a full three seconds watching the ball before remembering to run. Albright goes to third.

The cleanup hitter is Peter J. Jannetta, M.D., who is probably as close to being a jock as the profession has, by virtue of his history at Penn as a student athlete: four years on the swim team (MVP, in fact), four years on the lacrosse team, and a senior season with the football team "as an undersized end." He lofts a fly to right field that Hae-Dong Jho, whose youth in Seoul, South Korea, apparently did not include long afternoons on a softball field, loses complete track of. Both runners score, and Jannetta ends up on third, huffing slightly and grinning.

He scores on the next play when a ground ball to third is bobbled. As he heads toward the plate, Albright shouts, "Watch your head!" and Jannetta crosses his arms behind his skull. But there is no throw to the plate, and he scores this time unmolested, and his grin is, if possible, even wider. "I *love* being out here!" he says, clapping his hands, his musings in the parking lot forgotten. "Let's *go!*"

The banter level, particularly directed at the attendings by the residents, is high. Neurosurgeons suffer from any number of prejudices and stereotypes, including that they are humorless and don't know how to have fun. As with most stereotypes, there is a grain of truth, but a grain of truth that has a logical explanation. Imagine seeing a neurosurgeon in a hallway at Presby, perhaps the hall that leads from the Emergency Room to the lobby of the hospital. You smile at him and maybe make a joke; he does not respond. Maybe he is indeed humorless; maybe he doesn't know how to have fun. It is more likely, however, that he has just seen a patient that he could do nothing for, or that he has just told a family that a loved one is brain-dead, or that he has just done one or the other (or both) of those and is thus late for an operation that may take the better part of a day or night or day and night. Neurosurgeons on duty have, finally, horrible duties, and the nature of the profession is that they are on duty a huge part of the time. In the OR lounge on an operating day, it is easy to separate, say, a plastic surgeon from an neurosurgeon. The plastic surgeons, whose own field is packed with its own arcana and difficulties, almost never, statistically, have patients die; they almost never, statistically, perform surgery on patients who will die if the surgery is not performed. Even the heart-stopping drama of a long and complicated hand or limb reattachment, which falls within the plastic surgeon's bailiwick and which has its own aura of superhuman efforts and daring deeds, has, finally, a different effect on the surgeon's personality: plastic surgeons, if they are good, have lots of light at the end of their operative tunnels. The neurosurgeon is the one who is staring at a foam coffee cup as if it were a very dark and forbidding tunnel.

So, on a softball field on a sunny day, the neurosurgeons seem almost overly boisterous. They are off duty, and the residents say things that they would never say inside the building, and the attendings try and give back what they get.

"*Easy* out," one resident shouts at each attending who comes to the plate.

"Wooooooo," they holler when an attending takes a giant cut at a pitch, misses, and twists himself into a corkscrew. When an attending strikes out, the residents go into a frenzy of hoots, catcalls, wild applause.

When the attendings take the field in the bottom half of the first inning, there is more banter as well as a general exchanging of baseball gloves. One attending is halfway out to right field when he discovers that he needs a glove for his left hand, not his right. "Time out," he calls, although play has not started. "This mitt is backward." The residents jeer mercilessly.

The attendings team is fleshed out with two OR nurses, one of the audiology techs, two OR techs who calibrate and repair the operating microscopes. After some consultation at the mound, the infielders move to their positions, leaving Jannetta to pitch. The residents are thrilled.

"We've got your number," one calls at Jannetta.

The first pitch is high. "New pitcher," the residents shout.

The next pitch is a perfect strike, high and arcing as slow-pitch softball is meant to be, and the resident misses the ball by a foot. "That," Jannetta says, "was my knuckler."

There are many whiffs ("Feel the breeze," shouts Leland Albright), many pop flies, many anemic grounders all around. One of the OR nurses drops a pop fly, and Jannetta calls, "Good try." Some of the innings take a few moments, one half an inning takes fifteen minutes. An official score sheet would read like the chronicle of a very unpleasant operation.

"You swing like you cut," one resident shouts gleefully at another who has just struck out, and everyone laughs. Once, Jannetta gets two strikes on a batter and tries to slip in a fast one, a hard pitch neck high. The resident doesn't take the bait, and Jannetta grins his grin. On the sidelines, for the benefit of the first-year residents, Mark Dias tells his Jannetta story of the last play of last year's game.

In the late innings on this day, by the time the score has seesawed back and forth a few times, players have switched positions (Jannetta moving to third base), and there are the expected twisted ankles, scuffed knees, wrenched backs, and jammed fingers that accompany unaccustomed athletic endeavor. The banter is less boisterous. One of the residents has left, regretfully, to answer a page. "Last inning," an attending says hopefully as the staff neurosurgeons take the field. They are losing by three runs.

Howard Yonas is pitching for the attendings. Of all the people in the Department of Neurosurgery at Pitt, two names consistently come up as being among the nicest, most even-tempered, most interesting and pleasant to work with. One is Paul Nelson, and the other is Howard Yonas. Residents routinely pay Yonas the highest compliment a teaching surgeon can receive. "Thanks," they almost invariably say after working with him in a five- or ten- or fifteen- or twenty-hour operation. "Thanks. I really enjoyed that." Howard Yonas can make a twenty-hour dance with imminent catastrophe the kind of experience for which a resident can say "Thanks."

Yonas, however, is having a bad day on the mound. The strike zone this afternoon is an insoluble mystery. Since the game is played without an umpire and, hence, without called balls and strikes, each pitch out of the strike zone is an opportunity for a round of razzing from the residents. At the height of this, Jannetta, trying not to look too purposeful, saunters toward the mound. The residents are galvanized. They cannot believe the good fortune of Jannetta coming in as late-inning relief. Their good fortune has nothing to do with Jannetta's skill or lack of skill as a pitcher. Their good fortune comes from the residents' immediate collective recognition of what is one of Jannetta's most prominent personality traits, but one that is usually seen only in the operating room when he gets impatient (as he almost always does) with the pace of the operation: no matter how good-hearted and good-intentioned the intervention, Peter Jannetta is about to butt in.

One of the first residents to recognize this is Mark Dias. "The line here is 'I just want to throw a couple of pitches,' " he shouts with glee.

"Yeah," calls another resident. "He's saying, 'I just want to take a quick look.' "

" 'Let me take a quick look, and I'll turn it right back over to you,' " mimics a third.

"It's still your game, Howard. He just wants to look things over, and then he'll get out of your way."

"He'll be out of your way in no time. Just let him finish the game."

"Oh, he's going to finish up, all right. It'll only take him a second, and then next time you can do it all start to finish. He *promises*."

"That's okay, Howard," a resident shouts as Yonas, smiling, moves to third base. "It happens to us all the time. You'll get used to it."

"*We* have to," says Dias.

Jannetta, through all this, is grinning and shaking his head. "You guys are *always* complaining," he says, which brings a fresh assault.

"Why do we need to?"

"If you didn't come in, you wouldn't have to hear it."

"I cannot *believe* you are doing this."

"*I* can."

"So can I. He does it all the time. Why not during a softball game?"

"Show us how it's done, now."

"We'll just watch and learn."

"This is perfect—this is classic."

Jannetta ignores all of this, concentrating on his pitching. A grounder to second. A strikeout. A foul pop that Howard Yonas gets a glove on, bobbles, stumbles, and squeezes. Jannetta strolls off the mound. Sure. He intervened. He put out the fire, too, though.

This game ends not with a whack, but a whimper as the attendings go down in order. The residents have avenged last year's loss. But, as with last year, as equipment is gathered and the players and spectators snake back toward the hospital, the event that is told and retold, embellished, repeated for the sheer pleasure of contemplating it has at its center the Chairman of the Department of Neurosurgery. Once, on a Thursday afternoon, when the softball field lay deep in snow, Jannetta talked about the position he found himself in, within his profession. "Sometimes," he said, "someone has to be the lightning rod. Someone is going to be at the center of things. That's sometimes the only way that things can change."

Throughout his career, Jannetta has many times been accused of seeking to be at the loud and impassioned center of his profession. Someone watching him play softball might be inclined to think, if only for a moment, that some people are simply *destined* to end up in the center of things, waiting for the chatter to quiet down so that they can get to work.

12

Cranks

In November 1983, Jannetta traveled to Stockholm, Sweden, home of a hospital that contains what is arguably one of the most renowned neurosurgical programs in Europe—the Karolinska Institutets, called by almost everyone who isn't Swedish the Karolinska Institute. Much of the institute's reputation in the neurosciences is derived from its place as the professional home of Herbert Olivekrona, yet another of the "fathers" of contemporary neurosurgery. As a way of honoring both Olivekrona and his heirs in the profession, the institute created a prize named in his honor to be presented yearly to a neurosurgeon who has mapped new ground in the field. The first Olivekrona Lecturer was an American, John Mullan, M.D., who perfected a procedure for inducing thrombosis in giant intercranial aneurysms. In 1982, it was one of Jannetta's old colleagues, Charles Wilson, M.D., recounting his work with microsurgery for pituitary tumors. In 1983, it was Jannetta, whose topic was "Neurovascular Compression of the Cranial Nerves and Brainstem: Common Syndromes Related to the Aging Process." The dais at the Olivekrona Lecture is a very long way from that small meeting in Los Angeles nearly twenty years earlier that Jannetta was forbidden to attend. The distance is not best measured in miles, but rather in what has been gone through to get there. A child whose mother forbade him to play baseball and who ends up pitching in the World Series has come a long way, even if he grew up in the shadow of the stadium. The Karolinska Institutets is the World Series of neurosurgery.

But not everyone who makes it to the World Series receives a hero's welcome, and, unsurprisingly, this is also true in the world of neurosurgery. Although the Olivekrona Lecture was an acknowledgment of Jannetta and his work by a very well-regarded segment of the profession, it did not open all doors previously closed to him. It is probable that nothing could, because his self-assuredness, his persistence, his interpretation of his results, and, finally, the replication and reproduction of his work by others has continued to be galling to some prominent and vocal neurosurgeons, several of whom felt that they, too, had history and science and physiology and common sense on their side, just as Jannetta felt that these factors supported his theories. Science, particularly surgical science, is an endeavor in which certainty is rare and seldom comes easily. Negation—or hypothesized negation—of a theory is easier to come by, because where to prove a hypothesis the investigator must devise a theory that includes a dozen smaller hypotheses and stipulations, the challenger need only negate one of these smaller parts to shake the foundation of the whole. This is, for example, exactly what Robert Koch, the German bacteriologist and Nobel Laureate, had in mind when he formulated his famous postulates regarding experimental evidence required to establish a relationship between a given microorganism and a given disease. As all fledgling scientific investigators know, Koch's postulates demand that, first, the microorganism be observed in every case of the disease; second, the microorganism be isolated and grown in pure culture; third, the pure culture reproduce the disease following the inoculation of a susceptible animal; and, finally, the microorganism be observed in and recovered from the experimentally inoculated animal. A skeptical investigator who can show that any one of Koch's postulates was not demonstrated—even in one case—can call into question all of the associated experimental evidence as well.

Although microbiologists, especially those working with the AIDS virus (which has proven to be notoriously difficult to culture in the lab and even more difficult to entice to infect a lab animal), might disagree, Jannetta's work is in several ways much more susceptible to challenge because physiological systems differ from the mechanisms of infection in several notable ways. Most obvious is that in hypothesizing about a physical cause of a disorder, there is nothing from which to try and grow a culture in the first place and nothing with which to inoculate a lab animal. And even if there were a way of causing the physical change in a lab animal, trying to judge the presence or absence of something abstract like pain, or something transitory and amorphous like the twitch of a facial muscle, is absurd. (In a men's room in Scaife Hall there existed for a time a graffito in the form of a line of dialogue, penned either by a skeptic or an ironical neurosurgery resident: "Peter Jannetta to laboratory rat: Does it bother you? Does it ruin your life?")

Jannetta has found himself on the horns of this dilemma for the past twenty years. With fantastic regularity, case reports and series of cases appear in the professional literature, either in support of Jannetta's theories or in opposition to them. Articles that question the basis for Jannetta's work form a different kind of challenge than the challenge posed by physicians who grumble about him in the halls at medical conferences, because the grumbling at medical conferences is seldom vetted by a somewhat objective and dispassionate editorial board.

So Jannetta acts the role of patient correspondent, dutifully writing letters to journals in addition to publishing his own reports and follow-up studies. Letters to medical journals tend toward decorum rather than away from it. The tone is generally that reasonable people disagree. But if one party would just be patient while the other explains. . . . Most of the time, this is about all that a person can do.

In recent years, Jannetta has been able to add a few things to his journalistic armamentarium. The most persuasive has been the confirmatory work done by other surgeons at other hospitals and published in journals. Surgeons on four continents report on their work with microvascular decompression—much of it confirmatory, some not. Work at other institutions that supports Jannetta's theories goes a long way toward satisfying the surgical version of one of Koch's postulates: if surgeons in Tokyo and Buenos Aires and Boston and Barcelona are finding microvascular compression in patients with cranial nerve disorders and are finding that the patients are cured by microvascular decompression, it lends weight to the argument that these blood vessels are not just visible in cities where Peter Jannetta is working, but actually exist. It is of great help to Jannetta in doing what clinicians call "making your case in the citations"—being able to cite plenty of other reports where microvascular decompression is working.

Next, Aage Møller's work has gone a long way toward providing hard data on both cranial-nerve dysfunction and cure. As Jannetta publishes papers on surgical technique and outcome, Møller, his wife, and other researchers at Pitt publish papers that illustrate electrophysiological changes in the behavior of nerves that are compressed by blood vessels. What Jannetta lacked in the early years was a way of demonstrating objectively that he could make trigeminal neuralgia and hemifacial spasm and disabling positional vertigo go away. Predictably, there is a core of researchers who don't believe that the electrophysiologic data that Aage Møller gathers is worth two cents, but Møller's oscilliscope has made a firm believer out of many a skeptic.

But the skeptics still exist, and events like the Olivekrona Lecture seem, if possible, to harden the resistance to an objective evaluation of Jannetta's work. This is complicated by the fact that everyone tends to believe that he or she is being objective: Jannetta certainly does; and C. B. T. Adams, a Consultant Neurosurgeon (the British equivalent of an attending physician) at the Radcliffe Infirmary in Oxford, believes that he is, too. For nearly ten years now, though, the two have been conducting what most resembles a duel between pen pals in the letters columns of several neurosurgical journals.

When Adams and his colleagues Fabinyi and Kaye reported on a series of patients with hemifacial spasm in the *Journal of Neurology, Neurosurgery, and Psychiatry* (*JNNP*) in 1978 and 1981, their views on the subject—and on Jannetta—were already well known. Adams's view of why microvascular decompression works in cases of hemifacial spasm is not out of the mainstream. He adheres to the theory that decompression works by "persistent, but gentle trauma and fibrosis around the nerve," which is why he calls what he does not decompression, but "wrapping"—he wraps the nerve with an inert felt material and reports that he seldom finds any blood vessels that could be called pathologic. The late W. J. Gardner, at the Cleveland Clinic, reported this theory as early as 1962. Jannetta hears about "neurolysis" (which is what Gardner called it) all the time, and he has all the time maintained that the blood vessels are sometimes very difficult to find, very difficult to see, and thus easy to overlook. Adams has heard this for a long time, too, and matters came to a head in 1983 in "Matters Arising," the appropriately entitled letters column in the *JNNP*.

Jannetta, being Jannetta, was blunt. "I write regarding the papers which appeared recently in your journal concerning the treatment of hemifacial spasm by Fabinyi and Adams and Kaye and Adams," he began.

> I submit that these investigators have not fully understood the concept of vascular compression at the root entry zone of the facial nerve and have been performing the same neurolysis (using the surgical microscope) that Gardner pioneered many years ago.
>
> ... One of the authors of one of the above papers with whom I have discussed the operative techniques used in this series gives me to understand that the presence or absence of brain stem root entry zone vascular compression was not evaluated in these patients.

Medical journals, as a rule, have what is called a very long lead time—they are not edited and printed as though they were *Time* or *Newsweek*. Consequently, letters received by a journal about a contributor's article are routinely forwarded to the authors for a response, and long lead times permit reflection and percolation. In some cases, it permits a simmer to turn into a rolling boil. The reply to Jannetta by Adams and Kaye, in any case, is not the dry reading one usually associates with medical journals. "We are pleased to have the opportunity to respond to Professor Jannetta's claims that neither do we understand his concept of vascular compression at the root entry or exit zone as a cause of hemifacial spasm and trigeminal neuralgia, nor did we look for such compression at operation," they begin.

He gives no evidence for his first contention and his latter accusation is based on a conversation in Australia with a former colleague who assisted at only two operations for hemifacial spasm, one four years and the other at least one year before the alleged conversation took place. Hardly an impressive basis for his comments. We suggest that he misconstrues and perhaps misuses the politeness with which visitors and their ideas are normally received.

We have, of course, read Jannetta's papers carefully, and if he had returned the compliment, he would see in the first of our papers a precise description of our technique. . . . We expected to see vascular compression, but have failed to find evidence of this in most of our patients, and so report it.

They go on to list all or many of their difficulties with Jannetta's theory: "We note that Jannetta cannot explain why 'abnormal' vessels are seen in asymptomatic patients." "Jannetta claims the brain sags with age, thus causing veins to compress cranial nerves. . . . He also claims veins, coagulated and divided, may recollateralize and cause a recurrence of symptoms. We find all of this too speculative to accept." In a veiled reference to Koch, they say: "Morley suggests 'it only requires one case in which a nerve is not touched by a vessel (or tumor, etc.) to discredit the hypothesis completely.' " And finally: " 'Root exit or entry zone vascular compression is frequently subtle,' writes Jannetta. 'Well-trained neurosurgeons might not appreciate up to 30% of the abnormalities early on in their experience.' The inference is also subtle; that to be a well-trained *and* experienced neurosurgeon you have to see these abnormalities. Anderson warned against this approach and highlighted the eventual outcome."

Morley is a neurosurgeon writing in the now-famous book *Current Controversies in Neurosurgery.* "Anderson," however, was not trained as a neurosurgeon—he is really "Andersen" with an "e." One can imagine Adams searching the literature for such a citation. Under "References" at the end of the letter, the citation reads:

Anderson, Hans C, *Fairy Tales: The Emperor's New Clothes*. 1977:119. Victor Gollancz, pub.

In scientific circles, this is not considered to be keeping things on a high level. Although researchers are emphatically not immune from human foibles, scientific journals tend to try and pretend that they are. And Jannetta, perhaps because of the regular mention made of his charisma and charm, is sensitive to any intimation that his work is a fairy tale and his followers are under some sort of spell. (Once, the neurosurgeons had to move from one room to another to continue a meeting, and, as usual, the residents were somewhat strung out as they followed the attendings up the hall. Jannetta, because he walks as fast as anyone in the city, was at the head of the line, and a first-year resident, who later insisted that he was ignorant of any implications, mused that it was like following the Pied Piper. Jannetta was out of hearing range, but several other residents were not; and the looks they gave the resident could only be described as withering. There are very few things that the residents won't quip about, but one of them is that they've been hypnotized.)

Jannetta's response to Adams was, however, pretty much only what it could be: an avalanche of journal articles recapping fifteen years worth of cranial-nerve patients and, with Aage Møller, another avalanche of papers presenting the data gleaned from intraoperative monitoring of microvascular decompression surgery. And he kept up his letter-writing duties as well.

In 1985, there came a particular moment of frustration in this epistolary debate. Three Italian neurosurgeons, Carlo Pagni, Michele Naddeo, and Giuliano Faccani, from the University of Turin, reported in the *Journal of Neurosurgery* on a case of spasmodic torticollis due to neurovascular compression of the accessory nerve by a branch of the posterior inferior cerebellar artery. They relieved the compression and reported a cure. They also reported that to their knowledge, this was the first such case of spasmodic torticollis treated by vascular decompression.

In the fall of 1986, the "Neurosurgical Forum" section of the *Journal of Neurosurgery* carried four letters about this case report, including one from Jannetta, which referred to the "elegant" description by the Hamburg neurosurgeons Herrmann and Freckmann of eleven cases of torticollis caused by neurovascular compression, reported on in 1981. The Germans themselves also wrote, "Happy to find further support of our hypothesis of a peripheral factor in the etiology of spasmodic torticollis similar to that of hemifacial spasm proposed by Jannetta." A Japanese neurosurgeon also referred the authors to the 1981 article and went on to say that he had treated one case with good result and that he knew that Jannetta had had "at least five good results among 11 cases" of torticollis. And Peter Dyck, M.D., a Los Angeles neurosurgeon, in mentioning a similar case upon which he had consulted Jannetta in 1983, tried to give credit where he thought credit was due. "Pagni, *et al,* are probably the first to publish a report on this topic, yet I suspect Peter Jannetta is the godfather of this hypothesis. In the fall of 1983, I spoke with Dr. Jannetta and proposed my plan to him. I was encouraged, because, in two cases he had operated on, both patients had improved. Therefore, one must credit him with the 'Ursprung' of this notion."

The Italians, in their reply, graciously acceded to all the various other "firsts," even, in fact, going one better—they had received a letter from a surgeon who had done a similar operation in 1975. All hoped that further research in the field was forthcoming, etc., as researchers fascinated by similar problems always do. And that, everyone thought, was that.

It was not. In the April 1987 "Neurosurgical Forum," there was one more letter on the subject of spasmodic torticollis resulting from neurovascular compression. The letter was from C. B. T. Adams of the Radcliffe Infirmary.

> To The Editor: The Neurosurgical Forum in the November, 1986, issue of the *Journal* is dominated by the rush, indeed stampede, to get on the bandwagon of neurovascular compression causing spasmodic torticollis! Not only is there a stampede to get on but there is considerable jockeying to decide who should drive it. Dr. Dyck has ousted Dr. Pagni in favor of "The Godfather" Professor Jannetta. (Is this accolade religious or secular?)

Adams goes on to talk about what he considers to be fanciful applications of the theory of neurovascular compression: "Those troublesome veins around the olfactory nerves must cause intermittent distortions of smell and we are awaiting the first clinical description." "Consider those poor optic nerves trapped, nay strangled, between the ophthalmic and internal carotid arteries, and this must be the cause of a syndrome yet to be discovered." "We have in the posterior fossa the third, fourth and sixth nerves. These are thoroughly enwrapped by blood vessels. . . . Thus, hemiocular spasm is there waiting to be described by some neurosurgical neophyte seeking overnight fame and fortune."

"I have suggested in the past," Adams concludes, "that colleagues tempted to leap on this bandwagon should first read that important article by Andersen. One cannot expect people already sitting firmly there to read it, but those tempted to leap should first be sure that the king has indeed a suit of gold and is not in his 'altogether.' "

Jannetta has always been tight-lipped about certain criticism, be it explicit or implied. One of the big reasons for this is that he knows that he *needs* the academy, needs the establishment, needs to bore from within. When, early on, he recognized that he was going to be seen as a heretic, a crank, a charlatan by certain members of the profession, he knew enough about medical history to know that the worst move would be to isolate himself.

One of Jannetta's daughters, Carol, was at an impressionable age in the mid-1970s, when the controversies and criticisms surrounding her father and his work would occasionally spill over at home. As she recalls, he would come back from a medical conference in much the state that he is in when he reads a particularly virulent letter in a professional journal. Carol Jannetta had a civics class at the time, and she ran across a passage in a textbook that she copied out for her father and that she, and he, have both saved:

> The cranks are those who do not accept the existing order of things, and propose to change them. The existing order of things is always accepted by the majority, therefore the cranks are always in the minority. They are always progressive thinkers and always in advance of their time, and they always win. Called fanatics and fools at first, they are sometimes persecuted and abused. But their reforms are generally righteous and time, reason and argument bring men to their side. Abused and ridiculed, then tolerated, then respectfully given a hearing, then supported. This has been the gauntlet that all great reforms and reformers have run, from Galileo to John Brown.

"That," Peter Jannetta once said, "is what no one was ever able to tell Irving Cooper."

At some point in any conversation about Jannetta and his work, the name Irving Cooper will come up. It has to. It has to, because Irving Cooper stands as an object lesson to progressive thinkers in the neurosciences. Irving Cooper was a fine neurosurgeon, a progressive thinker. He had what all clinical investigators, if only privately, hope for: One Big Discovery. It was a discovery that eventually changed modern neurosurgery, a discovery that turned out to have ramifications for a changing profession far beyond the help he brought to his patients. But Cooper lived out his career with few accolades and little recognition; he never stood on the dais at the Karolinska Institutets; he never chaired the department of a major medical center. Irving Cooper, for reasons finally known only to Irving Cooper, tried to challenge his profession and was cut down.

Cooper's discovery was a relatively simple and highly effective treatment for the progressive neurological disorder known as Parkinson's disease. It depended on a relatively new technology at the time—stereotaxis, or "guided" surgery, in which a needlelike instrument is introduced, with radiographic guidance, into the brain. It also was a treatment that "shouldn't" have worked, given the state of knowledge at the time about the complex interconnections of neurobiology, neurochemistry, endocrinology, and neurophysiology. But Cooper found that it did seem to work, and he felt that the potential, particularly then (the 1940s and 1950s), was very great, because there was no really satisfactory treatment for Parkinson's disease. When he found the profession skeptical and unreceptive, he in essence went out on his own, setting up practice at a small clinic and counting on word of mouth and the attention of the media to convince his peers that his work deserved merit. He got both—plenty of patients and plenty of media attention; however, neither convinced his peers of anything except that he was to be considered, for all practical purposes, an untouchable. He tried harder; he tried to bully. When he found that the medical profession was not amenable to bullying, he tried to shame them, to overwhelm them, to jolt them into acknowledging his work. The high —or low—point in his efforts was probably a lavish and highly complimentary photo spread in *Life* magazine of a patient before, during, and after the surgery. Other physicians began to accuse him of fraud. Cooper developed elaborate schemes to try and objectify what he did: taking films of his patients before and after surgery; getting affidavits from operating-room visitors.

These methods were poorly adapted to changing something like medical opinion. In some ways, like encouraging independent verification by investigators at other institutions, Cooper almost certainly *delayed* acceptance of his ideas, because there was no faster way to institutional oblivion for a young researcher than fooling around with Irving Cooper's theories. As verification filtered in from overseas, where the intermural bias against him was more muted, Cooper's work gained a modicum of acceptance. And, on the threshold of grudging acknowledgment by the medical community, the chemical basis for Parkinson's disease was discovered, a pharmacological treatment—L-dopa—was developed, and surgical intervention for Parkinson's became limited to the small number of sufferers who could not tolerate the medication or did not respond to it. The era of acceptance for Irving Cooper ended almost before it began.

Late in Cooper's life, Jannetta looked him up at a medical conference in Florida and asked him why he had chosen the route that he did. Cooper's response was not illuminating; to his grave, he blamed the profession. In part, he was certainly right. In some sort of clinical Utopia, the personality, the methods, the *way* that new ideas are entertained by a community of professionals might not matter. Cooper never acknowledged that he was not practicing in that Utopia. Jannetta vowed that what had happened to Cooper would not happen to him. Just as he learned from the work of Walter Dandy and William Gardner, Jannetta also learned from Irving Cooper, because Jannetta recognized early on that his work and Cooper's were in some ways startlingly similar: for Jannetta, it was not stereotaxis, but the operating microscope that provided the technical advantage to formulating his ideas; where Cooper tried to objectify his results with films and affidavits, Jannetta has Aage Møller and his computer; and while Jannetta spends his share (or, as some bristle, much more than his share) of time in the newspapers and on TV, he does not do it at the expense of his share of time in the medical journals.

The difference that Jannetta's attitude (and his ability to control and measure his responses) has made in terms of acceptance of his work is extraordinary. The battles over trigeminal neuralgia and hemifacial spasm are for all practical purposes over and done, correspondents such as C. B. T. Adams notwithstanding. The fact that half a dozen different groups on three continents are actively exploring neurovascular compression as a cause of spasmodic torticollis is a good indication of how acceptable Jannetta's theories, at least at the level of working hypothesis, have become. The same could be said of disabling positional vertigo, which Jannetta and the Møllers first reported on in the *New England Journal of Medicine* in 1984. With each new syndrome, the level of early acceptance has increased, the number of other surgeons pursuing research in the area of vascular-compression syndromes has increased, the number of surgeons performing microvascular decompression seems to be approaching a critical mass. At a dozen medical centers around the country and another twenty overseas, residents are taught microvascular decompression as part of the armamentarium against cranial-nerve disorders. At medical conferences, Jannetta is more often than not a featured speaker, a featured presenter, a moderator, or the leader of a special group—positions generally reserved for the grand old men of the profession. He has on his wall the plaque from the Karolinska Institutets. Someone who did not know him well might expect him to be slowing down. He is not, for some very concrete reasons and also for some reasons that are perhaps not so concrete. The concrete reasons are simply that he has several applications of the theory of neurovascular compression up his sleeve, one of which he has begun to report on and at least one other that he has not. The less concrete reasons have to do, finally, with the kind of person that Peter Jannetta is and what he has become. And perhaps least concrete of all is the relationship in all of its intertwining complexity between Peter Jannetta and what he has made his life's work.

13

From Haddonfield

It is easy to forget that certain people are just that: certain people. When a certain person is engaged in an occupation that is particularly susceptible to generalization or stereotyping, and practices that occupation in a culture that pays particular attention to attachable labels while at the same time placing a high value on the belief that "understanding" someone is important for interpersonal and social relationships, individuals are tugged in two directions simultaneously. How conscious an individual is of this tugging is necessarily rooted in how easy it is for a label to be attached and how much a person is able to project his or her own personality beyond such labels.

Physicians in this country, as a societal group, have been scrutinized very carefully. Part of this is attributable to the exalted place they hold in a culture that openly seeks, if not to remain forever young, at least to remain forever healthy. Doctors have been given a mantle of power in many ways, and they have cheerfully assumed it in many others. We study their habits, the hours that they work, their relationships with their wives and their children and their siblings and their parents; we worry about their alcohol consumption and how much they sleep; we publish books that answer the question "Whom do doctors see when they're sick?" and we buy them. We make drama of their profession and absorb the fictional icons produced in those dramas into our lives: Dr. Kildare. Ben Casey. Marcus Welby. The little black bag. The house call. General Hospital. We ask what pain reliever they would take to a deserted island, what they recommend for upset stomach, for insomnia, for coughs due to colds.

On a real level, we support their education, their training, their research, their development of new machines and instruments and pills and procedures. We take sides in "the liability crisis," and we worry over genetic recombination, abortion on demand, euthanasia, the cost of a hospital room, organ transplantation, brain death, the artificial heart, *in vitro* fertilization, fiber in our diets. We make medicine a large part of our lives and, in doing so, make physicians into white-coated social phenomena.

Because physicians travel with so much social and cultural baggage, it is particularly daunting to try and sift through the events and circumstances that make someone a physician. When we ask the question "What made you the person that you are?" We expect a long and complex answer. When we ask "What made you a physician?" addressing particularly those in certain specialties, we expect less complex answers, because we feel we know so much already. With neurosurgeons, the answers so often have to be filtered through so much of what we believe is significant that the process inevitably runs the risk of becoming a matching exercise, a this-fits-and-this-doesn't method of trying to know a certain person.

With Peter Jannetta, the process is even more complicated, because so much of his professional and personal life has been shaped by the "serendipitous observations" he made in the mid-1960s. It is a fair bet to say that he would have been a very good neurosurgeon, because he has ended up being a very good neurosurgeon by any objective or subjective measurement. It is likely that he would have also ended up in the world of academic medicine, as opposed to private practice, because of his interest in the research side of medicine: it is a particularly Jannetta-like requirement that all the neurosurgery residents at Pitt spend one year in the laboratory. Surgery, as Howard Yonas says, is how a surgeon finally defines himself or herself. But there is a level of inquisitiveness, of exploring the unknown at Pitt, that is demonstrably attributable to having a chief who wants his department to actively expand the pool of knowledge in the neurosciences. The department, noted one hospital administrator who is conscious of the fiscal side of medicine, "has one helluva lot of Ph.D.'s"—the Møllers, Marvin Bennett, Walter Obrist, T. C. Hung, Robert Boston, Rosa Pinkus, T. K. Hung, Irving Nadelhaft, Robert Sclabassi. The department's research activities run from Alzheimer's disease through xenon CT scanning, and members of the department have joint appointments in areas such as Civil Engineering, Radiology, Pharmacology, and Otolaryngology. Residents interested in neurology can spend three months of a residency year at Queens Square Hospital in London (perhaps because Jannetta himself spent a month studying in London). It is tempting to conclude that Jannetta has created the department in his own image and to wonder how accurate that image is.

Jannetta himself has a whole bundle of labels for himself, some of which are mutually conflicting: his fondness, for example, for saying that he is "short-term impatient and long-term patient," generally said when he is being incredibly impatient. He scoffs when someone suggests that he is manic-depressive as he zooms through three brain operations, whistling, humming, and joking all the time, and then sits in his office with the door closed, strumming his banjo. Instead, he says with tongue in cheek, he is cyclothymic—that is, his cyclical periods of elation and depression are theoretically caused by the thymus, a glandlike body that is generally inactive in adults and, in any case, resides in the chest, a comfortable distance from the brain. For a period of years in the late 1960s through the mid 1970s, he worked what was for all practical purposes around the clock, going to the hospital in the middle of the night to do cadaver operations on the recently deceased, going to any medical conference that would have him to stand as a lightning rod for the skepticism of his peers, doing the preop and postop evaluations of patients that he brought to surgery, writing the journal articles about the cadaver operations, about the surgeries, about longer and longer follow-ups. His children remember this period as one in which he was either just leaving the house or just getting back. And yet when asked, off the cuff, how he did what he has done, he smiles and says, "I was lucky." In a profession where one proves oneself in the here and now of a tricky brain operation, he talks of some of his predecessors as though they are living collaborators of his and has in his office a lovely and ancient medical textbook about the brain that Albert Camma gave him, which he handles as though it were a first quarto Shakespeare. He says he has enough competition in his life without taking an intramural softball game seriously and then tries to slip in a high hard strike on an overmatched and bespectacled resident. He is proud of himself for being in control of his temper and his emotions in the operating room, and then he listens, incredulous, to the soundtrack of an operating-room videotape and a voice he does not even recognize as his own using language that he does not think he ever uses. Patient. Stable. Lucky. Rooted in the history of his profession. Noncompetitive. In control. Study a person closely enough, and you can see the exquisite tension between how that person sees himself or herself and what he or she appears to be.

Place that person in a milieu like neurosurgery, and the equation becomes much more complex. Neurosurgeons of Jannetta's generation are dramatically different from the generation immediately previous, just as the residents at Pitt now are dramatically different from their mentors: Chief Resident Rob Parrish, for instance, has, in addition to an M.D. degree, a Ph.D. in magnetic resonance imaging, a field that not only did not exist when Jannetta was in school, but that was preceded technologically by a field that also did not exist when Jannetta was in school—CT scanning. The Gamma Knife, which Presby has recently installed, is being used to treat arteriovenous malformations without surgery by obliterating them with radiation; it may eventually replace an entire generation of balloons, springs, wires, and glue that have been developed since Jannetta was a resident to replace the difficult and risky cutting and sewing that Jannetta learned.

It is possible to consider Jannetta's work in the context of this march of technology as being somehow almost inevitable, because if Jannetta has had one major collaborator, it has been technological advance. Before the advances of the postwar era in anesthesia and pharmacology, only the superstars of the specialty could work successfully in the cerebellopontine angle. The development of self-retaining retractors with malleable paddles eliminated much of the trauma to the cerebellum; the microscope changed forever what the surgeon could see; something as seemingly prosaic as "shadowless" lighting sources gave the neurosurgeons of Jannetta's time a clearer view of what they were doing than their teachers had had when they were learning.

Specific to microvascular decompression, the advent of certain technologies permitted Jannetta to demonstrate what his forebears could not. Walter Dandy made lovely line drawings and sketches of what he had seen in the cerebellopontine angle, but drawings, no matter how meticulously done, are not objective. Jannetta has color slides and color videotapes; he has a microscope with two sets of eyepieces so that an observer can see exactly what the surgeon sees; he has a video monitor in the operating room so that what was once reserved for the eyes of Walter Dandy is now viewed democratically. And then there is the next generation of data, the evoked potentials of the cranial nerves at work, developed with Jannetta for his work by Marvin Bennett, Aage Møller, and Robert Sclabassi. (Møller likes to joke that he can carry half a dozen brain operations in his pocket, preserved on a floppy computer disk.)

The people that Jannetta worked with early in his career unquestionably had some effect, too. He developed a marvelous rapport with Sol Erulkar at Penn, who was working on intracellular recording of nerve impulses in the spinal cords of cats. To do this, Jannetta had to use the operating microscope. He was encouraged to become involved in research in the first place by William Blakemore and Brooke Roberts. By leaving Penn and going to UCLA, Jannetta ended up in a place that had the first real microneurosurgeon, Ted Kurze, and soon Robert Rand. He brought to UCLA the curiosity and vigor he learned at Penn, which helped him face the criticism and skepticism he found there. Later, he took what can only be described as two major career gambles, trading the opportunity to be a small cog at a prestigious institution for chances at LSU and Pitt to run his own show. Since then, he has been suggested for a place as the biggest cog of all at two of the biggest neurosurgical machines in the country, and he has turned them down, going so far as to decline to formally acknowledge that the offers were made. "Nope," he said of one of the offers. "Too late."

It is reasonable and appropriate to paint Jannetta's accomplishments as one large collaborative effort, well salted with luck and, well, seredipity. For example, one of the reasons he moved to Los Angeles was daughters plagued by chronic kidney infections; he hoped that the change in climate would help them, which it did. Further, it is reasonable to attribute at least part of his success to the opportunities provided to a talented researcher by a profession in flux and transition. Most conservatively, there is an attractiveness to the argument that while Jannetta refined and adapted—even perfected—the technique of microvascular decompression, he invented and discovered nothing: Walter Dandy and William Gardner conclusively preceded him both in theory and practice. Jannetta himself makes certain that this is always clear, never sending a paper to a medical journal without the requisite footnotes crediting these two surgeons. It is possible to imagine Jannetta's work as the result of some sort of medical and societal confluence, a confluence that happened to find him at the headwaters.

If Jannetta were today simply the world's best surgeon for trigeminal neuralgia or for trigeminal neuralgia and hemifacial spasm (the two disorders treated by Dandy and Gardner), he would be much easier to evaluate as a member of a scientific profession and much easier to understand as a person: we understand and appreciate good work and good works; we readily assimilate practitioners in all endeavors who excel within the confines of their field, who thoughtfully apply the collective knowledge and experience of their peers and do a good thing well. But how, finally, do we assimilate a new thought and, by extension, a new thinker?

In a laboratory in Scaife Hall, Peter Jannetta, in conjunction with a former resident now practicing in Pittsburgh, Howard Gendell, M.D., and Drs. Wolfson and Segal, has figured out a way to give a laboratory animal a cranial-nerve disorder—and not any esoteric cranial-nerve disorder either. Through the use of an arterial balloon fed into the posterior fossa on the end of a catheter and inflated with a pump, Jannetta has been able to give apes high blood pressure.

The entire investigation of cranial-nerve compression as a cause of certain types of hypertension is in many ways a neat culmination of Jannetta the researcher, Jannetta the product of his generation, and Jannetta the person, because the three coalesce around an observation, a technological exploit, and a fundamental personality trait.

The original observation was made in 1973. A woman underwent microvascular decompression for glossopharyngeal neuralgia and suffered a severe hypertensive stroke two hours following an uneventful operation; she died three days later. Later that year, a man undergoing microvascular decompression, also for glossopharyngeal neuralgia, had extraordinarily high blood pressure following surgery—as high as $^{220}/_{110}$. He was given standard hypertensive medication for seven days following the surgery; the hypertension went away and never came back.

The glossopharyngeal nerve is the ninth cranial nerve and arises from almost the same point along the brain stem as the tenth nerve, the vagus. Both arise in an area of the brain stem where many of the cardiovascular system's "feedback" controls are located. These controls, or "centers," are part of the autonomic nervous system, which is dedicated to life-sustaining functions such as breathing, heart rate, blood pressure, and metabolism. Further, the left vagus nerve has unique autonomic duties: it is the major control of the left side of the heart.

The unusual responses of these two patients to surgical exploration along this particular area of the brain stem caused Jannetta and his colleagues to make a series of observations of blood vessels in this region in patients undergoing microvascular decompression for conditions such as trigeminal neuralgia and disabling vertigo. It also sent them to the lab, because, unlike pain or dizziness, blood pressure can be measured by anyone. If they could demonstrate that compression of the brain stem or the left vagus nerve caused some cases of hypertension, and if they could demonstrate that they could remove the symptoms by removing the cause, they would have a marvelous "animal model" of cranial-nerve compression, thus deflating the graffito artist's criticism ("Jannetta to lab rat: 'Does it bother you? Does it ruin your life?' ") as well as the criticism of those who think that Aage Møller's data is bunk and Jannetta's work deceiving.

In 1973, they were, however, a long way from demonstrating anything. First, if the theory were correct, Jannetta would have to separate the hypertension ostensibly caused by cranial nerve compression from the hypertension caused by dozens of other things. It is important to note that Jannetta was not, and is not, proclaiming a "cure" for *all* hypertension, just high blood pressure that is not caused by any of the usual suspect conditions, hypertension generally referred to, in classic making-the-unknown-sound-known medical lingo, as "idiopathic" (of no known origin) or "essential" (self-existing or having no known external cause) or "neurogenic" (having its origin in the nervous system, which is hardly as conclusive as it sounds; it is generally used when all other systemic causes have been ruled out—the nervous system gets blamed for a lot of things in this way). The neurophysiology of blood-pressure regulation is fairly well understood; branches of the vagus nerve are found in the carotid arteries, the aorta, and the heart. Blood pressure responds in predictable ways when these nerve branches are interrupted or interfered with experimentally; certain autonomic-nervous-system tumors or injuries can cause elevation or fluctuation of blood pressure. Data collected from heart transplant patients is of particular interest. A transplanted heart, because its vagal nerve branches have been severed when it was harvested, beats steadily, independent of autonomic control, so that, for example, a sleeping heart transplant recipient's heart doesn't slow down the way that a person's own heart, with its nerve connections intact, will.

Also, Jannetta's observations had been noted earlier in passing. His old colleague and mentor Ted Kurze observed as far back as 1964 the resolution of preoperative hypertension in a patient he operated on for hemifacial spasm. Attempts at developing animal models for the study of neurogenic hypertension had been made before as well. But persistent hypertension in a lab animal had been notoriously difficult to produce: either the hypertension produced was so severe as to be lethal, or the autonomic nervous system corrected for the hypertension and leveled the blood pressure out.

Jannetta's animal experiments differ in two ways. First, the ingenious balloon within a balloon in the posterior fossa allows him to create pulsing pressure on the brain stem and nerve rather than the constant pressure, say, of a solid implant of some sort. This pulsatile pressure mimics very closely the pulsing of an artery, which Jannetta thinks may act as a *stimulus* to the autonomic nervous system, as the beating of the heart and its consequent pulsations do. Second, the apparatus he uses to initiate hypertension can be "turned off"—deflated—causing the blood pressure to return to normal levels.

While the animal work proceeded, Jannetta came to a startling preliminary confirmation of his theory during a series of operations within the cerebellopontine angle. Patients who came to him with high blood pressure in addition to, say, trigeminal neuralgia or hemifacial spasm on the left side were asked by Jannetta if he could nose around a bit farther down along the brain stem. And if he found what appeared to be an artery causing pressure on either the brain stem or the tenth nerve, he asked (before the operation) if he could try and fix it. The patients, many of whom were taking large and complicated mixtures of antihypertensive drugs, invariably said yes.

Concurrently, in patients whose blood pressure was normal, he asked if he could nose around the brain stem to see if vascular compression was absent. The patients, since they were about to be opened up anyway, invariably said yes, too.

The results, perhaps predictably, put Jannetta in the headlines and attracted the approbation of a large segment of the medical community yet again. But Jannetta had learned something about himself and the medical community in the years since he first began reporting on cranial-nerve compression—or, to put it in a slightly more interpretative context, Jannetta was a different person when he reported on his initial observations regarding hypertension than he had been twenty years before. He had gotten all of his ducks in a row: clinical observations, laboratory data, patient follow-up. Jannetta had found, in addition to a very likely cause of neurogenic hypertension, something out about himself, because he formally reported on the origin and surgical treatment of hypertension in 1985, twelve years after he had first speculated on neurovascular compression as a cause of certain kinds of high blood pressure.

Twelve years, particularly in medicine, is a very long time; the first patients to be treated by microvascular decompression for hypertension had been followed for more than nine years. While Jannetta had suggested several times in that twelve-year period that this was something he was working on, both at medical conferences and in print (something that no clinical investigator should resist for one explicit reason and one implicit one, the explicit reason being to allow other researchers who are so inclined to begin investigations of their own and thus have the opportunity to contribute confirmatory and supporting data, and the implicit reason being that if you believe you're on the right track, you need to establish what you know and when you knew it), he had found it in himself to be "long-term patient" after all so as to present the medical community with at least the semblance of a *fait ac-compli*. By the time "Neurogenic Hypertension: Etiology and Surgical Treatment" was published in the one-hun-dredth-anniversary issue of *Annals of Surgery*, Jannetta, in fact, had already begun a second series of patients, this group being treated for hypertension alone.

Peter Jannetta spent the first two years of his life in what he refers to as "the Italian ghetto" of South Philadelphia. His parents were the children of Italian immigrants, and his father had been taken from school and put to work in a barber shop. He met Jannetta's mother when she was eight and he was fifteen, and has always said that he knew right then that he would marry her. He did so ten years later. When Peter was born, they were living in his grandparent's house in South Philly, which was not where Peter's mother wanted to raise her children. So they moved to Haddonfield, New Jersey, where his father opened up a hairdressing shop. First they lived in a rented house and then in an apartment over the shop. Jannetta's father went on to become president of the New Jersey Hairdressers Association.

Haddonfield in the 1930s and 1940s was a homogenous sort of place, a commuter suburb of urban Philadelphia. "We were not," Jannetta says years later, "Haddonfieldians." His mother, as a way of helping to compensate for the estrange-ment that Peter felt even as a child, would do things like travel to Leary's bookstore in Philadelphia and "empty a shelf," he recalls. "She was never particular about what she got but would just bring home an armload of books for me to read."

She signed young Peter up for piano lessons and maintains to this day that the primary reason her son became such a good surgeon was the manual dexterity he learned sitting on a piano bench. He developed an interest in painting and music, but never in Haddonfield; although he never complained, he also never felt that he belonged. As he grew older, he began to get into trouble. He would get into fights, including a fight with one of his high-school teachers. "I began to actively resent being an outcast," he says, "and actively resenting it just made me more of an outcast." There would be parties to which he was not invited. And at parties to which he was, he found it difficult to get along.

The family, which by then included Jannetta's two brothers and two sisters, made a big move in 1948, to York, Pennsylvania, where Peter's father and uncle opened a bar and restaurant. For Peter, then fourteen and a sophomore in high school, the move came at just the right time. Even now, York is somewhat bucolic, sitting in the heart of the Pennsylvania Dutch country; in the late 1940s, it was emphatically not a town with the complicated social stratifications that had made Haddonfield very hard for Peter to live in. He began to fit in almost immediately. He had been a swimmer at summer camp while growing up; at York, he would swim on the state championship swim team and make all-American; he tried out for, and got, a role in the school play; he began to do well in school. To the Haddonfield of his youth, a move to a place like York was not the "correct" move to make, but it was a move that allowed Jannetta to find his own level and to grow.

To Jannetta's father, there was only one suitable place for his children to attend college. Samuel Jannetta had a lifelong love affair with higher education in general and with Penn in particular, although he never made it there himself. (He did, while the family lived in Haddonfield, finish high school, college, *and* night law school at Temple University.) So Peter went off to Penn, where his degree in zoology—the "correct" degree for prospective physicians—masked his less parochial interests: anthropology, sociology, enough credits in English literature to have graduated an English major, had he so chosen. He had "always" wanted medical school, specialty unspecified, the "always" going back to his childhood in Haddonfield. He wanted medicine for the intellectual challenge, for the social and cultural world it functioned in, for the way that a tradition-heavy school like Penn imbued it with a sense of decorum and dignity. He took a class in medical school taught by the then-chairman of the Pathology Department, Dale R. Coman, who was also a painter, a sculptor, and a poet. And from the first day, Jannetta was enchanted.

Medical school is one of the more expensive-sounding areas of higher education. In real dollars, it is not much more expensive now than it was in the early 1950s, and Jannetta paid part of his way by doing what sounds like an almost fantastic cliché: Peter Jannetta's job in the summer of his second year of medical school was selling Fuller brushes. Something like serendipity intervened when he met William Blakemore, M.D., a cardiothoracic surgeon working, as were all cardiothoracic surgeons at the time, with the technique of arterial grafting, using arteries harvested from cadavers. Jannetta got a job in the lab for $25 a week, freeze-drying blood vessels for surgical research and use. Eventually, Blakemore set Jannetta up in a laboratory of his own, doing biological evaluations using rabbit aortas. Jannetta also entered the general surgical residency at Penn and received a fellowship in the Department of Surgical Research. When the National Institutes of Health began a program to encourage young physicians to stay in the academy and do research, Bill Blakemore, Jonathan Rhodes, and I. S. Radvin picked Jannetta, and together the four of them decided on neurosurgery.

"Neurosurgery at the time was a sort of traditionless specialty," says Jannetta. "The program at Penn was," he searches for a word, "complex. There was a well-established chief with well-established ideas about what one's interests should and should not be. But those ideas didn't have a lot to do with the ideas that I had. I was gaining a perspective on science of my own already from reading about scientific methodology from a sort of sociological point of view. Also, I would be entering the subspecialty training having already trained as a general surgeon, and I think that was in some ways sort of intimidating. I wanted to feel free to develop an area of my own."

So he went to California and found what was the closest thing that neurosurgery had to freethinkers—at least in the lower echelons. Jannetta's use of the word "traditionless" to describe neurosurgery in the early 1960s is idiosyncratic. There was a certain amount of tradition, but it tended to be tradition in the sense of ritual, not traditional in the sense of dogma. The rituals of neurosurgery were extensive. What was missing was a way of integrating new knowledge and new technology into established practice: contemporary medicine was born of an era that set its standards in a way similar to the way that legal practice sets its own: the concept of precedent was the ruling methodology in that some of Jannetta's teachers did things the way they did because that was the way they were always done. Research that supported established precedent fit into the conceptual framework; research that was not born of established ritual was greeted with skepticism and criticism. People like Kurze, Rand, and Alksne were, like Jannetta, of a different generation and thus in a unique position to separate ritual from dogma. This need to separate has stayed with Jannetta and has permeated the program he built: the only unacceptable reason to do something is to do it because granddad did it that way.

"It takes twenty years for a new concept to become accepted," Jannetta has learned to say. "It takes that long because the new people coming into the profession have to grow up with an idea and eventually replace the old guard." It was much easier to learn to say this than it was for Jannetta to learn it himself. In the intervening years were those very private times when he felt alone, or virtually alone, against a monolithic profession. And because he won—and there is no question that he has won—he has earned the right to say to a famous medical school, "Nope. Too late." He has probably earned the right to respond in kind to what C. B. T. Adams must consider marvelous whimsy, but, paradoxically, he does not; he no longer gets into that kind of trouble, no longer gets into the kinds of fights that make him an outcast. Metaphorically, he has moved again from Haddonfield to York, again from Penn to UCLA, again from UCLA to Pitt by way of New Orleans, where one of his daughters remembers with great affection her father playing the banjo in the Shakey's Pizza Parlor. "It was very strange to watch," recalls Carol Jannetta. "You could tell by just looking at him that he would simply lose himself in the banjo. He became a different person."

One Thursday afternoon, Jannetta roots around under a credenza in his office and pulls out his banjo case. He handles the banjo as though it were a delicate surgical instrument, tuning it and tuning it until it sounds exactly right. The door to the office is shut. He strums softly, reaches into the case to find a more suitable pick ("I know, I know, it's a poor carpenter who blames his tools," he says), strums again. "On the way into work today, I was humming a song I hadn't played in years," he says. "I learned this song in nineteen fifty, and I haven't thought of this song since I lived in New Orleans." And with a modest false start, he plays and sings a sort of Dixieland torch song called "Words." He plays it all the way through and then strums somewhat absentmindedly. He talks about his "pediatric piano lessons" and smiles at his mother's insistence that they were the reason he has become such a good surgeon. The telephone buzzes. He lays the banjo back into its case and reaches for the phone. "In another life," he says, "I could have very easily been a musician."

Epilogue

Change is fundamental to the workings of the Department of Neurosurgery at the University of Pittsburgh. But one thing that doesn't change is the steady flow of postcards, birthday cards, Christmas cards, and letters into the office as former patients dutifully let Peter Jannetta know how they are doing. His experience has taught him that roughly nine out of ten should be doing well, and in any small and arbitrary sampling, all—or none—may be feeling terrific, may be winners.

Stanley Risk is settled in the Southwest, where he is general manager of a television station. He has been pain-free since his operation.

Madeline Cooper is back in Philadelphia, back at work, completely cured of the symptoms of trigeminal neuralgia. Psychologically, she is still recovering, afraid when she bumps her head, aware every morning when she brushes her teeth of what she went through. Physically, she feels fine.

Xavier Williams, who came to Jannetta for treatment of hemifacial spasm and who, unbeknownst to him, had a tense time in the operating room, is fine. He owns a very successful automobile agency in the East, and his note card is elegant, with his name richly embossed on the front.

Janice Slater, who had five years of vertigo, was slow to recover. She had sporadic attacks of vertigo for almost eight months before it resolved completely. As is not uncommon, she finds herself brooding occasionally about what she went through and sometimes has dreams in which the vertigo comes back. During her waking hours, it has not.

Ellen Goldberg is doing well. The trigeminal neuralgia is gone. Her phone bill in the first month following surgery, as promised, made it into three digits, and, she wrote to Jannetta, "I enjoyed every penny."

Jannetta's work with spasmodic torticollis is proceeding slowly but well; he expects to report soon on his first series of cases. He has also just reported on the first group of patients treated for hypertension by itself, and the results remain highly encouraging. He is also extending the theory to two other conditions about which he is not ready to report and, hence, will talk about only informally. But when he is asked how it looks, he smiles his smile.

Aage Møller wrote a stiff letter to the *Journal of Neurosurgery* in which he refuted C. B. T. Adams's dismissal of the value of electrophysiologic data in understanding and verifying cranial-nerve-compression syndromes. His last paragraph read, "That Mr. Adams has presented these statements without presenting substantiating scientific evidence may be regarded as unusual in a debate in a scientific journal. What I find remarkable, however, is that a journal such as the *Journal of Neurosurgery* would publish a letter that expresses such skepticism in a way that ridicules another investigator personally." The editor wrote to Møller and said he would print the letter only if the last sentence were deleted, to which Møller agreed, albeit grudgingly, and the letter ran in the October 1987 issue.

Peter Jannetta has quit smoking and has cut his coffee consumption in half. In the winter of 1988, he was invited to a meeting in New Orleans, and his former colleagues and friends there rolled out the red carpet; he was welcomed back with open arms and open respect. When Jannetta was at LSU, Dr. Richard Paddison would tease him mercilessly about being an Italian in New Orleans, going so far as to install a pink flamingo on Jannetta's lawn, because Paddison insisted that no Italian home was complete without one. He and Jannetta took turns sticking pink flamingos into each other's lawns the entire time Jannetta chaired the department there. On Jannetta's visit, Paddison hosted a party for Jannetta, and when Paddison's wife opened the door for Jannetta, she saw, gleaming in the darkness—what else? A pink flamingo on the lawn, courtesy of the Chairman of the Department of Neurosurgery at the University of Pittsburgh. He returned from New Orleans looking as though he were on top of the world.

About the Author

Mark L. Shelton has been a science writer and editor at several hospitals and medical centers. He is currently associate editor of *Ohio Magazine* in Columbus, after having spent two years in a similar position at *Pittsburgh Magazine*. A native of Chicago, he is a graduate of Western Michigan University and the University of Pittsburgh. He divides his time between Athens, Ohio, and the Laurel Highlands of Pennsylvania. *Working in a Very Small Place* is his first book.